Village at War

Village at War
An Account of Revolution in Vietnam

James Walker Trullinger, Jr.

LONGMAN

New York and London

VILLAGE AT WAR
An Account of Revolution in Vietnam

Longman Inc., New York
Associated companies and branches, and
representatives throughout the world.

Developmental Editor: Irving E. Rockwood
Editorial and Design Supervisor: Diane Perlmuth
Cover Design: Dan Serrano
Manufacturing and Production Supervisor: Robin B. Besofsky
Composition: Book Composition Services, Inc.
Printing and Binding: BookCrafters

Library of Congress Cataloging in Publication Data

Trullinger, James Walker,
Village at war.

Bibliography: p.
1. Vietnamese Conflict, 1961–1975—Vietnam—Thôn Mỹ Thủy. 2. Thôn Mỹ Thủy, Vietnam—History.
I. Title.
DS559.9.T48T78 959.704′31 79-25406
ISBN 0-582-28181-4

Manufactured in the United States of America

9 8 7 6 5 4 3 2 1

Acknowledgments

Excerpt from the poem "Adam" on page xi from *Collected Earlier Poems of William Carlos Williams*. Copyright © 1938 by New Directions Publishing Corporation. Reprinted by permission of New Directions Publishing Corporation.

"Vietnam Message" on page xii from *Other Things and the Aardvark* by Eugene J. McCarthy. Copyright © 1970 by Eugene J. McCarthy. Reprinted by permission of Doubleday & Company, Inc.

Quotations in Chapter 5 from "Vietnam: A Family Goes to War" by James Walker Trullinger, Jr. Reprinted by permission of *The Asia Mail.*

Quotation on page 92 from Vietcong: *The Organization and Techniques of the National Liberation Front of South Vietnam* by Douglas Pike. Copyright © 1966 by the Massachusetts Institute of Technology. Reprinted by permission of the M.I.T. Press.

Quotation on page 138 from *The Winter Soldier Investigation: An Inquiry into American War Crimes* by the Vietnam Veterans Against the War. Copyright © 1972 by the Vietnam Veterans Against the War, Inc. Reprinted by permission of Beacon Press.

Quotations on pages 135 and 177 from *Screaming Eagle* by the 101st Airborne Division Association. Reprinted by permission of the 101st Airborne Division Association.

Quotations on pages 196–7 from *The New York Times*. Copyright © 1975 by The New York Times Company. Reprinted by permission.

Photo entitled "Captured Communist Weapons," number 68-0221-A, by The Pacific Stars & Stripes. Reprinted by permission of The Pacific Stars and Stripes.

Photo entitled "Beaucoup Vee-Cee Hue," by Dick Hughes, circa 1968–1969. Reprinted by permission of Dick Hughes.

All other photos by James Walker Trullinger, Jr.

Dedicated to Vietnam's and America's children. May theirs be a prosperous, free, and peaceful world.

Contents

Foreword

Underneath the whisperings
of tropic nights
there is a darker whispering
that death invents especially
for northern men. . . .

William Carlos Williams

Village at War is a report, a history of a Vietnam village, of its people, surprised and startled victims, first of twentieth-century colonialism by the French, then of Japanese occupation during World War II, followed by the post-war effort of the French to hold at least half of Vietnam, and finally of the American armed forces, who picked up where the French failed and carried on a war without clear definition of purpose, and with little or no understanding of the people against whom they were fighting.

The book is essentially a case study of disruption, showing how the series of intruders destroyed the order of village life. It concerns the economy which had never been more than marginally above subsistence level, but which met the limited material needs of the people, their need for security in property, and their right to work. *Village at War* also shows the disruption in family life, in community relationships, and in politics and government.

When the information in *Village at War* is added to the reports of misjudgment of persons and misunderstanding of political realities at high levels of government, both in Vietnam and in Cambodia, additional questions are raised as to how or why those Americans who advocated, who conducted and directed our military and political programs in those countries, could have been either so misinformed or so arrogant in their power.

Their folly is clear now, as it was to Doris Fleeson, a columnist, now dead, who wrote almost at the beginning of American military intervention that our intervention would not, could not, work. "We were," she said, "too big, too wasteful, too destructive. Our garbage, alone, would be too much for the Vietnamese to handle."

Village at War sustains the judgment of those who opposed the war from the beginning or soon after, when it became evident, as events showed time and time again, that those who were conducting the war did not know what was happening or what was going to happen. It sustains their recommendation to President Nixon that he end the war, and that if he did, no matter how badly things turned out, they would not criticize him. The book also sustains and underlines an answer I gave to that ultimate press question, the one which was to silence critics of the war, as to what one would do or say about Vietnam if elected President of the United States. I replied that I would send this message to them (essentially as it is in this poem) and act upon it:

Vietnam Message

We will take our corrugated steel
out of the land of thatched huts.

We will take our tanks
out of the land of the water buffalo.

We will take our napalm and flame throwers
out of the land that scarcely knows
the use of matches.

We will take our helicopters
out of the land of colored birds
and butterflies.

We will give back your villages and fields
your small and willing women.

We will leave you your small joys
and smaller troubles.

We will trust you to your gods,
some blind, some many-handed.

Eugene J. McCarthy

Preface

The village was a Vietnamese arena of intense human drama. It suffered a long, bloody, and devastating confrontation between two rival political forces. Those forces fought and fought hard, within the boundaries of the village itself.

During the fight, the village also had two names. Followers of one side called it *Thuy Phuong,* "Place of the Waters," while those on the other side gave it the name *My Thuy,* "Beautiful Waters." For years there was ambivalence, so it is simply easier to think of the village as having a composite name, *My Thuy Phuong,* "Place of Beautiful Waters."

In this book, I focus on My Thuy Phuong's long war—on continuity and change, sorrow and joy, life and death. I include profiles and the actual words of numerous villagers. There are many on my "cast of characters," real people like Binh the struggling peasant, Tri the warehouseman, Truong the grassroots revolutionary, Nghi the rice merchant, Minh the organizer, Phuoc the fanatical officer, and Te the village leader.

My purpose is to present the Vietnam War primarily as these and other villagers experienced it. For that reason, I include no theoretical discussion or comparisons with other villages, countries, or studies. It is my firm belief that if I were to aim for a global sweep or attempt to reach conclusions for social science, the village would be lost in a maze of theories, the voices of its people muted.

My interest in Vietnamese affairs stems from employment during 1969–1972, as a refugee relief worker in Danang, where my major preoccupation was assistance to homeless Vietnamese children, mostly shoeshine boys.

In 1974, I returned to Vietnam and decided to undertake a study of war in a contested village—My Thuy Phuong. I gathered most of the data for this study in the village itself, during the period November, 1974 through March, 1975. I left the village in late March because of chaos in the area and a desire to preserve research notes and films.

During the next five months, I conducted library and archival research at Cornell University, in Washington, D.C., and at a military base in Kentucky. I did most of the writing in Honolulu, Hawaii during 1975–1976, and some in Seoul, Korea during 1978–1979.

My Thuy Phuong was suggested as a research site by Vietnamese friends who described it as *atypical* of most Vietnamese villages in size, location, history, and so forth, but who nevertheless asserted that there was much to learn from its experience. I now share their view.

After initial introductions, walking tours of the village, and informal family visits, I conducted formal interviews and had informal conversations with villagers of all political stripes, provincial and local officials, and with some leaders of the local insurgent organization. All told, I had about 175 such interviews and conversations of varying lengths, and in some cases, extending over many days. I spoke with about fifty leaders and followers of the then incumbent regime, thirty-five on the insurgent side, thirty-five who seemed politically uncommitted, and forty-five whose political allegiance I could not determine. To capture important comments verbatim, I took notes during most of the formal interviews and immediately after many informal encounters.

I assured my contacts that in quoting I would not directly attribute anything they told me and not construct identifying family case histories without permission. However, I did tell them that I intended to identify quotes by profession of the speaker. Further, I assured the small number of villagers who agreed to in-depth profiles or family case histories that only pseudonyms would appear in the text. I wrote this book with all these assurances firmly in mind—and in force. This "ground rule" is behind the book's apparent paradox of many identified characters from the 1930s but few from recent years. Simply, many villagers were willing to talk specifically of individuals long gone, but feared personal complications if speaking in detail of those from the 1960s and 1970s.

I attempt to maintain balance throughout much of the text by including quotes which reflect divergent views on various subjects. In most cases, how representative the quotes are should be clear from context. And I repeatedly use the terms "villagers" and "people" in making small generalizations. The terms reflect consensus by at least two individuals I consider reliable, informed, and representative sources.

A comment now on social research in Vietnam. For most of the period 1965–1975, the Vietnamese and their war held the attention of numerous social scientists. During those years, many Vietnamese on both sides of the conflict grew to correctly understand that a great deal of that research was sponsored by the U.S. Government, and suspicion of all social scientists became widespread. To many Vietnamese the arms of the C.I.A. seemed very long indeed, and it was logical to distrust all foreign "researchers" as possible agents of that organization.

Identifying myself as a "social scientist writing about village life and the war," I encountered this obstacle of distrust and suspicion in My Thuy Phuong, but began to overcome it through identification in the village as a part-time volunteer teacher of twelfth-grade English in its school. That position also helped me overcome another initial suspicion, that I was a "bounty hunter," searching for remains of or clues about American soldiers missing in action.

Most villagers' reverence for teachers meant that many in My Thuy Phuong, especially the youth, viewed me as a very different sort of American—one who actually played a minor but respected role in their community. Another advantage in teaching was that students often accompanied me on walks through the village, and invited me into their homes, enabling me to make many valuable contacts.

I also gained access to many villagers through "understandings" with both sides in the war. Luckily, the former Republic of Vietnam province chief liked the idea of my research, and wrote me a letter of introduction to provincial, district, and village officials, most of whom fully cooperated with me. I won the trust of those officials and most of their followers in the village simply by assuring them of my desire to tell the truth about the war. When they asked for my opinions on Vietnam issues, I made vague, general replies. But such queries were infrequent and perhaps considered unnecessary because of the province chief's introductions.

I approached the revolutionary side with complete openness. After meeting with and presenting a written request and character references to a diplomat (serving in Laos) of the former Democratic Republic of Vietnam, and making assurances of honest analysis, the former Provisional Revolutionary Government of the Republic of South Vietnam apparently decided to "take a chance" on my research: insurgent forces never restricted or threatened my movement in the village or elsewhere, and I was able to meet with many supporters of the local insurgent organization. In conversations with those individuals, I honestly expressed my opposition to most American policies in their country. Note that insurgent followers were aware of my contacts, in offices and homes, with Republic of Vietnam officials. Those officials, incidentally, may have known of my contacts "on the other side," but never revealed as much to me.

I necessarily arranged all my meetings with leaders of the village insurgent organization outside village boundaries. Sites of those informal conversations were my home just outside of Hue, city market cafés, soup stands, public parks, sampans, moving motorcycles, shells of abandoned buildings, and mountain retreats. Careful arrangements insured that the meetings were undisturbed. Those interviewed and I frequently shifted sites, took circuitous and confusing approaches to meeting places, and took care that passers-by did not hear snatches of "incriminating" conversations.

Finally, I assured My Thuy Phuong's politically uncommitted about my research intentions through introductions from a number of generally neutralist or apolitical Buddhist monks and lay leaders, who knew me through introductions from a prominent monk in Danang, a long-time friend. Among those I met within village boundaries, frank conversations and interviews on political questions were possible after about two months of discussions on relatively mundane matters. All told, those conversations and interviews were long, and touched on many aspects of village life. Villagers patiently described and explained even the most mundane details of daily existence, usually with frankness and vividness, and often humorously. One-to-one, usually open-ended conversations in the fields, in private homes, or around tables of public refreshment stalls, touched on people's experiences, values, dreams, and fears.

To summarize, my identification as a teacher, the "understanding" of both sides in the war, introductions from Buddhist leaders, and a large measure of good luck permitted me to gain the trust of many villagers, and to hear many versions of My Thuy Phuong's story. In addition, the military activity throughout the area kept most villagers distracted, and allowed me to continue the last months of my research with little interference.

To supplement what I learned during interviews and conversations, I have amassed and drawn upon some documentary evidence. Involved here are very few documents from the village itself, but many Vietnamese, French, and American documents describing conditions in the province of which the village is a part. I obtained most of the Vietnamese and French documents in Hue and at the Cornell University Library. Most American documents came through the Freedom of Information Act, which gives citizens some access to classified U.S. Government documents. I include most references to the U.S. materials in the footnotes, so readers interested in official views on some matters should look there. And for those who might want to obtain copies of the U.S. documents, such as province advisory reports, I have listed complete data on whereabouts in the bibliography.

I hasten to add a word now on my values and this study. Like most social scientists, I understand just how difficult it is to achieve total objectivity in social research, for human values can influence perceptions and tilt research findings one way or another. I believe, however, that we can minimize value biases of various sorts if we make values clear at the outset, or even attempt to test them. In that spirit, I acknowledge that I opposed most U.S. policies in Vietnam, and in general prefer social, economic, and political policies which benefit the many rather than the few. I recognize that those values may have influenced my research in the village.

Another value that may have affected this study's objectivity was my belief that Vietnam's major political forces in 1974–1975 were the incumbent regime and the insurgency, and not the body of politically uncommitted, neutralists, and pacifists. Similarly, I believe that extended families, hamlets, and factions were relatively unimportant forces in the village.

While I include in the book some information on the "middle group" as it appeared in My Thuy Phuong and on extended families, my major focus is on the two contending sides in the war and their effects on village life.

There was simply too high a level of violence and too clear a left-right polarization for me to avoid emphasizing violence and the two combatant sides. I feel, however, that such an emphasis did not lead me too far from the truth about My Thuy Phuong, and that my recognition of the values mentioned above actually forced me to ask tougher questions of villagers, and of myself.

I would like now to acknowledge the assistance of many who made this study possible. Acknowledgment goes first to my friends in the village, whose names I will not mention. Especially helpful were my English language students of the Huong Thuy High School, who numbered about seventy. The Vietnamese visa sponsor was Dr. Le Thanh Minh Chau, the former Rector of Hue University, who secured the visa through his government's Ministry of Education. A high-ranking monk of the Danang Buddhist Association provided many important introductions and informal sponsorship in Hue. Many friends generously helped me get established in Hue, including several of Hue's shoeshine boys who shared my home, brought me great joy, and were informal guides. All shall remain anonymous here.

Ex-Colonel Nguyen Huu Due, the former Republic of Vietnam's military and administrative chief for Hue and Thua Thien Province, provided introductions to provincial, district, and village officials. A friend with the Saigon-based Buddhist Youth for Social Service helped me with invaluable advice and introductions in the Hue area. Three professors, one at Dalat University and two at Van Hanh University, also offered advice. The former first secretary of the former Democratic Republic of Vietnam Embassy in Laos was the individual who conveyed messages for me to the former Provisional Revolutionary Government of the Republic of South Vietnam.

There were many other research sponsors, whose names I *can* mention. Mr. Richard Hughes, of the Shoeshine Boys Foundation, helped with encouragement, advice, and living accommodations in Saigon. Two officials of the former U.S. Mission/Vietnam, Messrs. George Jacobson in Saigon and Albert Francis in Danang, helped with introductions to Vietnamese officials. My University of Hawaii doctoral committee members, Professors Robert Stauffer (chairman), Glenn Paige, Benedict Kerkvliet, Ben Finney, and the East-West Center's Dr. Gary Hansen offered considerable professional advice, encouragement, and assistance writing this study. Several staff members of the East-West Center were especially helpful, including Dr. Manuel Alba, Mrs. Mendl Djunaidy, Dr. Louis Goodman, and Miss Jennie Miyasaki.

A former teacher of mine at Cornell University, Professor George

Kahin, offered professional advice and encouragement both before and after the field work. Others at Cornell who provided research support included Mr. Giok Po Oey of the Cornell Library and Professor Frank Golay, Mrs. Peggy Lush, and Mrs. Helen Swank of the Southeast Asia Program. Several Cornell graduate students also assisted: Miss Hoang Thi Thanh Giang translated Vietnamese documents for me; Messrs. James Hinde and Louis MacKenzie translated French documents; and Mr. Paresh Majmudar drew the village maps. Dr. Jeffrey Race in Bangkok and Dr. Gerald Hickey at Cornell gave me suggestions for research approaches.

Several in Washington, D.C. assisted with introductions and gatherings of archival materials, including Dr. Richard Hatcher of the U.S. Army Adjutant General's Office, Mr. Frederick Brown of the U.S. Department of State, and Mr. David Cordingly, a businessman. And at Fort Campbell, Kentucky, Public Affairs Officer Mrs. Laura Chamberlain and Post Historian First Lt. R. Cody Phillips arranged several useful interviews with American soldiers and gave me access to military archives.

I would like to extend warm thanks to all those mentioned above. Special thanks and appreciation go to my family and to friends not mentioned above for so many kind thoughts and so much encouragement and patience. Finally, credit for whatever strengths this study may have goes to all who helped, while blame for its weaknesses is mine alone.

James Walker Trullinger, Jr.

Hue Area

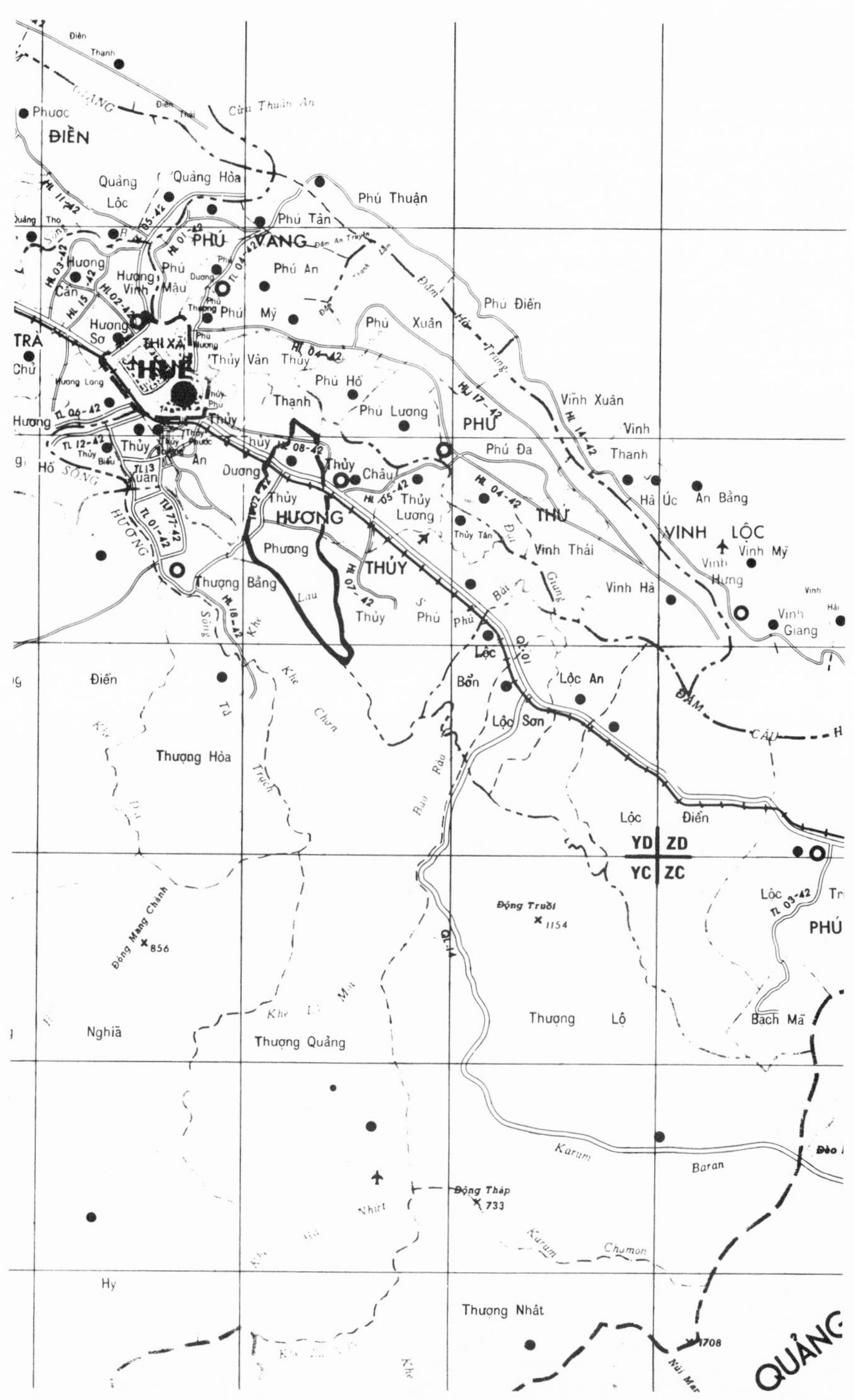

1

The Village

SETTING

The village of My Thuy Phuong (see Figure 1) lies about seven miles southwest of the Central Vietnamese city of Hue. It is in the lowlands between the mountains and sea of Huong Thuy District, in the former Thua Thien Province.[1] The village area is about 10.5 square miles, including extensive ricefields in the eastern section, flat drylands in the center, and rolling, sandy hills in the western area.[2] My Thuy Phuong is bisected by a railroad and by Highway One, a heavily travelled, asphalt, two-lane north-south line of commerce and military supply. French soldiers used to call part of this route "The Street Without Joy." Americans later named it "The Avenue of Horror."

According to 1975 figures, over 7,600 people, all ethnic Vietnamese, live in My Thuy Phuong, and there has been steady population growth over the years.[3] There are about 1,300 separate households, and over 50 percent of the population is under 18 years of age—meaning that the village is demographically young. Population density is greatest in the central area of My Thuy Phuong, near the highway. Along that route, immediately to the north and south, lie two other villages, similar topographically and demographically to My Thuy Phuong. Most homes in the village consist of two or three rooms, and are of cement and wood construction, with metal roofs. Fences or hedgerows surround nearly every home.

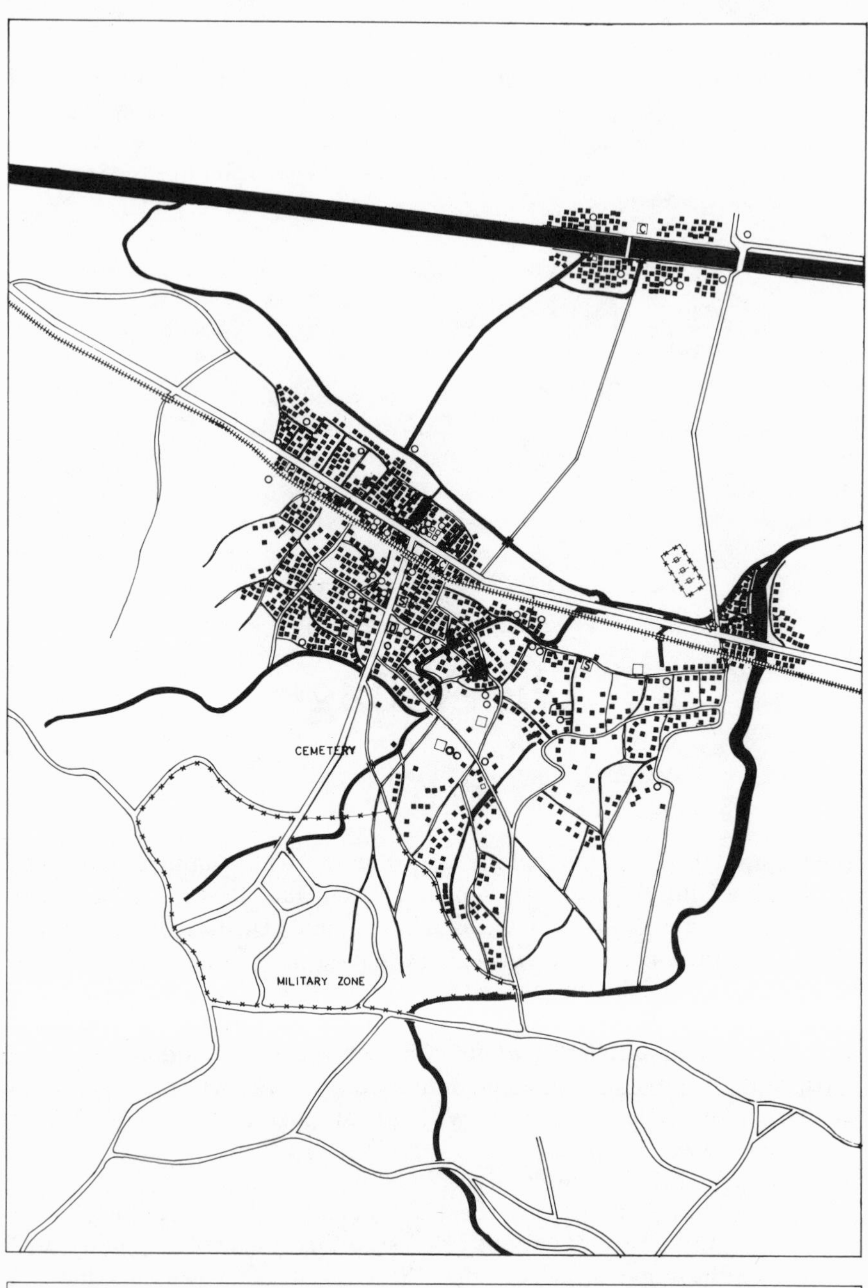
CEMETERY
MILITARY ZONE
HOUSE
SHRINE
GOVT. INSTALLATION
SCHOOL
PAGODA
CHURCH
DISPENSARY
RADIO STATION
RADIO TOWER
MARKET
MỸ - THỦY - PHƯƠNG

Figure 1

My Thuy Phuong's ricefields, about 1,161 acres in total area, are divided into rectangular plots of different sizes by narrow, slippery earthen barriers. These double as walkways. When rice seedlings are ready to transplant, or during harvests, the fields come alive. Hundreds of men and women work long hours, plowing, weeding, spreading fertilizer, worrying about the crop.

Numerous waterways crisscross the fields and wind through the inhabited sections of the village. Small boats carry people along the streams and canals, children play by their banks, and women wash clothes in their water.

Bamboo dips and sways with the breeze along paths that wind through the village's inhabited areas. Most of the paths are of dirt, but one in a low-lying area is completely "paved" with expended American artillery shells. Shade trees are abundant, surrounding homes and shrines, creeping up the low hills in the western part of the village, and making green My Thuy Phuong's predominant color. Only one small part of the village is drab. That is the congested, built-up area near the intersection of the highway and a road that runs southwest through the village. It is dusty, full of barbed wire and other junk of war, and has few shade trees.

In 1974–1975, about 67 percent of the village's total land area was communally held, including about 82 percent of the riceland. As detailed in subsequent chapters, control of communal land has shifted back and forth over the years, but the *amount* of such land has not varied much. This fact sets My Thuy Phuong apart from many other Vietnamese villages, which have seen large reductions in communal land areas.

About 80 percent of My Thuy Phuong's people earned livings from rice cultivation during 1974–1975. For generations, villagers have tilled, planted, fertilized, cultivated, and harvested the ricefields in two annual crops. The spring crop accounts for about 75 percent of total local rice production, and people consider it more delicious than fall rice.[4] Production and taste differences are due mainly to the higher rainfall during the spring growing period. The cool, rainy weather from November through March is more suitable for rice than the scorching days of summer, when the fall crop is growing. Weeding and fertilizing are periodically necessary during both growing cycles—weeding three or four times per cycle, and fertilizing once. The rice production schedule is as follows:

	Spring Crop	**Fall Crop**
Seeding	November	April 15–June
Transplant	December 15–January	May 15–July
Harvest	April 15–May	August 15–October

There are sometimes years when the rains come late, and sometimes there is flooding, but the peasants' routine rarely changes.[5] Most everyone in the village is up before dawn. Then it is to the fields, sometimes behind small flocks of ducks which feed in the canals and rice paddies. The peasants work all day, plowing, weeding, or harvesting. A few break for lunch and rest, but most cannot, and must work through until dark. Wives, children, and friends help out when they can, sometimes singing folk songs such as this one: [6]

> The sun in the east,
> I carry my hat,
> Go to the ricefields,
> Pull up the seedlings,
> They smile in the sun . . .

As the peasants go about their work, they use many traditional tools. For example, one or two peasants at a time sit on a bamboo framework partly shaded by canvas. Their legs move up and down in a regular, rhythmic pattern, like they are peddling a bicycle, and small wooden slats propel in an endless circular motion through a wooden trough. The slats force water uphill through the trough and into the fields. The mechanism is not terribly efficient, but it requires little maintenance, works, and has worked for years.

Water buffalo are among many villagers' most precious possessions. When not needed in the fields, young boys herd them. When peasants need to turn over the soil for a new planting of rice seedlings, their buffalo pull plows for hours through the mud. Sometimes peasants make up songs and sing as they plow:

> Oh buffalo, dear buffalo,
> Are you tired, dear buffalo?
> I will go with you, dear buffalo,
> I will go with you, dear buffalo . . .

My Thuy Phuong's areas of drier, sandier soils support about 104 acres of vegetable gardens, which bring extra income to many families. As with rice cultivation, whole families work together planting, weeding, and picking the vegetables, but only the women are concerned with sale of produce. Sometimes they sit for hours in the crowded local market, a grouping of covered open-air pavilions, just to make the equivalent of 20 or 30 U.S. cents profit for the day.[7]

The village also has about 50 part-time fishermen. Along a wide, deep village stream, huge stationary fish nets mounted on wooden stakes are periodically hoisted by groaning, straining villagers. Men or boys slowly row or pole small boats along the canals, and their hand nets, thrown or dragged, haul in a steady catch of eels and minnows. Occasionally in the nets there are good-sized fish or frogs.

Several hundred others have long worked at nonagricultural jobs. Some are traditional pursuits, and others more recent responses to changing technology or need. For years this group included about 100 people, 25 or 30 of whom were household heads working as officials or soldiers with both of My Thuy Phuong's political forces—in and out of the village. The tasks people performed for the two forces are described in later chapters.

In 1975, about 30 of the very poorest villagers could be seen walking miles every day to the mountains, where they gathered firewood. They cut the wood, tied it with palm leaf strands, and sold the bundles in and outside of My Thuy Phuong for small profits. About 100 of the poorest, including some wood gatherers, hired themselves out as field laborers or for work at odd jobs, earning wages equivalent to about 50 U.S. cents a day. And five to ten others worked in Hue at various heavy labor occupations, such as loading trucks in rice warehouses.

Also in early 1975, a number of tradesmen sold in shops or out of homes, two dealing in rice, one in bottled and canned goods, and four in school supplies. There was one rice wholesaler, who bought from local peasants. Fifteen tailors ran tiny, one-machine sewing operations, making nearly all clothing worn in the village, including uniforms for soldiers. Three families made small dresses and hats of colorful paper, which people bought for symbolic offerings on family altars to the spirits of deceased children.

There was a family that cut and sold large slabs of wood, and three others made cabinets and other furniture. And one enterprising family constructed little yellow tables and stools from discarded wooden ammunition boxes of American manufacture. Villagers sold most of the furniture made in My Thuy Phuong in the markets or to the shops of Hue.

The village also had many who worked at service occupations. A group of carpenters and bricklayers built houses on contract. There were also three rice mills, seven food and drink stalls, three billiard parlors, four barber stands, and a small beauty shop. Four homes took in laundry for soldiers. Two nurses gave injections for small fees, and the village had two midwives. There were four motorcycle repair places. Five three-wheeled Lambretta vehicles, owned by a few families, hauled people to Hue for a charge, and about five men took paying passengers by motorcycle on short trips. Three families had vehicles for trucking cut and uncut firewood to market.

Many of these retail and service operations were small, low-profit businesses, often run simply to augment incomes from other sources, such as rice cultivation. Most families survived by simultaneously working at two or three occupations. For example, one family in 1975 raised vegetables, sewed, and sold soup from a stall next to the family house, in addition to tending its rice paddies.

Now that the war has ended in Vietnam, it is probably a safe assumption that there have been some changes in this village occupational profile, which was made in early 1975. There are probably fewer billiard parlors, fewer gas-consuming vehicles in use, fewer laundries for soldiers, and fewer prosperous tradesmen. Other changes are sure to come in the years ahead. However, it is probably also safe to assume that My Thuy Phuong's economy remains primarily agricultural, that the nonagricultural sector remains diversified, and that most families continue working at several tasks to survive.

Most residents of My Thuy Phuong have a special attachment to Hue, Vietnam's former imperial capital.[8] A deep pride in the Hue region's traditionally important place in the nation is widely shared in the village, from the youngest school children to the most senior of local elders. It is so strong that it seems to cut across political, economic, and social differences. For generations, Vietnam's poets have described the city of Hue, and the meaning it has for most Vietnamese, including people in places like My Thuy Phuong.[9] They have written of its beauty, its charm, and its magic. In Hue, there is the Perfume River, running clear and clean. It winds through the city, flowing from the southwest, passing very near My Thuy Phuong. The hills, such as the famous one called Ngu Binh, are gentle and tall. And the landmarks, like the multitiered Thien Mu Pagoda, or the elaborate tombs of the emperors, are inspirations for many of Hue's people, and for many who live in the countryside: [10]

Romantic Perfume River
    with streets on both banks,
Look at the flow,
    so peaceful, so gentle.
The surface is a mirror,
    reflecting straight banks,
    the crossing bridge . . . .

Poets overflowing with love,
Sing of waiting river,
Blowing wind,
Waiting mountain,
Hanging moss . . .

There is something about the Hue region that most of My Thuy Phuong's people seem to love. Hue gives them a very special identity, and it breeds toughness and resiliency: [11]

. . . The people of Hue,
    are grave and quiet,
Sad when others are happy,
But full of confidence,
    seldom spoken . . .

Nearly every family in the village maintains a small plot of land for the remains of family members. The poorest have simple, round mounds of earth, and some of the more prosperous maintain elaborate cement grave complexes of archways, altars, and protecting walls.[12] Many feel obligated to keep the graves in good condition—weeded, painted, and repaired. Families burn incense at the graves, and arrange annual feasts to honor and remember particularly virtuous ancestors, usually fathers or grandfathers. In addition, many people make offerings to ancestral spirits on three specially designated days each year. Every day men, women, and children may be seen in the graveyards digging, carrying soil, cleaning up. "We are here to make the graves beautiful. We want our ancestors to be proud of us," commented an elderly peasant, who once a week came to the rolling, sandy hills of graves to pull weeds and burn incense at his family plot. "I have to come every week," he said with certainty.

There are countless other physical expressions of commitment and belief, scattered everywhere in My Thuy Phuong—the shrines. Some are old, crumbling structures, in need of repair or paint. But most are in good condition, maintained by families or by local committees and associations which contribute money and labor for their upkeep. Helping coordinate and officiating at many of the ceremonies at the shrines and in village homes is the prestigious local Cult Committee. Its six or seven members were, in 1975, among My Thuy Phuong's most respected men.

On or next to nearly every home in the village are small covered altars of wood, about two feet square, set on platforms, and usually full of offerings of fruit and sweets for the spirits of ancestors and home. Incense perfumes the air around these tiny shrines, to appease the spirits that most villagers believe frequent them. Practically every house also has at least one small indoor altar in the center of the main room. These honor more recently departed relatives and are usually crowded with photographs, incense, porcelain vases of plastic flowers, and offerings of bananas or other fruit.

The larger shrines, which honor hamlets, clans, or family name groupings, are sometimes of quite substantial cement and wooden beam construction, usually with graceful pitched roofs of red tile, which are decorated with Chinese-inspired lotus flowers, lions, and dragons.[13] Long, coiled, bouncing wires hold the dragons' bulging round eyes in place, and pieces of smashed porcelain dishes, stuck in the cement, give a touch of chaotic color to it all. Once or twice a year the shrine associations conduct important celebrations at these places, and people feast.

The most public and frequented of the shrines is a small, drab building of cement blocks called the *dinh,* which is a village meeting hall. My Thuy Phuong has always had a *dinh.* Villagers organize various types of functions there, such as meetings of peasants to plan improvements in the ricefields. They also conduct periodic ceremonies at the *dinh* in honor of the village spirit, or genie.

There is also a shrine in the middle of the ricefields, consisting of four slender supports and a roof. It honors the spirits of the soil and the spirits of rice. A few small trees grow beside it, and birds like to rest in the shade of its roof. The shrine has a volunteer caretaker. Every night someone goes out by boat to clean the simple structure, light a few sticks of incense, and sometimes leave offerings of fruit or other food. Many believe that the incense and the offerings bring good luck and good harvests.

At the base of a tree in the western part of My Thuy Phuong, a sort of banyan, is a small cement and wood shrine—an elaborate box, open in the front. It honors "the spirit of the tree," according to an elderly peasant woman who lives nearby. Every day she picks up fallen leaves around it, and once a week replenishes the oil supply in the tiny glass lamp that constantly burns in the shrine. "If the flame ever goes out," she said, "we will have bad luck."

The village also has tiny shrines by its hills, by many large rocks, and by other trees. One honors the road. Another marks a sort of sand dune, which some think is occupied by "spirits of death." Most of the shrines require some involvement—the burning of incense, placing of offerings, or participation in organized ceremonies or repair projects—and so are living forces in the lives of most villagers. The shrines provide believers with a direct and familiar way to communicate with spirits, and help preserve the logic and balance of forces, natural and supernatural, in their lives.

There is one other place of spiritual importance. That is the An Quang Buddhist pagoda, which in 1974 celebrated its renovation with three days of reconsecration, feasting, and a candle-lighting ceremony. It is actually a large, rambling collection of pavilions and courtyards, over 200 years old, located at the base of a hill near the railroad tracks. Four huge pillars and four lanterns mark the path that leads in from the highway, and trees shade and protect the pagoda from the elements. In early 1975, there were no monks living in the compound, and only occasionally did the monk assigned to Huong Thuy District visit the village, so a group of local elders governed the pagoda. A caretaker living nearby had the task of burning incense, weeding the pagoda gardens, and sweeping the old ritual hall.

In 1974–1975, an organization linked to the pagoda, the Buddhist Family Association, organized camps, hikes, local cleanups, and other activities for children and women. Only a few hundred were actively involved in pagoda affairs, but villagers estimated that as many as 90 percent of the populace identified with Buddhism, supported and came to the pagoda on important occasions such as the 1974 celebration, and sometimes looked to pagoda elders for guidance and leadership. However, most people did not actually describe themselves as Buddhists, but spoke of ancestor veneration as their "religion." And as noted earlier, most were moved to some degree by various animistic beliefs.

TIES TO THE PAST

To most people in My Thuy Phuong, there are events, personalities, and patterns of the far distant past that seem important. Let us briefly survey and discuss some of them in this section.

Nearly all villagers know of Vietnam's most important heroes in the long anti-Chinese struggle, people like the martyred Trung sisters and the strategist/emperor Le Loi.[14] They also know that when the first Vietnamese came to the area of My Thuy Phuong, the Chams were already there. The Chams were an agricultural people of a great and ancient empire that since the second century A.D. had ruled much of what is now Central and South Vietnam.[15] According to a nineteenth century Vietnamese treatise, in 1306, Vietnam's emperor wed his younger sister to the Cham ruler, and was rewarded with a large area of land that extended south from the present city of Hue.[16] The Chams farming there were few, and were edged off the land, including the area that is now My Thuy Phuong, by the more aggressive Vietnamese.

Joseph Buttinger writes that the earliest of those Vietnamese settlers arrived in the fifteenth century, marking the beginning of a southward expansion from the crowded areas of what is now northern Vietnam.[17] The pioneers, who were mostly youngsters and veterans of the imperial army, later sent for parents and others who had stayed behind. Eventually entire families pulled up stakes in the north and settled the My Thuy Phuong region.[18] Official records contain no information at all about village origins, and no one is sure just which section of northern Vietnam to claim as his family's. Most people cannot trace back genealogies beyond four or five generations, after which vagueness and fogginess prevail.[19] Illustrative is this statement by a peasant: "My great-great-great grandfather's father came from somewhere in the north."

Most villagers also understand that the rule of Vietnam's emperors deeply affected life in My Thuy Phuong. In the early days, the village was merely a collection of hamlets, which bore the names Gia Le, Gia Le Thuong, Thanh Lam, Lang Xa, Tho Vuc, Phuong Lam, Dong Hoi, and Loi Nam Gia Le Ha. (See Figure 2.) In 1975, these names remained in popular use. The emperor's court first officially touched the village in the sixteenth century, when it issued a proclamation that incorporated the hamlets into the rapidly expanding empire of Vietnam.

People like those of the My Thuy Phuong area were governed in the old days by local councils of "notables," usually five to ten men of greatest wealth, age, and education in each locality. In My Thuy Phuong itself, the council was chosen by consensus of men on the village rolls. According to Nguyen Khac Vien, the most important council members, and local leaders in their own right, were the scholars, men who aspired to the emperor's exclusive governing group, the mandarinate. But they could not pass the rigorous entrance test, given every three years.[20] The scholars acted as teachers, advisers, and men of ritual, and in many ways grew close to the people.[21] In My Thuy Phuong they taught in four tiny schools of thatched bamboo construction. These schools, totally supported by local contributions, brought a high rate of literacy to the village.[22]

HUE
DANANG
① GỊA - LÊ 1
② GỊA - LÊ 2
③ GỊA - LÊ 3
④ GỊA - LÊ 4
⑤ GỊA - LÊ 5
⑥ GỊA - LÊ - THƯỞNG 6
⑦ LỢI - NAM - GỊA - LÊ - HẠ
⑧ THỞ - VỰC
⑨ ĐÔNG - HỘI
⑩ LANG - XÁ
⑪ PHƯỞNG - LAM
⑫ THANH - LAM
TRADITIONAL HAMLET BOUNDARIES
MỸ - THỦY - PHƯƠNG

Figure 2

One of the major tasks village councils performed was collection of taxes for the emperor. Ngo Vinh Long writes that these amounted, at most, to 6 percent of the annual value of the rice harvests.[23] Other duties of the councils included finding recruits for the imperial army or laborers for public works projects, settling disputes, and distributing land.[24]

The council did not perform these tasks in the belief that all in the village were equal. In fact, My Thuy Phuong's social structure was very hierarchical. Notables were at the top, along with the elderly. Several in My Thuy Phuong confirmed Ellen Hammer's contention that people in such positions in the social order were free of taxation.[25] At a slightly lower level were men of learning and wealthy individuals not on the council. Everyone else was lower, ranked on the basis of landholdings and length of residence in the village. At the very bottom were newcomers to the village with no land.

There is a wide belief in My Thuy Phuong that the traditional council operated more or less *fairly* and *consistently* within the expected bounds of hierarchy. That is, villagers asserted that it never demanded in taxes more than what people, perhaps in patient submission, accepted as obligation. And most important, villagers contended, the council respected and protected everyone's position in the "pecking order," giving residents a feeling of belonging—psychological security.

In 1974, there was a family in My Thuy Phuong which kept a small box labeled *Xua*—"the old days." In the box was a carefully wrapped, crumbling brown piece of paper that was the oldest extant local record. It was a copy of a still older document, and it revealed that in about 1765 the emperor had his eye on one My Thuy Phuong hamlet:

> Two soldiers were transferred to the district to assist in tax collection in Gia Le, which had not paid all of its taxes that year.

This document suggests that something might have been going wrong for the emperor in the village. In fact, not long after the soldiers were sent there to collect taxes, the Vietnamese court faced a serious threat in nearly every corner of the empire. The year was 1773. Beginning in the village of Tay Son, far south of My Thuy Phuong in the province later called Binh Dinh, people rose up.[26] The rebellion spread everywhere, including the My Thuy Phuong area, and military successes destroyed the ruling Nguyen Dynasty and eventually the Trinh Dynasty to the north. A new regime came into being.

But in 1801, that regime fell to Vietnam's legendary unifying emperor, Gia Long. According to Alastair Lamb, Gia Long's victory was primarily based on small but significant amounts of advice, money, and materials supplied by the French, and on loss of peasant involvement in the Tay Son cause.[27] By 1802, this new Nguyen emperor had unified Vietnam, re-created much of the old dynasty, and in 1805 began to build the new capital of Hue. In Central Vietnam, where the Tay Son movement had its deepest roots, the experience left a rich legacy. Many of My Thuy Phuong's people, like those throughout the area, look back to the Tay Son rebellion and draw the conclusion that revolt and revolution are sometimes necessary.

On a more mundane level, many villagers also know that during "the old days," a number of important physical changes came to My Thuy Phuong. Many of the changes are recorded in a nineteenth-century Vietnamese study. First, in about 1815, hundreds of *corvée* laborers dug a canal and dike system.[28] Second, there were bridges. Laborers built these simple structures, of durable wooden construction, where village pathways approached streams and canals.[29] Third, the court directed that a secondary road be built in the village, at a time when a network of such roads grew all over Central Vietnam. Throughout the network lay *trams,* stations in a message-relay system that the court established to carry letters and decrees by horse and runner to different parts of the empire.[30] This was the Vietnamese version of the "pony express." It is unclear precisely when the court established the message-relay system, but the *trams* themselves were built in 1804.[31] My Thuy Phuong's road in the *tram* system cut through the village west into the hills, and to this day people call it "the *tram* road." In about 1835, laborers built three markets, simple covered pavilions, in the My Thuy Phuong hamlets of Thanh Lam, Gia Le, and Lang Xa.[32] Finally, there were improvements to the local schools.

This was where My Thuy Phuong stood in the mid-nineteenth century—physically changing, but at peace. In following chapters attention focuses on what happened in the village during a long test of its people's strength and determination. The test was brought on by the fundamental changes set in motion after white men came to Vietnam, and meant a bloody, devastating confrontation in the village, and throughout the nation, between forces of revolution and repression.

The purpose of this book is to spotlight that confrontation primarily as villagers experienced it—*not* to turn My Thuy Phuong into a testing ground for theories and strategies. In other words, this book is mainly for those who may have seen Vietnam on the 7:00 news and wondered, perhaps more than casually, "What's it like to live through hell?"

NOTES

1. This book is based on a dissertation submitted in 1977 to the Graduate Division of the University of Hawaii in partial fulfillment of the requirements for the doctoral degree in Political Science. Readers interested in examining more complete quotations, notes, and other supporting documentation gathered for the book should see the dissertation, located in and available through the University of Hawaii Library, Honolulu, Hawaii.

luctuations in the value of the piaster. Many villagers, for example, 974's piaster value (about V.N.$700 to U.S.$1) when describing ex- ; or salaries in the 1930s or later decades. In any case, amounts cited agers are stated here, unless other sources contradict and seem more e.

e only available piaster-dollar exchange rates on the free market are as s: (From "Annual Statistical Bulletin," U.S.A.I.D./Vietnam, no. 16, nber, 1973, p. 13; available in East-West Resource Systems Institute y, Honolulu, Hawaii)

Year	Piaster/Dollar
1962	97
1963	97
1964	131
1965	146
1966	180
1967	164
1968	190
1969	223
1970	397
1971	388
1972	439

nam" is the name used in this book to describe the country, although e 1804 numerous names were used—including Nam Viet, Dai Viet, Dai etc.

wo best collections of Hue area poems the author has seen are Thai Van n, *op. cit.*, and Vu Huong, Kieu Khe, Thanh Tung, *Co-Do Hue* (The Capital of Hue) (Hue: Sao Mai, 1971).

g et al., *op. cit.*, p. 35.

m, *op. cit.*, p. 246.

'Tombeaux Annamites dans les Environs de Hue" (Annamite Tombs the Environs of Hue), *Bulletin de la Societe des Etudes Indochinoises*, &2, 1958, pp. 130–134; available in Cornell Library. For an excellent e of information on art and design in the Hue area, including My Thuy ng, see *L'Art a Hue* (Hue Art) (Hanoi: Association des Amis du Vieux undated); the same text is reproduced in *Bulletin des Amis du Vieux* January–March, 1919.

e are three major name groupings in the village. "Nguyen Duy" is the st; next is "Nguyen Dinh;" the smallest is "Nguyen Viet."

ph Buttinger, *Vietnam: A Political History* (New York: Praeger, 1968), 30–31; Nguyen Van Thai & Nguyen Van Mung, *A Short History of Nam* (Saigon: Times Publishing Company, 1958), pp. 22–23.

Buttinger, *op. cit.*, p. 9; Khiem, *op. cit.*, p. 11; and "Dia-Phuong Chi; Thua-Thien" (Local Guide; Thua Thien Province) (Hue: Vietnam In- ation Service, undated), pp. 2–3, manuscript.

i-Nam Nhat-Thong-Chi; Thua-Thien Phu" (General Geography of Dai ; Thua Thien Province) (Saigon: Ministry of Education, 1961), no. 10, p. This is a treatise written between 1864 and 1875 for the emperor named Duc, and contains extremely detailed information on flora, fauna, geo- hic features, cultural attractions, etc., of Thua Thien.)

2. The population of Huong Thuy District in ing to Robert Jones III, formerly of the cember, 1970, there were 738,498 resider including 203,627 in Hue, according to "4 Geographic Directorate, 1971), map. Not other documents from Thua Thien/Hue, i

There are three major soil types in th One, dividing the village, there are prima (the ricefields), and regosols on white and flat. To the west of the highway there are acid rocks, and some white and yellow rolling, with one large hill. [Based on aut Soil Map" (Dalat, Vietnam: National Geo

3. While the village's population has grown in have been recent population shifts in the h here for each of the hamlets. (These figure Jones III.)

Date	Dong Tam (Thanh Lam, Tho Vuc)	Dong Tien (Gia Le 1, 2)
Jan. 1968	3499	3926
Jun. 1968	3499	3926
Dec. 1968	2559	3456
Jun. 1969	2554	3725
Dec. 1969	2559	3926
Nov. 1970	2335	3324
Jan. 1972	2490	3709
Mar. 1974	2700	3517

4. Total rice production figures for the village Thuy District, however, there was a per pea 296 lb., and in 1966 of 323 lb. (These number total paddy production for the district for peasants, taken at 30 percent of the district Phuong peasants reportedly had yields aver [See Vo Luan Han, "Thua Thien Agricultur the Result of Investigations of 411 Thua Thien Joint Development Group, 1967), pp. 11, 18 ernment contract agency, available in Cornel

5. There exists a ten-month record of rainfall i U.S. Army in 1968–1969. See "After Action 17 May–28 February 1969" (Camp Eagle: He Airborne Division, March 5, 1969), p. B–1– Museum, Fort Campbell, Ky.

6. This also appears in Thai Van Khiem, *Co-Do* (Saigon: Ministry of Education, 1960), p. 255.

7. In this book, most Vietnamese piaster amour proximate U.S. dollar equivalents. There is in cause villagers have often forgotten exact pia

wide used pens by vi relia

T follo Dece Libr

8. "Vi bef Nar

9. The Khi Old

10. Hu

11. Kh

12. See Fro no. sou Ph Hu *Hu*

13. Th lar

14. Jos pp *Vie*

15. Se Ti fo

16. "I N 23 Tu gr

17. See Buttinger, *op. cit.*, p. 46.

18. See *ibid.;* also see Frances FitzGerald, *Fire In The Lake: The Vietnamese and the Americans in Vietnam* (New York: Atlantic-Little, Brown, 1972), p. 45.

19. *Cf.* Gerald Hickey, *Village in Viet-Nam* (New Haven: Yale University Press, 1964), pp. 82–91.

20. Nguyen Khac Vien, *Tradition and Revolution in Vietnam* (Berkeley: Indochina Resource Center, 1974), p. 17.

21. *Ibid.*, p. 33.

22. *Ibid.*, p. 25.

23. Ngo Vinh Long, *Before The Revolution: The Vietnamese Peasants Under the French* (Cambridge: M.I.T. Press, 1973), p. 56.

24. For illustrative directives to villages from the Hue court, see *Muc Luc Chau Ban Trieu Nguyen* (Complete Table of Contents Nguyen Dynasty), Tap Thu I, Trieu Gia Long (Part I, Reign of Gia Long) (Hue: Uy-Ban Phien-Dich Su-Lieu Viet-Nam Vien Dai-Hoc Hue, 1960), pp. 4, 11, 18; available in Cornell Library.

25. Ellen Hammer, *Vietnam; Yesterday and Today* (New York: Holt, Rinehart and Winston, 1966), p. 217.

26. Thai & Mung, *op. cit.*, pp. 202–215.

27. Alastair Lamb, *The Mandarin Road to Old Hue: Narratives of Anglo-Vietnamese Diplomacy from the 17th Century to the Eve of the French Conquest* (Hamden, Conn.: Archon Books, 1970), pp. 145, 179–182.

28. "Dai-Nam Nhat-Thong-Chi . . .", p. 62.

29. *Ibid.*, p. 117.

30. *Ibid.*, pp. 103–104.

31. *Ibid.*

32. *Ibid.*, pp. 138, 140. Today in the village there is only one market, of cement and sheet metal construction, along Highway One in the Gia Le area of the village.

2

The Coming of White Man

DIVIDE AND RULE

In the late nineteenth century My Thuy Phuong's people saw their first white men. The French were becoming commercially and militarily active in Central Vietnam, part of their worldwide efforts to gain wealth and influence.

One of the earliest Frenchmen to visit the village was an explorer named Camille Paris. The year was 1885, and Paris was on a mission for the telegraph company. He went by palanquin, a sort of man-borne hammock, to Tourane (now known as Danang). In his journal, Paris wrote of the hamlets in My Thuy Phuong called Gia Le and Thanh Lam: [1]

> . . . October 23, 1885, entrusted with a mission for the telegraph company, I left Hue in a palanquin at three o'clock in the afternoon, accompanied by ten infantrymen commanded by a corporal: Thirty coolies carried my bags and those of the escort. Our little troupe walked sprightly, rifles over the shoulder, ears attentive; the route was less known [then] than today, and one could count in those days the Europeans who had gone that way. Prudence was therefore called for on our part; memories of the Hue incident were still fresh. I forgot about, as being a member of my escort, a mandarin from the citadel.
>
> This functionary appeared very concerned about our promiscuity and [looked] quite prepared to take off at the very first sight of a suspect lance. . . .
>
> At 6:30 we arrived at the village of Ya-Le [Gia Le], chance took us straightaway to the mayor's house. The weapons were immediately piled up, [and] the corporal placed a sentry at the door. . . .

The Annamites ran up from the surrounding areas to see our bivouac and streamed in. We had happened across them fifteen minutes earlier for they had bedded down in the rice paddies. But one of their group showed hospitality; consequently, they had nothing more to fear. It is a parade of pseudo-mayors, of quasi-literates, of so-called mandarins.

As it always came down to, at the risk of mistrusting their intentions, I made them all leave and gave a serious order to the sentinel. . . .

After a troubled night of "mosquitos and preoccupations," Paris and his entourage resumed their journey on the morning of October 24, 1885: [2]

The route is beautiful, shady, bordered with huts surrounded like that of the chief of Ya-Le. The natives take on a well-to-do air, their coats are clean and untorn. They own buffalo and farm yards. After a half-hour's walk, we arrive at Tham-Lam [Thanh Lam], a large village on the Arroyo River that one crosses by ferry. The market, called Cho-Vuc, is situated on the other side. But the ferrymen turned the corner of the alley at our approach and it is one of my coolies who mans the stern-oar.

It is impossible to know why the ferrymen fled. They were perhaps simply startled by the unusual sight of Frenchmen in the village, but there might have been other reasons for their flight. Perhaps they ran in fear, or because of hatred so deep that they wanted no contact of any kind with the Frenchmen.

It is clear only that France, at the time of Paris' procession through the village, was beginning to tighten its grip on the area. Until the late nineteenth century France had viewed Central Vietnam, which colonial administrators called Annam, as an area of little economic potential, not worth concerted commercial efforts or very much French "development" capital. Central Vietnam was poor and remote from the burgeoning commercial center of Saigon, the densely populated Mekong and Red River Deltas, and most of the profitable French plantations, so France at first left it to the mandarins and to its own traditions.

But in 1882, French ships moved on Hanoi and after some fighting defeated the emperor's forces there.[3] The next year a French fleet fired upon Hue, and French troops landed at the emperor's fort near the entrance to the Perfume River. The position quickly changed hands.[4] Out of it all came an 1883 agreement, signed with a group of mandarins in the Hue court, to make the French "protectors" of Central and Northern Vietnam. This was France's carte blanche for years of commercial and military activity in those regions.[5]

In 1885, the Vietnamese reacted. They unsuccessfully attacked the French garrison in Hue, and French troops retaliated by sacking the city. When word of the fighting reached the Central Vietnam populace, people rose up and attacked every French garrison and convoy in the area. Buttinger writes that the rebellion grew, at times reaching "the proportions of a truly national war of liberation." [6] The exiled Emperor Ham

Nghi and a group of his mandarins led the fight, which ended in defeat in 1888.[7] Resistance from then on was mainly under the leadership of scholars, but it too was unsuccessful, ending in 1895.[8]

Though this early resistance to the French ended disastrously for the Vietnamese, many in My Thuy Phuong, even in 1975, spoke proudly of it. And several elderly villagers were able to recite from memory long sections of an epic poem about the resistance, "Fall of the Capital."[9]

To consolidate their position, the French at first installed an emperor, named Dong Khanh, then dominated his successor, Thanh Thai, who was tolerant of the white men and their colonial cause.[10] The arrangement with "their" emperors permitted the French to freely proceed with commercial, cultural, political, and military adventures while they largely preserved the illusion of Vietnamese sovereignty. And then in 1897, the French ended this illusion by replacing the emperor's governing body with a council of ministers, which was headed by a Frenchman. Buttinger writes that "the final blow" came in 1898, when the French took over all tax collection and mandarins at all levels "merely became poorly paid employees of the French."[11]

From then on, according to Ngo Vinh Long, France gradually consolidated its control in Central Vietnam, in the hope that commercial ventures there—such as banks, rice exporting firms, plantations, and retail enterprises of various types—could become at least marginally profitable.[12] But that hope was never realized. French activities in Central Vietnam had to be supported by grants from the Ministry of Colonies and from the southern region, or Cochinchina, budget. People in places like My Thuy Phuong paid and paid, but it was never enough.

Several elderly villagers spoke of the changes brought by colonial rule, especially during the 1920s. People then were so impoverished they could not afford water buffalo. "My father was very poor," said a peasant. "He and my mother, and all of my brothers and sisters had to pull the plow. I had to help too, even when I was very small. In the old days, people did the work of water buffalo."

"We had always had enough to eat," according to another peasant, "but then we got poorer every day. We never bought new clothes, and none of our children could go to school. Everyone had to work. Also, there was no longer enough food." A peasant woman remembered, "Oh, the old days when the French were here were very hard. So many people were hungry, and did not have enough land. Taxes and rent were too high!" "It was very difficult for us," said a peasant. "When it rained everyone would be sick. We did not eat enough. My father did not have enough money for warm clothes or for medicine. Two of my little brothers died."

To understand these complaints, we must examine methods of French rule in the Central Vietnam countryside. Early this century, Hue court mandarins governed the region's villages for the "mother country." During those same decades, however, the French established commercial ventures in Hue and other Central Vietnamese cities, French bureaucrats arrived in considerable numbers, and a resident colonial administration began to grow, assuming more and more functions of government, and encroaching on the traditional village bastions. A French colonial official named Paulin Vial comments on mandarinal rule: [13]

> That is the only system that is compatible with our security, since it divides the natives by recognizing the autonomy of the village, a subject of great concern. The system has been experimentally introduced.
>
> The system has had good results. It gives satisfaction to the Vietnamese, and security to the French authorities, and will not permit the people to unite against us in a general action.

And in 1910, Louis Cury wrote these words on the impact of colonial commercial ventures in the area: [14]

> . . . capital money penetrated further and further into the community, and the equality which existed in the families before our arrival was broken. The democratic Annamite community evolved more and more into a plutocratic state. The social equilibrium . . . therefore changed and new elements . . . [came] . . . to superimpose themselves upon those which formed the older Annamite society.

Many major changes in "social equilibrium" came through the village council. As the colonial apparatus and French commercial involvement grew, the council gradually changed, a fact which had many consequences for nearly everyone.[15] First, the six or eight councilmen gradually became conscious that abuses of their traditionally defined authority would be tolerated by the French, and by the Hue mandarins, who were themselves growing corrupt. According to an elderly peasant, "They saw councilmen in other places getting rich, so they thought, 'Why not me?' "

One or two councilmen who apparently resisted the temptation to abuse their positions resigned from the body, only to be replaced by individuals primarily interested in personal financial advantage. As other councilmen died and retired, the council was gradually filled over the years with four or five of the village's larger landholders, a few prosperous local tradesmen, and others who seemed opportunistic and even more profit oriented than their predecessors.

The French levied heavy taxes on ricelands through the council. People said they paid as much as 20 percent of their harvests' value to the French, the same percentage Ngo Vinh Long says was collected throughout Vietnam.[16] On top of that, they paid a "head tax" for every member of every family.[17]

Several elderly villagers confirmed Ellen Hammer's contention that the French administration imposed taxes based on estimates of the total number of adult men in the village—regardless of their ability to pay. This was a change from the earlier, traditional system, whereby taxes were levied only on those listed on the village rolls.[18] The precolonial council had controlled those rolls, so there had been some defense against taxation. But under the French, the tax burden weighed heavily.

Along with other financial pressures (discussed below) the heavy taxes forced many families to abandon their traditional practices of bartering harvests and only occasionally using money for purchases of family supplies. People began selling crops through local tradesmen to French commercial enterprises, and sometimes borrowed money against anticipated harvests to pay taxes or meet other financial obligations. As monetization of the region's and the village's economies proceeded, a new local class of tradesmen emerged and grew prosperous. Peasants became vulnerable, as never before, to international fluctuations in commodity prices, and profit windfalls for peasants became rarer.

The village council's role in land management also forced many financial adjustments. About 67 percent of the total cultivated area was then communal land.[19] This included about 82 percent of the ricefields and 44 percent of the cultivated drylands. The council traditionally distributed communal land for renting, for periods of two to three years, on the basis of number of children and need in each peasant family. The council divided the land into parcels of about 5000 square meters (or 1.24 acres) called *mau,* and *mau* into units of 10 called *sao*. Traditionally, the council favored larger and poorer families in the distribution system, and few families farmed more than one *mau* of communal land, in addition to whatever land they owned themselves or rented from other individuals.[20] According to several elderly villagers, the council had honestly and fairly performed the land distribution and rent collection tasks for many generations. But as the membership of the council changed in the 1920s and 1930s, its members began renting the choicest and largest parcels of communal land to themselves, or to relatives and friends. And the council rented land to the majority of villagers at a high price. That is, individual councilmen pocketed excessive rents, and demanded bribes for land distribution. Also in the 1920s and 1930s, four or five families represented on or linked to the council pressured small landowners to sell out, and purchased their land at low prices. How this occurred in the 1920s is not clear, but details on such land pressure during the early 1940s are included below—possible clues to what happened in earlier decades.

Further complicating life in My Thuy Phuong, ownership of a few of the larger parcels of land shifted out of the village. For many peasants, rents increased at a far higher rate than income during the early decades of this century, and the few resident and absentee landlords lost some of their old sympathy for tenants, especially in years of bad crops or unexpected expenses. Furthermore, the landlords began cutting back on extra services, such as provision of farm tools to tenants.

Accumulation of the village's limited wealth in the hands of councilmen and their local allies accelerated when the French built up their colonial bureaucracy in Hue during the 1920s and 1930s, and lucrative "understandings" evolved between councilmen and bureaucrats. The council granted the four or five well-to-do families linked to the council large communal land parcels, with bribes to bureaucrats probably involved. And the majority in the village found mounting pressure to pay bribes to councilmen for lower tax assessments and larger communal land allocations. Several elderly peasants recalled that by the mid-1930s bribes became nearly unavoidable.[21] Those same peasants also recalled that family budgets grew strained in the 1920s and 1930s, an assertion supported by Pierre Gourou's research in the Hue area.[22] The peasants indicated, first, that increasing rents, bribes, and taxes forced most families to seek new sources of income. Some became paid field laborers. Others opened small local retail operations, such as soup stalls. And still others sought employment in Hue's shops, warehouses, and other commercial establishments.

Several villagers said that "many" frequently went hungry, almost never bought new clothing, and could not afford repairs to homes or purchases of agricultural tools. These were major changes from earlier decades, when such things were at least occasionally feasible. Tight budgets meant also that moneylenders, some not resident in the village, began to gain in influence, and credit terms tightened. With family budget problems, people who for generations had existed reasonably comfortably and happily at or above the subsistence level in the early decades of this century found themselves slipping below the line. Many then turned to the village's traditional institutions, the groups and individuals that had always before helped them survive. But they sadly found this traditional route transformed by some of the same forces that had touched the local council.

Traditionally, poorer villagers had turned to protecting patron figures in times of need, men almost invariably from higher status positions. Before the French, these were usually local notables, large landholders, or sometimes rich kinfolk. They provided dependent clients with favors and protection, such as loans, use of land, employment, and introductions in exchange for free labor, words of praise to others, and loyalty in local village groupings, such as kinship shrine associations.[23] Here are some examples of such patron-client relationships:

1. Early this century a flash flood devastated My Thuy Phuong's ricefields, which had just been planted. The event pushed many peasant families close to financial insolvency, but all managed to borrow for reseeding from several wealthy men in the area. Eventually, all the families recovered from the flood and repaid the interest-free loans. According to several elderly peasants, the families revered their patrons and for years voluntarily labored on the wealthy men's land at harvest time.

2. During the same period a family fell into debt, owing to the extended illness of the household head and a bad harvest. The family was rescued by a wealthy

neighbor, a member of the village council, who lent them a large supply of rice for sale, barter, and personal consumption. After the family head got back on his feet he repaid the loan in kind, and offered the patron his labor and respect.

3. In about 1910, a peasant got into a dispute over irrigation rights with someone from a neighboring village. He received help from a local councilman he had long assisted at harvest time. The patron introduced him to a powerful district-level official, who listened to the complaint and eventually settled the dispute in the peasant's favor.

These were reassuring relationships, beneficial to patron and client alike. But with the rise of the French bureaucracy and commercial institutions in the 1920s and 1930s, some of that changed. Illustrative are these comments, by a peasant:

> There was a rich family protecting my family for many years. Even before I was born they rented us land very cheaply, and gave us money when we had celebrations, like at Tet. But during the French time they raised the rent so high it was ridiculous. It was sad.

Another peasant recalled that his father suddenly changed his mind about a man he had long respected. "This was a member of the council," the peasant said. "My father had long been his friend, and he lent us rice when we needed it. But then the man said, 'No more. Now you must pay like everyone else.' " A tradesman thought back on the time his father was an influential patron in the village:

> There were many people here who liked to take advantage of my father and grandfather. My family owned much riceland then, and many farming people tried to borrow money and cheaply rent land from my family. For a long time my family did that to help the farming people, but then my father saw that he was losing too much money that way, so he stopped. Then he had to rent out the land like a businessman.

These and other comments suggest that local patron figures, many of whom sat on or were closely linked to the council, saw that their interests lay with the new political and commercial establishment. Despite continued lip service to village traditions, patrons began to abandon their clients and reap large financial gains at clients' expense. By the late 1930s, there were few if any of the original patron-client patterns evident in My Thuy Phuong. The prosperous and influential manipulated village land for profit, corrupted the local dispute resolution process, profited hugely on rice bought and sold in the village, lent at high interest rates, and exploited rather than helped peasants through contacts outside village boundaries. Precisely how they did these things is a topic of Chapter 3.

During the early decades of this century, the other side of the coin for most people was that local self-help groups found efforts less and less fruitful. The changes in these essentially redistributive welfare groups may be explained by the French-imposed drain of resources out of the village and by the natural process of population growth. There was simply too little to redistribute, and too many who needed it.[24] Three examples follow:

1. There had long been four or five credit pools in My Thuy Phuong. Each of these consisted of about 10 families which pooled small sums and lent them at low interest and for short periods within the group. But during the 1920s, financial pressure meant that most families lacked extra funds and could no longer afford these credit contributions. Most of the pools went out of existence.
2. Voluntary groups linked to the local Buddhist pagoda had long helped care for the aged and infirm. But early in this century dwindling contributions and lack of volunteers forced cutbacks in these activities—at the very time many families were beginning to feel critical needs for such assistance.
3. Several elderly villagers commented that as financial pressure worsened during the 1920s, less money circulated within extended families, and people gave less financial help to kin beyond nuclear family circles. Despite this, kinship ties remained strong, so of all the self-help practices in the village those within kin groups were about the last to be affected by changing economic and political conditions.

Another important change brought by colonial rule related to education of village children. Prior to the 1930s, several small schools had operated in My Thuy Phuong, supported by local contributions. But as family budgets tightened, contributions fell off, and village councilmen—most of whose children studied in Hue—seemed to lose interest in the schools. During the 1930s the schools closed, and most children had to depend on preoccupied, illiterate or barely literate parents for whatever education they received.

In summary, the early decades of this century were disastrous for most of My Thuy Phuong's residents, who had subsisted for generations in a world of production, tradition, and dependence. The changes brought by the French colonial regime forced upon them adjustments that were both far-reaching and, under France, irreversible. For decades the people endured it all, clinging to all they had left—weakened local traditions, families, and a hope that things would somehow improve.

FIVE MEN

It was in a milieu of dissatisfaction that a revolutionary movement emerged in My Thuy Phuong. A few of the village's most elderly residents remembered that at first hardly anyone dared openly criticize the colonial regime, or bring complaints to the village council. In fact, during the 1930s there were only five or six occasions when people brought complaints about land manipulation and other abuses by procolonial neighbors before the council. In every such instance, councilmen dismissed the complaints, and complainants often suffered reprisals—such as eviction from rented land, rent increases, or even detention on false charges by colonial police. Sensing that recourse to official channels was futile, most everyone grew quiet, for that was the safer course.

But despite the general quiet of the 1930s, there was some whispered criticism. People identified the chief critics as five men, of varied backgrounds and interests. Gradually, during several years of conversations and developing friendships, these individuals together, and perhaps at first unwittingly, laid the groundwork for the day when a revolutionary movement would emerge in My Thuy Phuong.

The most distinguished of the five men was Nghi, who in the late 1930s was about 50 years old and who was a member of the prestigious Cult Committee, mentioned in Chapter 1. Nghi was a tradesman who operated a tiny shop in one room of his home near the market. He had never attended school but had been taught in the closing years of the nineteenth century by an elderly man, a traditional scholar, who tutored a small number of children in his home.

Another of the five men was Thi, who at the time was about 35 or 40 years old. Thi served as a low-paid clerk in the French provincial offices in Hue, and every day commuted by bicycle from My Thuy Phuong into the city. In the village, his family farmed a small plot of land, lived in a small, simple wooden house, and had very few material possessions. People remembered that Thi was well educated, and as one peasant said, "always full of opinions on everything."

They also recalled a third man, who in the late 1930s was considerably younger than either Nghi or Thi. This was Minh, then about 30, who was the son of one of the village's larger landholders. Minh was somewhat estranged from his father, and for some reason rejected his father's wishes that he behave as a subservient son, loyal to the large landholding class. Minh had received some schooling, perhaps at a private school in Hue. He was good-humored and, in the words of a peasant related to him, "frighteningly intelligent."

Villagers described Minh in terms of a contrast between father and son. One elderly peasant said, "His father was a typical rich man, and did not care much about the people. But the son was completely different. He seemed to be interested in the poor people, and always had ideas about how poor people could live better." Minh left home in his mid-twenties, married, and found work as a tradesman in Hue and the village area. He bought and sold local produce, moving from one market to another to take advantage of price variation. In his travels Minh developed friendships in many other villages, and became aware that his home village's economic and social problems were not unique.

The next of the five was Truong, who owned about three *mau* of riceland, and farmed it with the help of his several sons. In the late 1930s,

Truong was about 40 years of age, and was a middle-level peasant in terms of income and landholdings. He was illiterate, but maintained a lively interest in current affairs, and reveled in the long, rambling conversations that he sought out and often dominated in the village. Many remembered Truong's inquiring mind and quick sense of humor.

Finally among the five men was Tu, about 40 years old in the late 1930s. He too was a peasant, cultivating about one or two *mau* of communal riceland. People remembered Tu because of his association with the above four individuals, and also because of his active role in maintenance of the Buddhist pagoda and organization of celebrations and ceremonies both there and at one or two local shrines. Tu had never attended school, but like Truong had been tutored by a local scholar. Tu spent most of his energy working the fields, but all of his free time went to the pagoda, to the shrines, and to the conversations and friendships with the other four men.

Usually the conversations among the five men were after dark, when work was done, and when gatherings were not as obvious to the unfriendly eyes of colonial security agents. The men met over small glasses of rice wine, beer, or tea. They all gathered as frequently as possible, but often only two or three could come. Those who attended passed on opinions and reactions to those who could not or dared not attend. A peasant described the conversations among the five:

> First they talked about the problems and difficulties of life—like taxes, land problems, and corruption among local authorities. They talked about their own personal problems, their families' problems. But that was not all! After a little while they also talked about the village, then later about problems outside this place. They talked so much, and after much talk they clearly understood all about the Westerners. They knew what France was doing in our fatherland. They understood why Westerners were here.

In other words, the five spoke at first of mutual frustrations, and of how life had gradually become more difficult in the village. They spoke of most of their own families' difficulties—of lost income, reduced economic opportunities, and personal tragedies. It was not long, however, before this personal focus gave way to "larger" issues. Slowly, the plights of the village, region, and the nation became subjects of conversation. According to people who recalled those discussions, they were exciting, horizon-expanding experiences for the participants. "Those five men kept talking about bigger and bigger matters," said a tradesman. "The more they talked, the more interested they became in important political matters."

Joining the men in some of their conversations, often merely as listeners, were many men, women, and children. One peasant, who as a child was present for some of the conversations, recalled the exchange of new ideas:

Everyone knew that there were people in our village who were beginning to criticize the Government, and everybody knew that it was dangerous. But we were glad that somebody was doing it. It gave some of the people hope just to think that some people cared about their problems.

At the time, most villagers remained preoccupied with the daily struggle for subsistence. However, many were seemingly fascinated by first-, second-, and third-hand reports of the five men's conversations. A peasant recalled the local mood in the late 1930s:

> Many people heard new ideas against the Government. These were matters that were very dangerous at the time. We knew that a few people were passing ideas, and talking about what was going to be done to oppose the French. We also began to hear about movements in other parts of the country, but we did not know very much. We had a small idea that things were beginning to change, and everybody was happy that change was coming.

Another peasant commented, "It was an exciting time. It was exciting because people were actually speaking criticism against the French. Although they did not do it too loudly, they were speaking, and people were beginning to listen. And to agree." There are indications that the early discussions came under the scrutiny of local colonial security forces. On one occasion in about 1939, police arrested Minh and Truong, and took them to a police compound in Hue. There the police held them at the Thua Phu provincial prison for five or six months. When finally freed, they returned home, where many viewed them as heroes.

To better understand local reactions to Minh, Truong, and the other three men, it is useful to know what ordinary people looked for in local leaders, and how they saw themselves as followers. So let us briefly digress and examine comments made by villagers in 1974 and 1975 on leaders and followers, reflecting views which, many suggested, had not appreciably changed for decades.

According to a peasant, "A leader is a man who is honest, and who must be well educated, and close to the people. He must have qualities that we admire, and he must be strong." Another peasant added, "I only admire leaders who are men of purpose. Their purpose must be to serve the people, and they must do it in a way that helps the people. They must be honest, and they must try to get the support of the people." Still another peasant spoke: "The leader must be a man who is educated but who does not act like he is a king. He must be a man we can respect for many reasons." The image of the traditional mandarin was distasteful to many villagers. A tradesman said, "There was nothing good about the mandarins. These were usually men who were selfish and stupid. We want leaders who are good people, and who work only for the people, and who are not corrupt."

Another tradesman stated:

Too many of our leaders act like kings. They are simply stupid. They think we are stupid and simple, and think we do not see how corrupt they are in front of us. They are men who are not dedicated to the people. The leader must be a good man, and must act in a strong way only for the people.

And a peasant spoke of leaders and followers:

We will support programs that help us, and we will support a government that has good programs and leaders. Most important, we think, are the leaders. How can we support a government that is led by bad men?

A young soldier had this comment:

Why do we follow a political party or a government? We do it because we think it is best for us, but we also do it because the leaders are good. Leaders are very important in Vietnam. Without good leaders in every position in the government, the government cannot be good.

And according to a teacher:

The Vietnamese people always look for good leaders, because we feel that a government with good leaders must be a good one. We also feel that a government with bad leaders is a bad government. I do not mean only the leaders in Saigon. I mean leaders in the provinces, in the army, and even in the villages. Without good leaders a government cannot succeed.

If these and other comments from 1974–1975 are indeed as applicable to earlier decades as villagers suggested, we might conclude that traditional leaders were competent, had just, good purposes in their lives, lived guided by those purposes and yet remained sensitive to others, discrete, and humble. Leaders were also intelligent, and had common sense and courage of conviction. People combined all of these characteristics in a traditional concept called *uy tin,* which we might view as a Vietnamese combination of prestige, charisma, *chutzpa,* and *raison d'etre.* In general, villagers far preferred men of *uy tin* as leaders. The comments quoted above and in later chapters also suggest that people enthusiastically followed such men, but only when doing so seemed to serve individual, family, and community interests.

Note that villagers often described the five early critics of colonial rule as men of *uy tin.* They seemed to naturally attract followers by their intelligence, personal abilities, and actions.

PARTY CELL

The five men had for years been aware of a shadowy organization which was trying to mount resistance throughout Indochina to the colonial regime. This was the Indochinese Communist Party, or I.C.P.

According to published Vietnamese accounts, throughout the 1930s the Thua Thien/Hue branch of the party actively endeavored to organize both urban and rural residents against the French. It set up 16 party cells in the area. According to a Hanoi publication, 500 members of underground youth and women's organizations and trade unions supported 76 active I.C.P. members, there were a number of anti-French student and peasant demonstrations, and the party began to circulate several small newspapers it published in the area.[25] Some elderly villagers and Hue residents confirmed that there were indeed some such party activities at the time, but suggested that they came sporadically. Newspapers, for example, were irregular in publication.

During 1936–1939, the I.C.P. belonged to an umbrella organization of anticolonial groups, the Indochinese Democratic Front. According to Hue residents, the Front never had much political impact in the Thua Thien/Hue area, primarily because barriers of distrust divided its members, making coordinated political actions difficult to accomplish. In My Thuy Phuong, the Democratic Front had no discernable impact at all, for people recall nothing of it, and the five local leaders rarely if ever spoke of it.

It was in about 1939 that the I.C.P. first touched the village. Some party pamphlets and newspapers reached the hands of the five men. The materials took a Marxist-Leninist perspective, focusing on class warfare and imperialism, describing other successful revolutionary movements, and calling for such a movement in Vietnam. At first, the men kept the literature among themselves, passing it back and forth, reading it, and thinking about it. Then they began to meet covertly to discuss the ideas in the literature.

At about the same time the men were beginning to study the tenets of Marxism-Leninism, one or two I.C.P. members visited the village. People were not sure who those men were or exactly when it was in the late 1930s that they first appeared. One peasant suggested that perhaps they were related to someone in the area, or worked with some villager, such as Thi, the French civil servant. Another peasant stated that Minh and Truong were the ones who first brought I.C.P. organizers to My Thuy Phuong—men they had met in prison. Others confirmed that Minh and Truong had indeed become acquainted with party members while imprisoned, but were unsure whether this contact led to the first visit of Communists to the village. It is clear only that after the party members visited My Thuy Phuong, the five men became associated with the party. Minh actually became an I.C.P. member; the other four did not officially join, but began to support the party just as actively as Minh.

Beginning in about 1939 or 1940, the five men began to receive publications and very general guidance from the I.C.P. They began to draw inspiration from party pamphlets, especially those about revolution and the French, quoting from them first among themselves, and then to their neighbors. Gradually the five men became more and more involved in the workings of the I.C.P. Their contacts with party members in Hue and in other villages near My Thuy Phuong became frequent, and the party selected one of them, Minh, to attend special training meetings, organized covertly in Hue. The meetings, according to villagers who knew Minh well, focused first on ideological matters—Marxist-Leninist tactics and I.C.P. positions. But of most immediate importance to the village, the party trained Minh in Communist organizational techniques. When he completed the I.C.P. training, Minh and his four closest friends began to organize for revolution in My Thuy Phuong.

Their first step was to establish a party cell in the village. The cell was, in effect, a formalization of the five men's position as emerging revolutionary leaders, for they were its members.[26] Many years later, one of the five men told two friends that the five had considered themselves equals within the cell, but that Minh had served as chief contact man with district and provincial I.C.P. organizations.

Each cell in Thua Thien Province operated independently, although the party occasionally assisted and loosely coordinated all cells. That is, I.C.P. leaders at provincial level occasionally passed general messages to the cells, including printed materials for political discussions and guidelines on organizational techniques. However, more explicit I.C.P. influence over its My Thuy Phuong followers was difficult, according to villagers' brief comments, owing to the party's own organizational problems in Thua Thien/Hue. It suffered pressure from colonial security agencies. Many I.C.P. members in the province had personal and ideological weaknesses. And many throughout the area were suspicious of the party.

My Thuy Phuong's cell members, with but general tactical guidance and help with printed materials from higher I.C.P. levels, undertook an organizational effort in the village. The cell became a proselyting unit, focusing on individual members' families, friendships, and contacts. In the years 1939 through about 1942, the cell members sparked a large-scale duplication of the same phenomenon that had initially drawn them to the party.

Villagers illustrated the I.C.P. proselyting strategy during that period by describing one cell member's activities. That individual was Truong, the middle-level peasant. Proselyting targets were two men Truong knew well, neighbors who were peasants. According to a peasant related to one of the targets:

> My uncle was a very good friend of that man [Truong]. They were neighbors, and had grown up together as boys, so my uncle trusted him like a brother. I don't know how they became involved at first, but I do remember my uncle used to say that before he understood politics he trusted only that man [Truong]. So it was because they were friends that my uncle followed.

Gradually, Truong acquainted his two companions with the ideals and programs of the party, educating them first on the realities before their eyes. The peasant just quoted had this additional comment:

> My uncle used to come home and tell us, first, about some of the bad things happening here, about the people being slaves of the French. He only talked about this local place, and some of the things that were important to all of us. Later, he understood what was happening in all of Vietnam, and understood the bad things the French were doing all over the country.

The peasant's term "bad things" referred to excessive local rents and taxes, councilmen's land manipulation, and corruption. It also meant the majority's growing impoverishment and loss of influence in local affairs.

In effect, Truong guided his two fellow villagers in rapidly grasping and accepting I.C.P. positions and tactics. He did so in almost the same step-by-step, gentle fashion that he had himself experienced, beginning with a focus on subsistence problems—or "life and death" issues.

NOTES

1. H. Cosserat, "La Route Mandarine de Tourane a Hue" (The Mandarin Route From Tourane to Hue), *Bulletin des Amis du Vieux Hue,* January–March, 1920, pp. 67–69. Note that in many of the French, Vietnamese, and American documents quoted in this book there appear occasional spelling and grammatical errors. While the author recognizes that such errors are distracting, so is frequent use of the expression *sic.* The errors are thus included without comment.
2. *Ibid.*
3. Joseph Buttinger, *Vietnam: A Dragon Embattled* (New York: Praeger, 1967), p. 1202.
4. Auguste A. Thomazi, *La Conquete de l'Indochine* (Paris: Payot, 1934), pp. 162–163, 165–166; available in Cornell Library.
5. For a summary of terms of the 1883 agreement, see *ibid.,* p. 166. The text of the agreement is included in Georges Taboulet, ed., *La Geste Francaise en Indochine* (Paris: A. Maisonneuve, 1955–1956), pp. 807–809; available in Cornell Library.
6. Buttinger, *op. cit.,* p. 127.
7. *Ibid.,* p. 128.
8. *Ibid.,* pp. 128–130.
9. See Nguyen Khac Vien, ed., *Vietnamese Studies,* Hanoi, no. 23, p. 428; hereafter, issues of this journal are cited as "Vien, no. 23," "Vien, no. 37," etc.; none of the issues is dated.
10. Buttinger, *op. cit.,* pp. 440–441, n. 22.
11. *Ibid.,* p. 15.
12. Long, *Before The Revolution,* p. 102.
13. Quoted (without indication of original source) in Toan Anh, *Lang Xom Viet-Nam* (Vietnamese Villages) (Saigon: Phuong Quynh, 1968), p. 107.

14. Louis Cury, *La Societe Annamite; Les Lettres—Les Mandarins—Le Peuple* (Annamite Society; Letters—Mandarins—People) (Paris: Faculte de Droit de L'Universite de Paris, Jouve & Co., 1910), p. 108.

15. See Anh, *op. cit.*, pp. 95–97, 116–119.

16. The most comprehensive study in English of the French impact is Long, *op. cit.* (see pp. 67–68). An excellent Vietnamese language source is Pham Cao Duong, *Thuc-Trang Cua Gioi Nong-Dan Viet-Nam Duoi Thoi Phap Thuoc* (The Situation of Vietnamese Peasants Under the French Period) (Saigon: Khai Tri, 1967); available in Cornell Library. Also see Samuel Popkin, "Corporatism and Colonialism; the Political Economy of Rural Change in Vietnam," *Comparative Politics*, April, 1976, pp. 431–464.

17. See Long, *op. cit.*, pp. 63–64.

18. See Hammer, *Vietnam: Yesterday and Today*, p. 115.

19. See Nguyen Van Vinh, *Les Reformes Agraires au Viet-Nam* (Agrarian Reforms in Vietnam) (France: Librairie Universitaire Uystpruyst, 1961), p. 34. Also note that in 1974–1975 the amount and use of communal land in the village was about the same as in the 1930s, despite the trend in some other areas involving transformation of communal land into private plots.

20. According to villagers, distribution also varied with soil quality. Each *sao* was divided into 10 parts, and councilmen distributed the land under complicated formulae. In determining family size, only those over 15 years of age were counted. Determinations of family wealth were apparently much more subjective; there was no set formula. A family of 10 (all over 15) would be rented about one or two *mau*. Each of the village's three major name groupings was also given a parcel of land (several *mau* each, at most), so people could also rent from this source.

21. See Long, *op. cit.*, pp. 68–71 for a general discussion of local corruption.

22. See Pierre Gourou, *L'Utilisation du Sol en Indochine Francaise* (Soil Utilization in French Indochina) (Paris: Centre d'Etudes de Politique Etrangere, Travaux des groupes d'Etudes, Paul Hartman, 1940), pp. 412–414.

23. See Phuong, Tran, et al., *Cach Mang Ruong-Dat o Viet-Nam* (Land Revolution in Vietnam) (Hanoi: Nha Xuat-Ban Khoa-Hoc Xa-Hoi Viet-Nam, 1968), pp. 9–48; available in Cornell Library.

24. *Cf.* Long, *op. cit.*, pp. 92–97.

25. Vien, no. 37, pp. 50–54.

26. People asserted that all five men belonged to the cell, despite the fact that only one of them was actually a party member—a puzzling assertion, and possible indication of the I.C.P.'s lack of influence in the province during the 1930s.

3

Rule and Revolution

BUILDING THE VIET MINH

Dissatisfaction and occasional agitation turned into organized resistance in 1941. That was the year the anticolonial Viet Minh organization emerged in My Thuy Phuong and elsewhere.[1]

These are the words of a peasant who at age 15 began to help the Viet Minh:

> When did I follow the Viet Minh? Oh, that was when my father told me to join him. He said, "Son, it is your duty to come with me." I didn't know for sure what he meant, but I went with him because he was my father. That's the way it is in Vietnam. The family is very important.

Others told similar stories, suggesting that family ties attracted many in My Thuy Phuong to the revolutionary movement. Another peasant recalled:

> My uncle helped start the Viet Minh in this area, and he came to us first. We respected him, so listened carefully to him. I didn't know about politics, but everyone in our family always had respected him, so my mother and father didn't stop me when I went with my uncle. After a year or two, my father came too!

Reflecting on the colonial regime and the Viet Minh, still another peasant looked back:

> Many people here used to be protected by rich relatives or big men in the village. But that was a long time ago. Under the French that became very difficult. . . . Some of us [later] became very loyal to some of the Viet Minh leaders. These were men who could not help us with money too much, because these were men who were poor. But they could help us with opinions, and as friends, and we went to them for guidance and help.

Several others commented on changing political attitudes in the village. According to a small tradesman, "For many years the people had no power. But with the Viet Minh the people began to see their own strength." A peasant stated, "The big men always controlled everything. We were sometimes very afraid of them. But we saw that begin to change when the Viet Minh began to become active. We saw how afraid they were of the Viet Minh and of the poor people who followed the Viet Minh."

Another small tradesman recalled:

> Slowly we began to understand everything better. But first of all we studied our local area. We saw how the French used the village chief and the rich people to get richer. We saw that the French did only bad things in the village. We saw how the rich, who liked the French, had more land, and we saw how the poor were exploited.

Members of My Thuy Phuong's I.C.P. cell took the lead in organizing the Viet Minh. They tried to attract men of prestige and influence to anticolonial ranks.

One early supporter was a local small tradesman, widely respected because people considered his prices fair, and because he served on the Cult Committee and was active in pagoda affairs. The tradesman said he joined the Viet Minh because he "hated the French," and through his friendship with Thi, one of the five men described in Chapter 2. He remembered:

> I felt that my love of country had to come before any selfish desire for money, so I joined the Viet Minh. There were so many people who joined for the same reason. Many of us knew that there were Communists in the Viet Minh, but the Viet Minh was not a Communist organization. If it was Communist, then there were too many of us who did not like Communism who were members.

Thi invited the tradesman to join the local Liberation Committee, the small group which set Viet Minh policy for the community.[2] The tradesman shared in decisions about political meetings, leaflets, and other Viet Minh activities. Several others became local Viet Minh leaders. Included were three young men from prosperous families. "These young men were very idealistic," according to a peasant. "They worried about the future of our country, and said that they were joining the Viet Minh to fight for a free and independent Viet Nam." The three began to spend long periods away from their families, assumed humble, softspoken manners, and visited homes of young people to recruit for the Viet Minh struggle. Through such visits, and despite their wealthy origins, the three became well known and popular in the village, and their evident nationalism and devotion to the Viet Minh cause inspired many young people. The example—and the *uy tin*—of the three attracted many to the movement.

As the local Viet Minh leadership group began to take shape in 1942, the party cell members welcomed into leadership positions three or four others who might have been expected to support the pro-Japanese colonial administration, but who did not. Included among these converts were three colonial civil servants, two of whom were village councilmen. Prior to the formation of the Viet Minh, I.C.P. followers regarded such men as enemies, but between 1942 and 1945 local Communists welcomed all who opposed colonial rule to Viet Minh ranks.

The civil servants' ties to the Viet Minh were of necessity covert, as they continued working in their official positions. One among them, who worked in a colonial office in Hue, took advantage of his position to gather intelligence on French and Japanese activities. The two sympathizers on the village council did likewise. All these individuals helped set Viet Minh policy for the village, sharing with most other Viet Minh members a deep and burning feeling of nationalism. A peasant close to the local leaders indicated that ideological differences separated the leaders, but such differences never really surfaced: [3]

> The Communist [Party] cadres during that time did not talk much about Communist ideas of socialism. They only said, "We are all nationalists. We must unite to fight the French." They did not want to frighten the people. But, you know, they never forgot their Communist ideas.

To the peasant, "Communist ideas" referred partly to concepts from class analysis and imperialist theory that the local leaders had learned through early study of I.C.P. pamphlets and newspapers—such as calls for a socialist revolution and worldwide struggle against imperialism. Other "Communist ideas" related to land redistribution and reform of the village council. Before 1945, all of these concepts were soft-pedalled in My Thuy Phuong as the Viet Minh reached out for broad support.

BURDEN OF EMPIRE

"They had to be servants of the French, and who respects such people?" These were the words of a peasant who was discussing local councilmen. During the 1940s, most of the councilmen came from *the same families* which had grown influential during the 1930s. They represented only about 3 to 5 percent of My Thuy Phuong's people. And it was mainly the profit motive that brought them to the council. Another peasant recalled, "Councilmen did nothing except take our money and get rich." Still another peasant said, "They always looked down on us and took advantage. Only bad men and stupid men wanted to be councilmen. The good men would not do it."

During the 1940s, the growing dependence of councilmen on the central bureaucracy was obvious to many in the village. "Who were these men?" asked a tradesman. "They certainly were not Vietnamese," he answered, "even though they looked like us. But they were not Frenchmen either. They were both, but they were neither." To understand these complaints concerning the village council, it is necessary first to focus briefly on activities of the French administration which collaborated with the Japanese in Vietnam during 1940–1945. Beginning in about 1942, control over villages tightened, part of Japan's efforts—administered by the French collaborators—to tap Vietnam's human and natural resources for the war effort. During those years, My Thuy Phuong residents had to pay higher taxes, give a larger percentage of rice harvests for outright governmental use, and provide conscripts to labor on construction projects, such as fortifications or roads. According to villagers, some conscripts perished. In addition, inflation devastated the local economy, clothing was in short supply, and food shortages developed.

The colonial bureaucracy also set specific requirements for village council elections and qualifications for candidacy. Beginning in 1942, people elected members of My Thuy Phuong's council from lists of candidates approved by the bureaucracy. The authorities did not permit men insufficiently "in touch" with governmental policies for the area to stand for election, and often required bribes of approved candidates. According to Toan Anh, the authorities also began to appoint all village chiefs.[4] Villagers indicated that this practice continued until 1945—when colonial authorities again permitted people to select their own chiefs, but only from lists of approved candidates. Finally, the authorities usually removed or sometimes even arrested World War II-era councilmen and village chiefs who differed too dramatically with governmental policies.

Through the 1940s, a central issue in My Thuy Phuong related to land. As noted in Chapter 2, during the early decades of this century, communal and privately owned land became vulnerable to unfair manipulation by those who served on the village council. More such manipulation occurred after 1940. First, there was corruption in the collection of taxes on the village's major product of the land—rice. Councilmen pocketed a portion, occasionally as much as 5 or 10 percent, of local rice tax revenues.[5] They did so with little fear of censure or prosecution by colonial bureaucrats, who apparently tolerated such practices as one of the necessary costs or "evils" of empire. Possibly they even shared in the taxes.

Many councilmen continued after 1940 to award larger parcels of communal land to themselves, or to relatives and friends, for renting.

Others simply took more than their fair share. Where one or two *mau* might have been due them under the traditional formula, councilmen sometimes took ten or more *mau*. There are no land records remaining to verify these allegations about land abuse, but several estimated that after 1940 and continuing until 1954, 90 percent of My Thuy Phuong's peasants were "poor," cultivating 40 to 50 percent of the communal and privately owned land, in plots averaging one *mau* or less. Roughly 8 or 9 percent were more prosperous "middle peasants," with about 10 percent of the land and larger plots. And about 1 or 2 percent were "rich owners," cultivating about 30 to 40 percent of the land in parcels of many *mau*.[6]

As in the 1920s and 1930s, corruption of the village's traditional land system meant that people who for generations had depended upon communal lands to bring in extra money no longer had that income.[7] Peasants asserted that rents rose on communal and privately owned land, from an estimated 1920s level equivalent to about one-twentieth the value of the harvest to a figure after 1940 sometimes reaching one-fifth harvest value. In making these post-1940 estimates, peasants included calculations to reflect the higher bribes required to rent communal land. However, note that various scholars offer far higher figures for colonial-era taxes.[8] To make matters worse, after 1940 the village council more often than not settled land disputes in favor of councilmen and their relatives and friends. Extra income and additional influence in the village thus flowed to the small procolonial group.

Members of the colonial *Sûreté,* policemen assigned to Huong Thuy District, enforced decisions of councilmen and other governmental authorities. Usually one or two policemen worked in the district at a time, and over the years about ten rotated through Huong Thuy police assignments. In the village, these policemen wielded considerable influence. With the help of councilmen, they collected taxes, and could charge individuals with crimes, arrest, and detain. They could also draw upon police personnel assigned elsewhere for assistance in the village, and they occasionally did so.

A peasant recalled:

> The policeman came around with the landlords to force us to pay the rent. Once we had a very bad flood, and the crop was lost, but the policeman came anyway. He said that if we didn't pay he would arrest us, or take the land and rent it to someone else.

Another peasant claimed that he was arrested when he could produce no money for rent of his ricefields:

> I was held for a week in the [village] office. They made me sit in the corner, and my family had to bring me potatoes to eat. Finally, my son borrowed some money from friends, and they let me go. But I had to give the policeman some money for himself, even after I paid the rent.

Local policemen were arbitrary and cruel in collection of taxes, and in forcing compliance with governmental decrees. A few former landlords and officials of the colonial apparatus hinted at landlord-police cooperation, and many people were sure it existed, although no one could prove allegations that it did. However, it does seem likely that the enthusiasm policemen evidently had for their work grew out of some form of self-interest. Even without illegal monetary rewards, policemen learned that promotion, power, and prestige within the colonial bureaucracy accrued when they effectively performed assigned tasks. Like councilmen, they learned that the bureaucracy permitted those who helped manage colonial affairs in the village to reap ample rewards. Most were evidently dedicated to the colonial apparatus.

Such dedication and involvement extended beyond a handful of policemen and councilmen. There were a number of others in and of the village who supported the colonial cause. Among them were five or six large landholders, each of whom owned up to about 30 *mau* of riceland. They were not excessively wealthy, but certainly much more prosperous than the vast majority of their neighbors. Most of them lived in substantial homes, ate and dressed well, and often sent their children to private Hue schools. Most of the large landholders were also members of or closely tied to the village council, through which they found support for manipulation of land.

Peasants described an instance of land manipulation from the 1940s which illustrates how such manipulation occurred during the *entire* period from the 1930s to the 1950s. The peasants recalled how two or three large landholders, with adjacent pieces of land, decided in about 1944 to cooperate in a move to increase holdings of ricefields. To do this, they abandoned their long-standing practice of permitting freedom of movement along paths that wound across their fields. For many decades, the large landholding families had permitted other families to reach their own smaller parcels of land by these routes, and they could herd water buffalo through for plowing. But that year the large landholders, who actually had sharecroppers working their land, erected barriers by the paths. They effectively fenced out those who worked land on the "interior."

As people recalled it, there were loud protests by peasants of the then restricted zone, who filed brief written appeals with the village council. But as the protesting peasants probably expected, the council upheld the large owners' right to control movement along the paths, and directed the police to arrest and fine trespassers. The effect of the fences and of the council rulings was extreme. There was immediately further impoverishment of the small landholders and their tenants, about 10 percent of My Thuy Phuong's residents. Later, the inevitable occurred. The small owners sold out at low prices to the large landholders. Then they returned to their land, but only as tenants, and *their* former tenants became sharecroppers under them or the large landholders.

Most large tradesmen, who bought and sold products and supplies in the village, during the 1940s joined the large landholders in supporting the colonial apparatus. Several of them actually resided in the village, and others lived in Hue or nearby villages. However, all of them had ties to the commercial and governmental institutions of Hue, all found support in those institutions for money-making activities, and all reaped considerable profits from the peasants of My Thuy Phuong. These were profits *after* deduction of the various colonial market taxes and license fees.

As indicated in Chapter 2, by the 1920s and 1930s the tax and rent burden had become onerous for the peasants, and the tradesmen sensed an opportunity. They began to manipulate the price of rice and other products of the land. In the 1940s, this manipulation by large tradesmen continued. There is little mystery to the tradesmen's *modus operandi,* for to maximize profits they simply relied upon supply-demand fluctuations for products such as rice. Moreover, they depended upon peasants' lack of knowledge of and access to alternative, nonlocal commercial channels. When prices were high, they sold existing stocks through commercial outlets in Hue. When harvests were in and abundant supply drove prices down, they replenished stocks through large purchases.

There were other large tradesmen who operated in My Thuy Phuong. One man, who lived in the village, sold fertilizer to the peasants. He too waited until the demand for the product was greatest, and sold it at substantially inflated prices. Even a few of the smaller tradesmen reached for excessive profits, such as those who sold necessary household items. They also set high prices whenever possible. One small tradesman, for example, raised the price of patent medicines to extremely high levels during one particularly severe rainy season in the 1940s, when influenza was sweeping the village.

Among those closely aligned with the colonial apparatus in and around My Thuy Phuong after 1940 were, finally, the moneylenders. As noted in Chapter 2, these individuals became active when traditional patrons and self-help lending institutions failed to save villagers from increasing financial burdens. Without exception, the moneylenders did not live in the village, but came from Hue or adjacent villages. Among them were a few Chinese. Like the rice and fertilizer dealers, they preferred to operate when peasants were most pressed by debts and had little cash, such as during the long months between harvests, when savings usually dwindled and incomes fell off.

Few of these individuals actually went around to the peasants, but waited at home for the needy to come to them. The amounts they lent varied widely—sometimes enough to pay a few months' overdue rent, or for purchase of land, equipment, or even water buffalo. The moneylenders, according to villagers, were unconcerned with where the money went, but only that people repaid them, and with substantial interest. Monthly interest averaged 12 or 15 percent of the original amount borrowed, so profits for the lenders were enormous.

Through the 1930s and into the 1940s, village councilmen, large landholders, prosperous tradesmen, and other members of the procolonial group grew more aware than in preceding decades of shared economic and social interests. And awareness of common political interests emerged as well. As illustrated above, cooperation among members of the procolonial group became common, taking the forms of collusion in tax and rent collection and resolution of land disputes, of price fixing, and of selective law enforcement. Complementing these financial "partnerships," friendships among such villagers grew.

Ties between members of the procolonial group also assumed a cultural dimension. Western ideas that appeared with the colonialists deeply affected many of the village councilmen, tradesmen, and large landholders. Several studied at French-curriculum schools in Hue or elsewhere, and found themselves attracted to "modern" ideas they encountered in classes, in French books, and in occasional meetings with Westernized, urban Vietnamese. Many became convinced that Western culture was superior to Vietnam's, and that those who reflected Western culture were inherently superior to those who did not. They accepted, in other words, most of the premises of France's *mission civilisatrice*—its "civilizing mission."

A former rice dealer named Nghi, who in 1974 was 65 years old and living in Hue, illustrates the background, lifestyle, and type of thinking that motivated most members of the procolonial group. Nghi's early years were spent in a variety of French-supported schools, where teachers employed French language for instruction. He studied the French classics and European history, but learned very little about his own country's literature or history. Nghi worked for many years for his family's rice firm, which though based in Hue, bought exclusively in My Thuy Phuong and other nearby villages. He knew the village well, and several of his closest friends were village councilmen.

Nghi traveled occasionally to Saigon and Hanoi to meet with representatives of other firms. "When I visited those cities, I was very impressed with the efficiency of the French," he said. "They were very modern, and better than the Vietnamese." Slowly, Nghi grew convinced of the superiority of practically everything French over Vietnamese practices, products, and institutions. "French culture and history is so much higher than Vietnam's," he said. "That's why I have always wanted to go to Europe. We Vietnamese are very undeveloped in the cultural area, you know, even though Vietnam does have a few good poets and musicians."

The tradesman's fascination with Western culture led him to furnish his house in what he considered a Western "vogue." Light weight, vinyl-covered furniture of what approximated Western design cluttered the main room of his house. A large clock, which he said was "beautiful with the furniture," and other treasured momentos—a radio, a table cigarette lighter, a few small French language books, and an empty cognac bottle—were on display in a glass-fronted case in that room. Next to the case was a small refrigerator, unplugged, with a blue plastic doily on top.

But much more important than home furnishings and general cultural preferences is Nghi's attitude—which he said has never changed—toward the rural people of his country. "The people need strong leadership," he said. "They do not understand business and must be told how to save money and spend it wisely." And what of the West? "I learned that European culture is superior to Vietnamese culture," Nghi recalled. "It is modern, but it always depends on a small number of highly educated men to lead the poor, and to help them understand modern things."

EVE OF REVOLUTION

World War II gave the Viet Minh valuable time to lay more groundwork for revolution.

My Thuy Phuong fit the pattern seen throughout the province and other parts of Vietnam.[9] Insurgent leaders at provincial level passed instructions for various types of actions to the village branch. Usually such instructions came in secret written messages or by word of mouth, and were very general in nature—such as "increase recruiting efforts" or "heighten political efforts among the people." This left great flexibility to local movement leaders. These were the five men associated with the I.C.P., the tradesman, the three young men, and the three colonial civil servants. The leaders discussed and collectively interpreted instructions from above. However, sometimes they ignored instructions, depending upon prevailing conditions in the village. If police operations were frequent, for example, they did not "heighten political efforts."

During World War II, only about 5 percent of My Thuy Phuong's people, mainly prosperous villagers, supported the central government. But there was also a small number of financially hard-pressed people included in the 5 percent. The regime or its prosperous supporters *paid* such needy villagers for loyalty and services to the council, police, and individual families. Another 15 to 25 percent of the people were during World War II committed to neither central government nor Viet Minh. These were mainly apolitical peasants—individuals very concerned with subsistence problems, but hesitant to look for political solutions to them. Such avoidance of politics meant that the uncommitted were often vulnerable to pressures from both the local procolonial group and the Viet Minh, a fact which eventually prompted many to make commitments, usually to the revolution. Finally, during the World War II years 70 to 80 percent of My Thuy Phuong's people supported the Viet Minh. About 50 percent of such people were very firm, active supporters. They frequently attended Viet Minh meetings. The other 50 percent consisted of passive supporters, less likely to participate in local Viet Minh activities, but still generally supportive of the Viet Minh cause.

To spark interest during 1940 to 1945, the Viet Minh circulated leaflets and newspapers, organized political meetings, and tapped informal local communication channels. The leaflets, newspapers, and political meetings focused almost without exception on colonial rule, and on the twin themes of injustice and independence. They identified the Viet Minh with the Allied objectives of defeating Japan and Germany. The leaflets and newspapers were usually printed on flimsy, inexpensive paper, sometimes on the backs of sheets already used for other purposes, but were nevertheless popular. They were so popular, in fact, that many of My Thuy Phuong's illiterate had relatives or friends read the materials to them. There are available no Viet Minh leaflets or newspapers previously circulated in My Thuy Phuong, but people recalled two specific leaflets. One was two pages in length, and listed a number of anticolonial actions in different parts of Vietnam "to support the Allied struggle." The other was a one-page discussion of Vietnam's long struggle against Chinese domination, drawing parallels with the anti-French struggle.

The meetings organized during the early Viet Minh years were of two types: formal and informal. The formal meetings were less common, chiefly because of the presence in the village of a variety of threatening security agents. But when they occurred, they were at night. Groups of as many as 50 villagers gathered in local shrines or other public places. People heard of the meetings through friends, neighbors, or relatives. Viet Minh leaders usually organized the meetings hastily, to lessen the chances of colonial police finding out and stopping them. Over the years before 1945–1946, there were five or six large meetings, only one of which was disrupted by police.

Typically, a local Viet Minh leader chaired the meetings. They began with a series of introductory remarks on subjects of national or regional interest. Usually after the general remarks, there were questions and answers and informal discussion on local and national issues. A tradesman said:

> Sometimes people who came to the meetings did not seem to understand the discussions about politics, or the leaders' speeches about politics, so during the discussion period we tried to explain some of those matters. You must remember that very few of the people then could read or write, so their knowledge about the world was not very high, and sometimes their questions were about very simple matters. We always tried to answer if someone asked a question like that, because we knew that it was not that person's fault that he did not know.

Sometimes in the discussion phase of these meetings people raised specific questions about the Viet Minh. According to a peasant who attended many of the meetings, "The people would ask about what the Viet Minh was going to do about the Japanese, for example, or what the Viet Minh hoped to do about taxation. There were many questions the Viet Minh cadres could not answer." Other questions posed by people during the meetings concerned possible Viet Minh responses to corruption by village councilmen, excessive rents, and price manipulation by large tradesmen in the area.

The meetings stimulated informal political discussions everywhere in My Thuy Phuong. A peasant woman commented on the mood of the village as the movement began to gain strength:

> Everybody was talking all the time about the Viet Minh. In the market we usually knew who to trust, so we would give those women little opinions about the Viet Minh. We had to be careful, because sometimes the police might hear, so we never said that we agreed with those ideas, and we never said that we liked the Viet Minh. We only said, "This is a new idea, and it is different, something new. What do you think about it?"

The "new ideas" discussed in the market and elsewhere involved such matters as local land distribution, corruption of the village council, and France's economic exploitation of the entire nation. One of the village's Viet Minh organizers asserted that insurgent strength increased slowly in the early 1940s:

> It was like the people were waiting for an answer. When they heard the new ideas of revolution, they thought to themselves, "This is a good thing. This will get rid of the French, and mean independence and democracy and a better life for us." The people were thinking those things, and speaking. First they just thought to themselves, then spoke more and more, and finally it was very free and open. Nearly everybody supported us, and the government men knew that everyone was against them. They did not dare do anything about it.

A teacher, who during that period was a student in Hue, often visited his parents in My Thuy Phuong. He remembered the mood of the village. "It happened in about one or two years," he said. "The Viet Minh suddenly became very strong and very popular. They had almost everyone on their side. It was very exciting."

The Viet Minh organizers built on this excitement, letting it feed on itself. Many were receptive to Viet Minh ideas, and with that the local leaders' boldness and confidence grew. And as the pro-Japanese colonial regime increased its pressure for taxes and conscripts, the Viet Minh simply gained ground. Among its more popular acts were those connected with the "Storm The Rice Stocks, Relieve The Famine" campaign of early 1945. While My Thuy Phuong villagers did not participate, many other Viet Minh branches in the region seized rice warehouses and redistributed rice to families hardest hit by a severe famine.[10] A peasant commented on the mood of his village on the very eve of revolution, 1944–1945:

> We knew the war was coming to an end, and we knew the Japanese were going to be defeated by the Americans. We were also sure that the Americans would not let the French come back to Vietnam. We were all hopeful that Vietnam would be independent soon.

A peasant woman said:

> I was a little girl at the time. But I can still remember how much everyone liked the Viet Minh. In my family, my mother and sisters and I spent our time late at night making little Viet Minh flags. We worked on them together. We sewed all the red flags with the yellow star, because we knew that the people would want them to celebrate the Viet Minh victory. And we were pretty sure that the Viet Minh was going to take over the country.

The Viet Minh appeals, especially early appeals focusing on subsistence issues, psychologically prepared many to demand radical solutions to the local social and economic difficulties created by decades of colonial rule. But there are indications that during World War II My Thuy Phuong's few I.C.P. members and other more radical Viet Minh leaders deemphasized such demands to concentrate on nationalistic, anti-Fascist appeals. These came in meetings, pamphlets, and through conversations among friends and neighbors. Such appeals attracted people of varied political persuasions to the Viet Minh's broad nationalistic umbrella. In fact, some joined who otherwise felt threatened by calls for redistribution of social and economic power.

During World War II, the Viet Minh movement thus went further than the French colonial regime had ever gone toward creation of a strong political force in the village. As noted above, during the war years about 70 to 80 percent of My Thuy Phuong's people supported the Viet Minh cause—a reflection of similar strength throughout the entire area.

NEW COURSE

For the Viet Minh, a major change came with the end of the war. The Japanese surrendered on August 15, 1945. After that event, the Viet Minh moved boldly. It proclaimed independence, established Hanoi as the capital of the new Democratic Republic of Vietnam, and named Ho Chi Minh President. In the days after the Japanese surrender, the Viet Minh took over My Thuy Phuong and other rural parts of Thua Thien Province.[11] People recalled that it was on about August 18 that local Viet Minh leaders set up a temporary People's Committee in the village.[12] Somewhat later, the Viet Minh set up a provincial revolutionary committee in Hue.[13]

In My Thuy Phuong, according to a peasant, "Everyone took a holiday for a few days when Hue was liberated by the Viet Minh. Everyone tried to go into the city to see how beautiful everything was with the new Viet Minh flag." A small tradesman recalled that all the schools were closed in celebration, saying, "Our teachers were so happy. They told us we must go out to celebrate our independence day. They said that when we are old men we will remember this day, and we must remember it as a day of celebration, not as a day of studying." Many in the village, however, continued to work in the ricefields and vegetable gardens, and at other professions. Foremost among those who stayed at work were the local Viet Minh leaders. One of them said:

> We were very happy, but we were also full of worries. We knew that we were going to be very tired in the next few years, because the revolutionary government had very little money, and the people expected us to do many of the same things the French had done. We knew we had to set up a revolutionary administration, and we knew that it would require hard work.

The 1945 backdrop against which the local movement leaders began to operate must be elucidated. With the end of the war, there began a period of extensive diplomatic maneuvering, involving the Viet Minh, France, Japan, Britain, Chinese Kuomintang forces, and America. Japanese forces remained in Vietnam waiting to surrender; France insisted on a reassertion of its claim to Indochina; the British, Americans, and Chinese played minor roles; and the Viet Minh attempted to hold onto the country it had won. As Vietnam's future was being negotiated between France and the Viet Minh, and as the Viet Minh began emasculation of rival political groups, the Nationalist and Dai Viet Parties, a Viet Minh government emerged.[14]

In the village, among the first Viet Minh acts after the declaration of independence was to organize several large meetings in and around the *dinh,* the communal hall. Nearly every man, woman, and child willingly attended these gatherings, which were marked by speeches by local Viet Minh leaders, attempts to explain what had happened in Vietnam, and evocations of what one colonial-era councilman called "a cooperative spirit."

At the first of these meetings Viet Minh leaders also announced that villagers soon would choose a new local ruling body, the People's Village Assembly, and should begin thinking about personnel choices for that body. At subsequent meetings, the leaders outlined assembly electoral procedures. They required villagers interested in assuming the 20 or so assembly positions to submit their names to the temporary committee. When election day came, villagers discovered that the only candidates were incumbent "temporary" council members and those who had been active in or openly sympathetic to the Viet Minh cause. The local authorities seemed to honestly administer the balloting and vote count. The resultant assembly in turn chose a five-to-six member Village Administrative Committee from its members. Those selected for this key executive body were My Thuy Phuong's most important Viet Minh leaders. Several in the village described the assembly and its administrative committee in quite positive terms. For example, a peasant said, "It was one of the most popular councils we ever had."

One of the reasons for that popularity was that a number of prestigious unelected individuals, such as members of the Cult Committee, regularly sat in on assembly meetings as *ex officio* members. The new assembly's and administrative committee's chief function was to widely popularize revolutionary government policies. A peasant recalled:

> The assembly was sort of like the old councils, because it was not too free, and took orders from the higher levels. But its orders were to help the people, so we

all supported it. It was better than the old councils because it was very democratic. People could talk and discuss very many matters.

This comment was typical of several others, and suggests that the principle of democratic centralism—wide-ranging discussion on policies set at higher levels to build consensus on those policies—marked assembly and administrative committee deliberations.

It was not long before the Viet Minh began to set a new course for the village. Directives from higher revolutionary government levels reached the village during 1945–1946, reflecting the new government's interest in supporting village assemblies as both symbols and the substance of its authority in the countryside.[15] However, local Viet Minh leaders had to depend almost entirely on indigenous resources as they began governing. "All the Viet Minh government had was the support of the people and new ideas," commented a peasant. "At that time the Viet Minh had no money, and did not know how to administer programs, so their problems were very large."

In the first open Viet Minh village meeting, the leaders outlined in general terms the program they hoped to follow. According to a tradesman, "They told the people that the Viet Minh government was a government of the people, and that sacrifice was needed. They said that all the people must unite to support the government." A man who was a councilman during the late 1940s recalled, "The Viet Minh said their program was for continuing revolution." The new administrative committee moved immediately to encourage wide participation in local affairs. As implied above, local leaders especially encouraged discussion among village assemblymen during assembly proceedings. Large village meetings, open to all, came as often as twice weekly, and also became forums for participation, where Viet Minh leaders encouraged open discussion.

The new government organs operated for only one and one-half years before being forced into exile. During their brief period of operation, there were no acts of reprisal against former Viet Minh enemies. But the local Viet Minh structure attempted to spark significant local social and economic changes. Here are the main accomplishments of the 1945–1946 government:

1. There were adjustments in local land tenure practices. The assembly lowered rents it considered excessive, and redistributed communal land overconcentrated in the hands of certain families. It gave landless peasants first priority in the redistribution, followed by peasants with little land, and full-time village Viet Minh activists with little land of their own. However, the rent adjustment and the redistributions were not as extreme as some might have wished, possibly a function of what villagers described as the local leaders' desire to attract wide support, even from former opponents.[16]

   Some of the local land tenure changes came at the recommendation of a Farmers' Committee of about five peasants, formed by the village assembly. This cell-like functional group, which several described as "popular" and "active," helped involve peasants in local revolutionary government affairs.[17]

2. Reform of the tax structure was more drastic. The village's Viet Minh leaders received word that the new government had abolished the head tax and taxes on small landholdings, moves that were quite popular.[18]

3. The new authorities endeavored to control area moneylenders. District and village-level officials attempted to regulate interest rates. One peasant recalled that the authorities set annual interest ceilings of about 30 percent on amounts borrowed from private individuals. Others noted that at one point in 1946 the local assembly actually began making small, low-interest loans to the neediest.

4. The Viet Minh attempted to control corruption. "I remember one time the Viet Minh found a cadre who had been corrupt," said a peasant. "They made him confess in front of all the people and say he was sorry. Everyone knew that no cadre dared be corrupt." Some villagers differed on the nature of Viet Minh rule during this period, but none disagreed that the anticorruption efforts were effective and popular.

5. Finally, My Thuy Phuong's assemblymen organized the young people, through a local committee similar to that of the peasants. One peasant recalled:

   > At that time I was about 15 years old. I remember that they organized many young people in the area. We had political study meetings, and participated in demonstrations for the revolution. There were also occasions to sing and hear speeches. But the most important activity was in education. Many young people taught children who were not in school, and some young people taught adults how to read. There were many free classes at that time, and the Viet Minh let the young people do all the organizing and teaching.

With the few exceptions noted above, people's comments on these revolutionary programs were brief. According to a peasant, "The people liked the Viet Minh government very much, because it was honest." A small tradesman said, "Everyone supported the Viet Minh at that time. Everyone liked to have a democratic government." And a peasant stated, "That was the best administration we ever had here. It was a short time, but many people were happy to support the Viet Minh. The Viet Minh was close to the people."

NOTES

1. For background on the Viet Minh, see Buttinger, *Vietnam: A Dragon*.
2. The term "Liberation Committee" was used during the World War II period.
3. Others stated that Viet Minh messages also emphasized anti-Japanese ideas.
4. Anh, *Lang Xom,* pp. 116–119.
5. Taxes collected for the French were of several types. There were real estate taxes, taxes on products of the land, and a "head tax" and *corvée* tax on residents. See Paul Cordier, *Notions d'Administration Indochinoise* (Indochinese Administrative Notions) (Hanoi: Imprimerie d'Extreme Orient,

6. *Cf.* Yves Henry, *Economie Agricole de l'Indochine* (Indochina's Agricultural Economy) (Hanoi: Gouvernement General, 1932), quoted in Long, *op. cit.*, p. 27. In 1952–1953, the colonial government reported that in Central Vietnam (Annam) 53 percent of the families were landless, and 47 percent had some land (see Vinh, *Les Reformes*, p. 45).

7. The most comprehensive studies in English on the French impact are Long, *op. cit.*, and Truong Chinh & Vo Nguyen Giap, "The Peasant Question (1937–1938)" (Ithaca: Southeast Asia Program, Department of Asian Studies, Cornell University, January, 1974), data paper no. 94.

8. See, for example, Anh, *op. cit.*

9. *Cf. Hue Anh-Dung Kien-Cuong* (Heroic and Strong Hue) (Hanoi: Ban Lien-Lac Dong-Huong Thanh-Pho Hue, 1971), p. 27.

10. *Cf.* Tran Van Dinh, "The Vietnam People's Army," *Indochina Chronicle*, (Berkeley) no. 31, February 28, 1974, p. 9.

11. See Truong Chinh, "Mot So Van-De ve Cach-Mang Thang Tam" (A Number of Problems Concerning the August Revolution), *Hoc-Tap* (Study-Practice), September, 1963; a North Vietnamese publication, quoted in *ibid.*

12. A committee at district level supervised the village committees; above it was the provincial committee. Also see John McAlister, *Vietnam: The Origins of Revolution* (New York: Knopf, 1969), pp. 264–265.

13. See Vien, no. 37, pp. 60–61; also see "Thirty Years of Struggle of the Party" (Hanoi: Democratic Republic of Vietnam, undated), p. 95, cited in McAlister, *op. cit.*, p. 193.

14. See Buttinger, *Vietnam: A Political History*, pp. 218–271; also see Douglas Pike, *Vietcong: The Organization and Techniques of the National Liberation Front of South Vietnam* (Cambridge: M.I.T. Press, 1966), pp. 43–46.

15. The Viet Minh's national policy toward village councils is described in Anh, *op. cit.*, p. 121; also see McAlister, *op. cit.*, pp. 265–266.

16. *Cf.* Buttinger, *Vietnam: A Political History*, p. 233.

17. *Cf.* McAlister, *op. cit.*, pp. 263–264.

18. See Buttinger, *ibid.*

4

Battle

UNDERGROUND

A protracted colonial reassertion in Thua Thien/Hue began in March, 1946, when 750 French soldiers and a large number of French civilians arrived in Hue.[1] The Frenchmen had come to "relieve" Kuomintang forces, which were there to arrange for the surrender of Japanese forces. During long months of indecisive French-Viet Minh negotiation, the French gradually and with difficulty usurped the Viet Minh regime's *formal* authority in Thua Thien/Hue, replacing it first with their own, and later with a royalist administration they completely dominated.[2]

By late 1946, the Viet Minh provincial administration was in "exile," from which it directed revolutionary activities in Thua Thien/Hue, retaining much *informal* authority within the populace.[3] This was a strategic retreat, a Viet Minh attempt to avoid an immediate fight with French security forces, and a way of preparing for battle. The same pattern held for My Thuy Phuong. By late 1946 or early 1947, the Viet Minh assembly was no more, and the administrative committee for the village was underground. Aboveground was an eight-member council, composed chiefly of villagers sympathetic to the colonial cause. The Viet Minh administrative committee became, in effect, the guiding organ for anti-French activities in the village, and people called it The Resistance Committee.[4]

The colonial reassertion was fraught with difficulties, owing to widespread anti-French sentiment. So it depended upon outright force. That meant many thousands of American-equipped French troops appeared in Central Vietnam after 1946.[5] Augmenting them were African Foreign Legionnaires and Vietnamese soldiers serving in French ranks. There had long been colonial troops in Thua Thien/Hue, based in small garrisons near the mouth of the Perfume River and in the emperor's walled citadel. But after 1946, the French military presence in the area increased substantially, as did the French commitment to training Vietnamese "volunteers." [6] The French constructed a military installation near Hue, and colonial units based elsewhere in Vietnam undertook operations in the area. From the late 1940s until 1954, there were extensive colonial military operations in the region, such as sweeps in the coastal lowlands north of Hue, near Highway One—Bernard Fall's "Street Without Joy" area.[7] And military operations even occurred in and around My Thuy Phuong.

According to villagers and others who had knowledge of French military activities, the operations came periodically to the village. Those were joint operations by French troops, non-French Legionnaires, Vietnamese soldiers, and colonial police. More often, French troops passed through the village in supply convoys or on their way to battle elsewhere. And occasionally soldiers on leave visited. A woman had this memory:

> Bastille Day was the day we feared most, because the French and Africans always got very drunk to celebrate. I was in school then, and our teacher made the boys escort the girls home. Sometimes the Frenchmen tried to rape the girls, so we had to be very careful.

In the face of colonial pressure in the village and elsewhere in the area, provincial Viet Minh leaders began to plan their battle. In 1945, they had not been ready to fight the colonialists. But in 1946–1947, the situation was different. On March 25, 1947, the Viet Minh organized a provincial conference of resistance cadres, which some Viet Minh leaders from the village probably attended. After the conference, the Viet Minh issued a document that summarized the anti-French strategy. It resolves: [8]

> To continue the armed resistance, resolutely fight the rural puppet authorities and traitors, strengthen the people's confidence in the Government, the Party and the national resistance following the line: a long resistance of all the people in all fields.
>
> To step up production, practice thrift, conceal food and belongings, establish resistance bases for a long struggle.
>
> The cadres of various levels should go back to their bases, return to the plains, and cling to the population; holding firmly to the resistance bases.
>
> To consolidate the leadership of the Party, the Front, the administration, simplify organization, maintain steady communication in order to guarantee the effectiveness of the directives, decisions and policies issued.
>
> To reorganize the army, militia, guerrilla units, security services, restore military activities within a short time, put the accent on guerrilla warfare while creating conditions favorable to mobile warfare.

The Viet Minh battle strategy, in other words, was to have essentially two phases. First, the Viet Minh was to continue efforts to broaden and deepen loyalty to the movement. Second, and complementing the first phase, the Viet Minh was to mount a direct assault against the local colonial apparatus, involving noncooperation with the colonial authorities and steadily mounting military pressure against French forces. The direct assault actually began in the province before the March, 1947 conference—in the early morning hours of December 20, 1946.[9]

People described the first phase of the Viet Minh battle plan as it affected My Thuy Phuong—the Viet Minh attempts to win their political allegiance. A peasant stated:

> The Viet Minh were very clever at propaganda. They kept telling us many, many times that they were going to win, and that victory would soon be theirs, and would be a victory of all the people. We heard this from our friends and neighbors, and from everyone.

Others also indicated that anti-French messages came again and again in Viet Minh leaflets and discussions, most of which people believed and accepted. Especially popular were those that focused on high French taxes, corruption, and land distribution. Such "subsistence messages," however, were overshadowed by nationalistic, anti-French appeals—which aimed at broadening the Viet Minh's base of support in the village.

There were also continued Viet Minh political meetings. Because of the danger of informers, the open community meetings that had marked the 1945–1946 independence period were no longer possible. Instead, two or three times weekly the Viet Minh organized smaller meetings, similar to those of the period 1939–1941. On one or two occasions, police swept into the village to break up gatherings, sometimes arresting Viet Minh leaders. Despite the dangers, the meetings persisted. And meetings became more interesting as the years went on. That is, local leaders became more adept at delivering speeches and organizing discussions, and higher Viet Minh echelons provided better written and more detailed "study materials."

As noted earlier, the second phase of the Viet Minh battle strategy partly involved a noncooperation movement. Here targets were the *same* procolonial villagers and the *same* types of local abuses and inequities that had been so oppressive in earlier years. Under colonial police and military protection, the small minority again grew ascendant, at least in an economic sense.

Through meetings and informal contacts, Viet Minh leaders focused on people's relationships with the French-supported village council, colonial tax collectors, and recruiters for the colonial army. "Nobody wanted to help the French," remembered a peasant woman. "Nobody wanted to support the rich men in this place. Nobody wanted to pay taxes. So what we did was pay as little money as possible." Another peasant added, "The Viet Minh did not have to force us to do this. None of us wanted to help the French." Viet Minh followers thus withheld cooperation from the colonial apparatus, except when absolutely unavoidable.

Paralleling the noncooperation movement was a concerted Viet Minh effort to discredit those who cooperated with the colonial regime. The Viet Minh accomplished much of that in the political meetings, which on occasion aired specific local complaints against specific individuals, usually men of local authority or wealth, such as large landholders, local military officers, or influential councilmen. There is also some evidence that the Viet Minh employed rumors to discredit procolonial individuals and others regarded as possible opponents. For example, in the late 1940s, the Viet Minh began a specific denunciation campaign aimed at the colonial police. According to a peasant, "They attacked a policeman by name, and said he was a cruel agent, a puppet of the French, and that he was corrupt. They said that he had had his own mother arrested, killed, because she criticized him." The policeman's mother had indeed died very suddenly and unexpectedly, so some in My Thuy Phuong believed the rumor.

DIRECT ATTACK

The most important part of the Viet Minh attack was the military effort. In the village that effort consisted primarily of small guerrilla operations which slowly intensified over the years. Villagers said that "several" from My Thuy Phuong departed for duty in the main force Vietnam People's Army, but for most people the military struggle was in the village itself.

What eventually became a highly effective guerrilla force began as a group of people interested in causing the French some trouble. The guerrilla force originated in about 1945, when the Viet Minh village committee responded to a directive from the provincial command ordering establishment of a village-level "defense force." [10] Several peasants emerged as the backbone of that new local force. Those men, who had little knowledge of weapons or of military tactics, went into the jungles of Thua Thien Province for about a month of intensive training, presumably with guerrilla teachers. The men, in turn, attempted to convey what they had learned to others in the village, and slowly built a local force of about 20 full-time guerrillas and "many" part-time armed supporters. In addition, hundreds of unarmed men, women, and children over the years assisted guerrilla activities as runners, lookouts, and providers of food and hiding places. A tradesman, whose father was a poor peasant in the 1940s, stated:

> When I was only 10 or 11, I remember how exciting it was to join them. All of my friends and many relatives were fighting, and I wanted to go. But they had a

rule. They said that you had to be so big to be a guerrilla, so if you reached a certain measurement on their bamboo pole they said you could go. I was so afraid I was too short, but I was lucky. I was tall enough.

Others confirmed that the Viet Minh set high standards for height. That was to insure that no harm came to the youngest children. The first several guerrillas began to work closely with local leaders in training self-defense members at a jungle "classroom." Training lectures stressed the overall military strategy, which was to drain French resources through small annoyance attacks, gradually isolate the enemy, and in the end destroy him. A peasant recalled, "Everything they said was very political. 'The guerrilla is fighting for a political reason,' they said. They taught the men why they were fighting."

Over the years, there were three clear instances of Viet Minh pressure against people allied with the colonial regime. The first of these involved one of the area's more infamous moneylenders, a man far from sympathetic to the Viet Minh cause. According to a peasant, "The Viet Minh shot that man, and everyone was very surprised. The Viet Minh said that he died because he was a servant of the French, and did not work for the people." Another of the Viet Minh victims was a Vietnamese soldier serving in French colonial ranks, a sergeant. People knew him for his corruption, and for his cruel temper. He actually lived in the adjacent village, but spent a great deal of his time helping coordinate police operations in My Thuy Phuong and the surrounding area. A Viet Minh sniper gunned down the sergeant as he pedaled his bicycle through the village.

In a third instance, the Viet Minh gave a warning to one of the village councilmen, who was a large landholder. They viewed the man, well known for his influential role in council deliberations, as a major local enemy. One night an explosive charge leveled the front part of the man's house. The councilman was unhurt by the blast, but deeply frightened. Shortly thereafter, he resigned his council seat, moved to Hue, and rented his land to several local peasants. The Viet Minh then had one less opponent in the village.

The main north-south highway through My Thuy Phuong presented many tempting targets of opportunity for the local guerrillas: French military vehicles. Throughout the anti-French war, action along the highway constituted the major Viet Minh military thrust in the village. According to a peasant, "It happened so often. The road was never safe for French soldiers." The Viet Minh guerrillas, usually in groups of two or three, sniped at French jeeps and trucks from concealed positions along the highway. The Viet Minh carefully planned the sniping forays. Usually snipers stayed close to one another, often on the same side of the highway. They were adept at careful but rapid selection of targets. As a French truck came into view on the horizon, the guerrillas had only a matter of seconds to decide whether or not to shoot.

The sniping incidents were frequent along the highway, and became so frequent, in fact, that the French periodically organized large military operations in My Thuy Phuong to destroy guerrilla units. Villagers remembered that in about 1949 there was a one-day operation. They have forgotten or never knew its precise dates, numbers of soldiers, and unit names. But they described it as typical of others the French organized in and around My Thuy Phuong during the years 1946–1954. Here is a reconstruction of the operation.

Before sunrise, several hundred French and African infantrymen, heavily armed with carbines, grenades, and knives, came in open trucks to the village. They immediately fanned out along Highway One, and proceeded to cross the ricefields, using the narrow paths dividing rice plots. They moved out to the furthest extremity of the village, the hamlets set in the ricefields. When the French forces reached the edges of the hamlets, they formed what they called a "perimeter." That is, they moved to completely encircle the area, to prevent movement out by any residents. When the troops were in place, other armed men began to move in, including more Frenchmen and African Legionnaires, Vietnamese soldiers, and a few Vietnamese policemen.

These soldiers and policemen moved quietly from house to house, apparently trying to cause as little commotion as possible. They entered homes without knocking, and pulled residents out of bed. Their next step was to demand identification papers, search all cabinets and drawers, and pry loose floor boards. They also searched clothing, and with fixed bayonets probed the large jugs that stored family rice supplies. The soldiers and policemen looked for concealed weapons and any types of printed materials, such as anticolonial leaflets or books, that might have linked people to the local revolutionary movement. They also looked carefully for concealed entrances to tunnel complexes, pretty good signs of resident Viet Minh sympathizers or possibly guerrillas. While soldiers and policemen were searching homes, most people did not dare resist or even complain about the inconvenience of it all. According to an elderly peasant, "We always were very still and didn't speak much when the French troops came, because you could never know how they would misunderstand your words. It was very frightening!"

During the operation that day, colonial forces detained about 50 men, women, and children as they moved through the village. Colonial soldiers moved the detainees under armed guard to a central part of the village, and later took them away, probably to a French base camp for interrogation. The soldiers did not bind hands, but closely guarded the detainees, and occasionally nudged them with rifle butts. People who attempted to move through the barricade of armed French soldiers around the hamlets ran a high risk of being shot, and several met that fate. A peasant remembered, "My brother did not know we had to stay home, and he was shot going out to the ricefields. He was carrying a hoe, so maybe they thought he had a gun."

But that day others with weapons considerably more lethal than hoes tried to penetrate the French perimeter. Four or five local guerrillas, armed with carbines, decided to flee rather than risk arrest in the house-to-house search. Their plan was probably to kill one or two Frenchmen, then flee through the hole created in the military line. The guerrillas crept slowly past houses and fences up to within about 10 yards of the French line. Soldiers stood about 10 yards apart along the edge of a path. One guerrilla took aim and pulled off a shot. A French soldier screamed and collapsed where he had stood. The guerrilla then fired at a second Frenchman nearby, who was by then crouching. He fired again and again, but could not find his mark.

Time soon began to run out for the guerrillas, who probably felt that escape was difficult, and perhaps impossible, as long as that second French soldier remained alive. Hearing shouts from other parts of the French line, two of the guerrillas decided to risk it: they ran toward the French perimeter. The shooting had alerted other Frenchmen, and the area swarmed with alert, advancing troops. It is unclear precisely how it happened, but there was a fierce exchange of gunfire, and the two guerrillas were killed. Soldiers of the perimeter then immediately captured, disarmed, and detained the remaining guerrillas, who had chosen not to run the gauntlet of death. Colonial soldiers dragged the guerrillas off, probably to their base camp, and no one in the village ever saw them again.

After the death and capture of the guerrillas, the search of the ricefield hamlets proceeded uneventfully. By late afternoon, the French lifted their perimeter, and the troops left. The colonialists undoubtedly measured and expressed their results that day as statistics—numbers killed or detained, and numbers of weapons and documents seized. But the Vietnamese viewed the day's military activities very differently. First, the military operation had many small costs in the village. There was an entire work day lost while it proceeded, and small losses of personal property to thieving colonial soldiers. Second, the death of the guerrillas during the operation deeply affected many in the village. "We all knew them," a peasant remembered, "and they were friends. We were sad to see them dead." Several spoke also of the ways village life began to change after the first large French military operations. According to a peasant woman, "We could never be sure about the French, they were so cruel. We were afraid they would come back, but never knew when they would." Terror and uncertainty thus began to haunt the village.

Sensing the change in mood between 1946 and 1954, local landlords, large tradesmen, and councilmen used threats of additional operations to increase their personal wealth and influence in the community. Threats "to bring the French soldiers" accompanied shakedowns by local officials or pressures by tradesmen or landlords. And councilmen and policemen, citing "security requirements," discouraged meetings and other cooperative efforts by groups of people, including groups that traditionally brought in harvests or built and repaired community facilities, such as irrigation canals or the *dinh*. The significance of such moves was not lost on one peasant, who commented, "The big men and the Westerners were afraid the people would unite against them. And their profits were larger if the people were divided."

STAND AND FIGHT

In 1948, three local Viet Minh leaders travelled far from the village boundaries. The Viet Minh provincial organization had selected them for training at a resistance base camp in the hilly Hoa My jungle area. The men journeyed to the camp on foot, travelling by jungle trail, and occasionally pausing along the way at preestablished rest points. A North Vietnamese publication included a description of the base camp, and of two others like it in the Binh Tri Thien region of Quang Binh, Quang Tri, and Thua Thien provinces:[11]

> Relying on remote and difficult mountains, the resistance bases were the seats of the leading organs and the liaison services with the central government and the places where important meetings were held. Gradually army workshops, logistic departments, pharmacies (manufacturing medicines on the spot for the army) and military hospitals were set up there, and, along with them, cadres' training schools, and workshops for printing pamphlets, newspapers, documents, books. . . .
>
> The supply of food to the base was made by local agricultural farms, which grew rice, maize, sweet potatoes, cassava and vegetables and practiced animal breeding, fishing and hunting.
>
> Army units came there for training, relaxation and replenishing their forces and attending political courses. From there they returned to the plains and other theatres of operation.

At the camp, the men joined a military study group, formed to train other leaders from other villages. The training sessions lasted about two months, and were organized by main force Vietnam People's Army soldiers, who fought the large battles against colonial forces. Trainees slept in lean-to jungle structures, or in hammocks, and ate the simple fare of the People's Army. Typically, the training sessions included lectures on Viet Minh doctrines and blackboard talks on military strategy and local leadership techniques. Experienced Viet Minh soldiers also provided training in actual combat techniques.

When the three men returned to the village from the base camp, they found that pressure from French security agencies had increased in Thua Thien/Hue. Throughout the province, colonial forces had killed or jailed many Viet Minh guerrillas and other followers. And provincial Viet Minh leaders found that village-level revolutionaries in the area were often so preoccupied with colonial police and military efforts that they ignored instructions from above.

In the village, colonial forces arrested and killed a number of Viet Minh followers during the late 1940s. This pressure caused some less committed Viet Minh supporters to abandon the movement for safer, uncommitted political stances. In addition, Viet Minh leaders lost some freedom of movement in the village. However, in the village and throughout most of the province, the Viet Minh effectively adjusted to most of the setbacks brought by colonial pressure. In later sections of this chapter, we discuss those adjustments.

When My Thuy Phuong's Viet Minh leaders returned from their training in 1948, they found more than problems in the local movement. They also discovered that in their absence an important new leader had emerged, a man named Te. Let us now focus on that new leader, for his is partly the story of My Thuy Phuong's revolutionary movement.

We must first briefly return to the early 1940s, when Te was about 25 years of age. He was married and had two young children. The Te family lived in the southern part of the village, near the bridge, in a modest two-room home of cement and wooden walls and red tile roof. The home had been built by Te's father, who in the 1920s and 1930s was a modestly successful tradesman dealing in cloth. Te neither owned nor rented any riceland, nor did he have business holdings. His home was simply furnished, and his family lived frugally. Despite the comfortable inherited home, the Te's were financially only slightly better off than most other villagers. In social and cultural terms, however, they differed dramatically. The difference can be attributed to Te's educational background and chosen profession. In the 1930s, he attended a French-supported secondary school and graduated near the top of his class. His favorite subjects were literature and history. In the late 1930s, Te returned to My Thuy Phuong, fully imbued with an interest in Western literature, and especially in poetry. He secured a teaching position in the small district school, located outside the village. He taught lessons in European history and literature, and earned a small but adequate salary. To augment that income, he also taught part-time in a private elementary school in Hue, and his wife tended a small vegetable garden near their home.

Te had been greatly influenced by many of the Western treatises, novels, and poems he had read in high school, and thought of himself as something of a Vietnamese "renaissance man." Like many other Vietnamese students of French schools, he loved the richness and depth of Western literature and contrasted it with Vietnam's traditional literature, which he began to think of as "poems for the emperors." But a number of Western ideas about democracy and national self-determination also struck him, and he grew aware that Vietnam had been denied these "rights."

Over the course of a few years, Te's awareness of social conditions in the village area heightened considerably. Although the colonial regime's curriculum outlines were supposed to guide his literature and history lessons, he began to slant his teaching. According to one of his former students, this was "to make the students think about freedom and democracy."

Outside the classroom, students and neighbors began to visit him, to seek out advice and opinions, and Te began to find an important place for himself in the village. Gradually, he slipped into the role of advisor and informal "advocate" for some of the village's disadvantaged. As his reputation spread, as a young man of education who for some reason wanted to help the poor, many brought their problems to him. "They told him about landlords who were raising rent, about the Government taking taxes, and about how poor they were," his wife recalled. She and Te's friends emphasized that in the late 1930s, Te never advocated revolt or noncooperation as ways for the poor to deal with the local colonial apparatus. But despite that hesitance, word of his interest in the poor soon reached the local authorities, and repercussions followed.

Two or three members of the local council visited Te at home and suggested that he consider running for that body. But Te hesitated, claiming that his duties as teacher kept him too busy. The councilmen then dropped strong suggestions that his talks with the peasants were causing them problems in the village. A peasant recalled:

> The men told him that some of the farmers had come to the council and asked for their rent to be lowered, and those farmers had mentioned his name. The councilmen said he should be careful what he told people, that new ideas were dangerous when the people did not really understand them.

Te apparently understood the significance of the invitation to join the council, and the warnings. His wife stated, however, that, "The people were suffering, and he could not make them go away." In 1941, colonial authorities dismissed Te from his position as teacher in the district school, and soon thereafter he lost his part-time job in Hue. According to those who knew him, Te understood clearly what had happened to him, and saw a period of coming financial readjustment. He rented an additional small parcel of land, and his wife increased the area under vegetable cultivation. Te himself began occasionally tutoring the sons and daughters of a few wealthy families in Hue and Huong Thuy District, and his family adjusted satisfactorily to the drop in income.

Te's wife said that the local procolonial group was "killing" her husband, for those villagers feared him as a threat, or saw him as one of their own who had somehow lost all sense. During most of the 1940s, Te maintained his vegetable plots and continued to offer advice to peasants and former students. Te's wife stated:

> He was very interested in the Viet Minh. Once he went to a Viet Minh meeting. But his philosophy was just to live a simple life and not participate in politics. After many years, however, he changed his mind. He saw that just giving

> opinions to people was not as good as working for them and fighting the Westerners. He also saw that the Viet Minh was very good, and very strong, so he followed the revolutionary side.

Te made that decision in 1948. Because of his reputation as a man of compassion and intelligence, local Viet Minh leaders welcomed him to the Viet Minh ranks, and soon invited him to join the covert Viet Minh village council. Te concentrated on recruitment to revolutionary ranks of the peasants he had been helping over the years. Some of his recruits became trusted, dedicated guerrillas.

As their abilities improved, the Viet Minh guerrillas augmented sniping attacks by organizing several ambushes along the highway. Some of these involved many guerrillas and local Viet Minh supporters. Two peasants described how the insurgents organized an ambush of a convoy one day in about 1948. Ten or twelve guerrillas took up positions in the predawn hours on both sides of the highway. This was in the section of the village where the route is bounded by ricefields on one side and by the slightly elevated railroad bed and a small strip of rice paddies on the other. Guerrillas divided into four groups of two or three men, two groups per side of the highway, and separated by several hundred yards. On both sides the guerrillas dug small, shallow trenches for extra protection from the expected hail of French bullets.

Several unarmed individuals cooperated to support the ambush. Three or four women carrying market baskets took up positions near the highway, at the north and south ends of the intended ambush corridor. The guerrillas expected that several minutes before the French targets crossed the range of fire the women would begin stopping pedestrians and those travelling by bicycle. Their job was to prevent injury to innocent passers-by. Two children played crucial roles during the operation. One boy, no older than seven or eight, sat on top of his family's water buffalo south of the ambush strip, but near the highway. His task was to wave his arms in a certain pattern when he spotted the expected target approaching through the adjacent village. He was the advance lookout. Another boy ten or twelve years old, sat by the roadside some distance to the north, and had been instructed to wave if danger appeared in the forms of approaching police, army patrols, or convoys from the north.

A peasant who assisted the guerrillas said, "The little boy on the water buffalo gave the signal, and the women had done their job, too. There was nobody on the road who might have gotten hurt." The guerrillas apparently knew precisely when to begin firing, and at what. A convoy came into sight—about 10 trucks, equally spaced, and moving at a high rate of speed. Within seconds the first trucks had entered the ambush corridor, and were approaching its center, but the guerrillas held their fire.

The peasant recalled:

> The Viet Minh waited until the trucks were about half way up the road. Then everyone began firing at the first two trucks. The first two trucks were hit very hard, and had to stop. One of them went off the road, and you could see that one French soldier was dead inside. All the other trucks then had to stop.

The guerrillas then concentrated their fire on the tires of the stalled trucks, and on any French soldiers who were riding on them. Many of those soldiers tried to take cover in and around the trucks or in the ditches off to the side of the road, where accurate guerrilla fire cut some of them down. Hiding was practically impossible.

People did not know how many Frenchmen died that day in the village, nor was it clear whether there were casualties on the Viet Minh side. The peasants quoted above recalled only that most of the damage occurred in a minute or two, after which the guerrillas retreated. According to others, guerrilla results that day were a hopelessly immobilized French convoy, a heightened sense of pride and accomplishment, and enhanced reputation in My Thuy Phuong as a powerful fighting force.

Under mounting Viet Minh pressure, the French came up with a "solution" for Vietnam in 1949. They signed an agreement with Emperor Bao Dai permitting him to establish a government and an army. But it was a government in name only, for under the agreement the French retained military and civil control, leaving little but opportunities for corruption to Bao Dai and his administrators.[12] In effect, the Bao Dai regime was only a cover for French colonial rule.[13] My Thuy Phuong's proximity to Bao Dai's home town of Hue and most people's deep affection for the old capital seemingly had little effect on political attitudes.

As a peasant put it, "No one here respected Emperor Bao Dai. He was just a playboy and a puppet of the Westerners. When he tried to make a new government, everyone knew it was really the French behind him." Many others knew absolutely nothing of Bao Dai's political moves, indicating that they brought no new programs, personnel, or political messages to the village. The only significant changes were entirely negative—heightened activities by security agencies and rampant price inflation. And during the Bao Dai years, the *same* sorts of abuses by the *same* procolonial minority that had existed for years continued apace. To most villagers, Bao Dai and the French were one, local enemies unchanged.

Beginning in about 1949, a major Viet Minh military intensification complemented the highway ambush and sniping tactics.[14] To support that intensification, in the late 1940s or early 1950s two or three men informally called tax collectors began operating in the village. These individuals, who were close to local Viet Minh leaders, attempted to gather contributions from every sympathetic or potentially sympathetic family. Usually collectors paid nocturnal visits to homes, but they rarely used the word "tax." Instead, the men asked for "donations." Tax collectors usually said they needed the money to buy supplies, especially food and weapons, for local guerrillas. While on their rounds, collectors generally reminded people of the Viet Minh struggle and were not coercive. In response, villagers usually gave small sums of money and sometimes stocks of food, such as uncooked rice.

Related to the nationwide expansion and improvement of the Vietnam People's Army and to a Viet Minh shift to a more aggressive "annihilating" phase of attack, in about 1950, the village's 15 or 20 guerrillas began to stand and fight in response to French military probes. Two peasants recalled the local response to a French military/police operation in about 1951. They described that guerrilla attack as typical of others organized in the early 1950s. According to the peasants, the strength displayed by the local Viet Minh forces during that day's encounter was in part due to the extremely effective Viet Minh intelligence system. Word arrived by way of a secret courier that at a certain time, on a certain morning, a certain number of French military and police units could be expected in the ricefield hamlets. The Viet Minh hierarchy instructed the local organizers simply to "prepare." There was only about two days' advance notice, but that was more than enough time for the guerrillas. First, they hauled in weapons and stocks of ammunition from a hidden arms cache. Then local Viet Minh leaders began to plot strategy.

The leaders set a meeting of local guerrillas for a place in the hills southwest of the village. Children notified guerrillas of the evening rendezvous in messages they brought to guerrilla homes and places of hiding. All attended the session, during which local leaders thoroughly explained what they had planned. The battle itself went almost predictably. On schedule, the French forces arrived, and began the long trek out through the ricefields toward the hamlets, which frightened, forewarned residents had almost completely evacuated. The Viet Minh guerrillas had completely hidden themselves at different points throughout the rice paddies near the path being followed by colonial soldiers. As the French were moving through the ricefields, the guerrillas opened fire. From every side guns blazed, and all along the French line soldiers dropped. In panic, the colonial soldiers began returning the fire, but shot wildly, unsure where to direct their fire. Within minutes the French forces pulled back, leaving behind about 10 dead. The heavy French barrage following the initial Viet Minh attack lightly wounded one guerrilla and no guerrillas were captured.

The final intensification of the Viet Minh military thrust brought local guerrillas to the point of attacking a French outpost at a place called Hoa Da Tay, about five miles southeast of the village. The outpost was actually a heavy cement aboveground fortification, occupied by what villagers said was "a small number" of Vietnamese colonial soldiers. On three separate occasions most of My Thuy Phuong's guerrillas joined others from Huong Thuy District area in assaults against that point. One night in about 1953, guerrillas surrounded the fortification. Barbed wire and mines completely ringed it, but those proved minor obstacles to several of the guerrillas—highly trained sappers. Armed with grenades, satchel charges, wire cutters, and other tools, the sappers quietly cut and worked their way through the barbed wire and past the mines, creeping unnoticed close to the base of the fort. There they placed the satchel charges, then slithered back by the same route they had taken to enter. Some minutes later the charges exploded, a signal that unleashed a hail of bullets and mortars from the waiting guerrillas.

That night—and during the two other attacks at Hoa Da Tay—heavy gunfire from the outpost defenders, who were apparently well armed and numerous, answered the guerrilla onslaught. However, guerrillas did not attempt to capture the outpost. They only blanketed it with fire. Here is what one peasant said about the attacks:

> There were Vietnamese soldiers in that place. Can you understand how frightened they were during the attacks? We did not mind. We did not want to capture that place, but only to scare the puppet troops. We knew that if any of them died, the other puppet troops would find out about it, and they would be sad, and there would be deserters. We knew that those who were not killed would be very afraid, and would talk to others about how strong the Viet Minh was. So we felt that this would weaken the French army, and would help to make the French leave Vietnam.

Paralleling stepped-up guerrilla actions in the early 1950s were intensified Viet Minh political thrusts. The Viet Minh's frequent use of class-oriented messages in the village, which several attributed to a local increase in I.C.P. influence, sparked several incidents related to land. On two occasions Viet Minh leaders organized groups of 20 to 30 peasants to protest village council corruption in land distribution, which was occurring in the same ways as in the 1940s. The leaders operated covertly, not even as representatives of the Viet Minh "farmers' affairs committee," and got the peasant groups to file petitions with the councils. The protesting peasants also spoke at small Viet Minh gatherings against colonial land policies. On another occasion in about 1951, the Viet Minh supported about five or six tenant farmers who were facing stiff rent increases. Local insurgent leaders simply sent word to the landlord that the increases were too high and would not be paid. There was of course an implied threat in the message, and the landlord replied by rescinding the increases.

The training and expansion of the local Viet Minh leadership group and continuation of Viet Minh proselyting attracted most villagers to the movement. People variously indicated that after 1945 "everyone followed the Viet Minh," "95 percent liked the Viet Minh," "the Viet Minh was very popular," and "this was a Viet Minh village." These comments and other evidence indicate that between 1945 and 1954, about 5 percent of the village's people supported the colonial cause, about 80 percent supported the Viet Minh, and the remaining 15 percent assumed uncommitted positions but leaned toward support of the revolutionary movement. An estimated half or more of the Viet Minh followers were reliable, active supporters, and the remainder were not as reliable, so might be considered passive supporters of the insurgency. And My Thuy Phuong's uncommitted felt pressures from politically committed neighbors similar to those which uncommitted people experienced during the World War II period.

It is also noteworthy that as the Viet Minh grew strong throughout the province, including the village, there were changes in the role played by the I.C.P. within the movement. According to Hue residents knowledgeable about I.C.P. history in the region, party discipline generally improved between 1950 and 1954, and the party began to play a more dominant role within the Viet Minh. Under I.C.P. pressure, Viet Minh proselyting efforts became more explicitly class-oriented, and most top Viet Minh decision-makers in the province were party members. This last fact partly resulted from several purges of Viet Minh ranks in the area. Several Hue and village residents indicated that after 1950, the Viet Minh command removed about 20 Viet Minh leaders throughout the area, ranging from guerrilla commanders to village and regional officials. The command may have killed or "made available" to French security forces one or two of those removed. However, most were simply stripped of rank and allowed to remain active in the movement.

In the village, to make explicit what is implied above, the I.C.P. was quite influential, operating as it did through its members—who led the Viet Minh locally. Party policies were reflected in the village through the actions of those men and the local Viet Minh branch. Villagers suggested that beginning in the early 1950s, I.C.P. influence became more pronounced locally, reflecting the region-wide pattern mentioned above. As noted earlier, there were subtle shifts in Viet Minh political messages away from those solely nationalistic in content and toward those with a focus on class struggle. Further, the village's Viet Minh branch purged three men and one woman. Two of those purged were guerrilla leaders suspected of harboring "rightist thoughts." The local Viet Minh command reduced them in rank. These were men of relatively prosperous families, who apparently never captured the full trust of the village's Viet Minh leaders. The other man and the woman purged were husband and wife, both responsible for "farmers' affairs." Several indicated that their error was failure to aggressively exploit peasants' dissatisfaction with the pro-French council's corruption in communal land distribution. The couple's purge came at the direction of the village's Viet Minh leaders, probably a result of I.C.P. directives to more aggressively exploit politically volatile land issues in the anti-French struggle. The man and woman were removed from their positions and lost influence in the movement, but remained active, especially in supporting local guerrilla actions. There were never purges within the village's small group of I.C.P. members, and no purges within the Viet Minh branch beyond the five just mentioned—two more indications of the movement's great strength in My Thuy Phuong.

In 1954, many deeply felt that strength. A peasant noted, "When we heard that Ho Chi Minh had agreed to negotiate in Geneva, we were all happy, because we knew that it would mean victory over the French." A peasant who was formerly a Viet Minh guerrilla said, "We knew that the French were losing and wanted to leave Vietnam. So we began to get ready to welcome the victory." And another peasant described the mood of My Thuy Phuong with these words: "Everyone was so sure that the French were going to leave. It was so happy. None of us thought that the Americans would make things so difficult for us. None of us thought that the Americans would start to fight the war the French had lost."

NOTES

1. Vien, no. 37, p. 68.
2. Villagers did not know the exact date of French reoccupation of Hue. It likely occurred between March 6 and December 19, 1946. (See Vien, no. 23, p. 216; no. 7, p. 243.)
3. It is stated in a North Vietnamese publication that the Viet Minh administrative offices were transferred from Hue to the countryside between March 6 and December 19, 1946. (See Vien, no. 23, pp. 216–217.)
4. Throughout all Vietnamese villages, this name was later changed to "Committee for Resistance and Administration" and "Military and Administrative Committee." (See Pike, *Vietcong*, p. 47.)
5. See *The Pentagon Papers, As Published by the New York Times* (New York: Bantam, 1971), p. 15; *The Senator Gravel Edition; The Pentagon Papers; The Defense Department History of United States Decisionmaking on Vietnam* (Boston: Beacon, 1974), p. 9.
6. See *The Marines in Viet-Nam; 1954–1973; An Anthology and Annotated Bibliography* (Washington, D.C.: History & Museums Division, Headquarters, U.S. Marine Corps, 1974), p. 9; Vien, no. 37, pp. 68–69, 75, 95.
7. See Bernard Fall, *Street Without Joy* (New York: Schocken Books, 1972), pp. 144–173.
8. Vien, no. 37, pp. 71–72.
9. Buttinger, *Vietnam: A Political History*, p. 269.
10. See Tran Van Dinh, "The Vietnam People's Army," p. 8.
11. Vien, no. 37, p. 73.
12. Buttinger, *Vietnam: A Dragon*, pp. 667–734.
13. *Ibid.*, p. 762.
14. See Vien, no. 37, pp. 68–69, 81. In 1949, a Binh Tri Thien division was formed to "coordinate its actions with those of other divisions operating all over the country with the aim of raising the level of battles of annihilation." (Vien, no. 37, p. 87.) By 1954, besides the Binh Tri Thien division, there was a regiment of regulars in Thua Thien, and another in Quang Tri, one or two companies in each district, and "from one platoon to one company of sufficiently armed guerrillas in each village." (Vien, no. 37, p. 103, 88–89, 90–95, 97–99.)

5

Two Families

Let us break the chronology in our story of revolution in My Thuy Phuong and briefly return to about 1950. We do this to trace the lives of two typical village families, another way of "charting" the Viet Minh rise. Here are the family cases.

THE BINH FAMILY

The first family consisted of nine people. For years they lived in a two-room wooden house in the central part of the village near the highway. In 1950, the family head, Binh, was 50 years old. He owned about three *mau* of riceland, and rented about one and one-half *mau* of communal land. His wife, who was 40 years old, occasionally worked as a field laborer for other villagers, making the equivalent of about 30 U.S. cents for a day's work of harvesting or cultivating. She also took care of the six children living at home, who ranged in age from two to seventeen. Another child, a girl, was married and living with her husband's family.

During the 1940s, Binh had gradually managed to save and borrow enough to purchase his riceland. But he remained heavily in debt, dependent upon bountiful harvests to pay all the bills. To bring in a bit of extra money, Binh worked at odd jobs in the village, occasionally helping a group of men erect frames of houses on contract, or hiring himself out to labor in others' vegetable gardens or ricefields.

None of Binh's children ever studied higher than elementary school. In 1950, the two sons who had finished school worked with their father in the fields, and themselves looked for odd jobs. The younger children attended a local elementary school, which was supported by local contributions and the colonial government.

Once or twice a week the two older sons walked several miles up into the hills west of the village to cut firewood. They tied it in bundles, and carried huge loads back to the village for later sale. The work was exhausting and dirty, but the extra income helped the family stay afloat financially, and even put aside small amounts for savings. As Binh described it, about two-thirds of his family's income during the 1940s came from rice production, and the rest from odd jobs family members could find, such as field work or wood-gathering. Expenditures were many. Rent and taxes, according to Binh, amounted to almost half of what the family grossed every year. And purchases of fertilizer and other farming supplies drained off another quarter of the gross. The remainder went for living expenses, one quarter of gross family income. Binh was acutely aware of his high fixed expenses—the taxes, rent, fertilizer and supply costs—and worried about having enough left for family living expenses in years of drought, floods, or high inflation. "We always had to pay the rent and taxes first of all," Binh noted, "and if we didn't, we would get in much trouble."

Binh recalled that in 1950, trouble came on several fronts. First of all, that was a year of heavy floods, which came just after rice seedlings had been transplanted to the fields. Floodwaters swept away most of the seedlings, and Binh lost valuable growing time and money because the flood forced him to reseed. To complicate matters that year, there was a searing, scorching drought during the dry season. "There was no water for anything to grow," he said, "and most of the crops died. Even wells in the village were dry, and we had to go far away to carry in drinking water." The Binh family's income dropped sharply that year, and was further drained by the serious illness during the rainy season of two or three of his children. Medicine was expensive, but Binh felt he had to buy it at any cost. "The year before one of our babies had died of a bad cold," he remembered, "and I didn't want that to happen again. . . ."

To put the Binh family's 1950 experience in perspective it is important to understand that people in Vietnam, as in many agricultural countries, have for generations faced the risks of natural calamities, and have usually demonstrated great resiliency recovering from such blows. For the Binh's the difference in 1950 was that the family was denied some of the advantages its ancestors had possessed when faced with floods, droughts, or illnesses. In 1950, some members of My Thuy Phuong's procolonial group saw and moved to exploit Binh's misfortune, and self-help institutions were too weak and potential patrons too disinterested to help. A generation earlier that probably would not have been the case.

Binh remembered what happened when taxes and rent for the communal land came due. "Councilmen came around for the rent," he said, "and told me that they wanted the same amount as usual. But they came right after I had bought some seed and supplies, and I had no money.

How could I pay them?'' Like others before him Binh then felt compelled, under pressure from creditors, to seek a loan. ''I knew no one in the village with extra money,'' Binh said, ''so I had to go to a moneylender to borrow. He gave me enough for the rent and the taxes, but I had to repay at a very high rate.'' That monthly interest charge was about 12 to 15 percent of the total originally borrowed. The initial loan apparently satisfied the village officials, and it gave Binh time to recover his losses. But when the summer drought almost wiped out his harvest, Binh found the pressure from creditors unbearable. He recalled, ''The moneylender wanted his money, food was more expensive, and I had more expenses coming up.'' The burden of debt finally brought Binh to the point of selling his land. But even that drastic step invited and brought financial exploitation by some procolonial neighbors.

Other peasants in the village had found themselves in similar circumstances that year, so many were interested in selling out. The price of land dropped and the chief buyers, the village's already large landholders, profited handsomely from the misfortunes of families like the Binh's. ''I had no choice,'' Binh recalled. ''We needed the money so badly, and I knew the police would make me pay the taxes and land rent on time, so I had to sell my land. If I hadn't sold, we would have been very hungry.'' Binh indicated that he was unable to borrow money for taxes and rent, for he was already heavily in debt. He also said that resisting the police demand for taxes and rent would have brought arrest for him and problems for his family.

The year 1950 was thus a turning point for Binh and his family. Natural calamities and exploitation by members of the procolonial group transformed the Binh's from marginally successful small landowners to a family of tenant farmers. ''After we sold the land,'' Binh said, ''I had to rent land, and we never had as much money as before.'' That lack of money affected the family in other ways. Its diet, which had occasionally included meat and other more expensive food items, became less varied and less balanced. The Binh's almost completely eliminated meat from family meals, and reduced portions in size.

There were other significant changes for the family. Two of the older children dropped out of school. Books, writing supplies, and school clothing simply cost more than they could afford, and Binh needed extra help in the fields. Binh's wife reduced the already infrequent purchases of cloth for clothing, and the family drastically cut expenditures for annual feasts honoring ancestors. In short, many necessities and important ''extras'' drained out of the family's life. And for Binh himself, deepening cynicism and resignation about future prospects tempered and replaced his earlier happiness and optimism. ''I began to feel that there was nothing I could do for my family, to make life better for them,'' Binh said. ''The harder I worked, the poorer we became, and the richer and more powerful the politicians became.'' To Binh, the ''politicians'' were members of the village council, policemen, and others loyal to the colonial regime.

Binh's son recalled that over the years his father was gradually exposed to anticolonial ideas. They came to him through friendships with the teacher/leader Te and fellow peasants. Slowly, the questions of family economics expanded in Binh's mind to the larger questions of French control over the village and country. He listened to Te and his friends, and in the early 1950s finally joined the Viet Minh. Binh became involved in small activities directed against the French, carried messages for the Viet Minh, and sometimes served as a lookout during Viet Minh military operations. His son spoke of Binh's political activity during those years:

> My father was very happy to be helping the Viet Minh. He told us that if the Viet Minh wins, Vietnam will be independent, and there will be a better life for everyone. He helped the revolution in many ways. You could see how very happy he was to be a very small part of the revolution.

Binh and other villagers had an uncomplicated vision of a "better life." It meant economic prosperity and peace in the countryside.

THE TRI FAMILY

In 1950, a man named Tri lived with his family in one of the hamlets in the ricefields. He was then 47, his wife 39, and their 8 children ranged in age from 1 to 20. The family occupied a wooden house on a small fenced parcel of land. Tri's parents lived with him, occupying a simple one-room house directly alongside the Tri home. Two children had by 1950 moved away from home—the eldest son to join a unit of the colonial army, and a daughter to marry. None of the children except the son in the military had ever attended school.

Owning no land of his own, Tri depended for income almost exclusively on rented ricelands. He rented about one *mau* of village communal land, and jointly rented another *mau* of privately owned land. The joint venture was with one of his neighbors, who shared the labor and the profits. To supplement what the family made growing rice, Tri's wife operated a tiny soup stand in front of the family home. She sold noodle soup, as well as small pastries and soft drinks, and made daily profits equivalent to about 25 or 30 U.S. cents.

In the 1940s, high taxes, high rents, and steady inflation began forcing the Tri's into a cycle of indebtedness and sacrifice. When the drought of 1950 occurred the cycle broke, and the Tri family faced disaster. "I had already borrowed a lot of money," Tri said, "so could not borrow any more. When they wanted me to pay the rent for the land, I just had nothing left." By that point the large Tri family was living on the tiny earnings of the soup stand. It provided just enough money for one family meal per day, a sort of rice porridge served with sauted greens and occasionally fish. Tri's wife prepared a tiny snack of rice in the mornings for the smaller children. There was rarely any money left for "extras," such as medicine for sick children or cloth for clothing.

With pressure from creditors becoming unbearable, Tri made what he described as "the saddest decision of my life." He decided to give up his land. He did so under considerable pressure from the landlord and village councilmen, all of whom were unmoved by his pleas for compassion and time. Within a week of failure to meet his payments Tri relinquished the land, and a week later the council and his former landlord rented it to someone else. The fact that Tri had recently planted and fertilized the land compounded his financial loss and heartbreak, so his final investment of time and money bore no return at all.

At first Tri was shocked to see new tenants farming the land he knew and loved, but soon grew wiser about his plight. Tri began to understand for the first time that his financial future probably did not lie in My Thuy Phuong. "I saw that I could no longer be a farmer," he remembered. On that day of painful realization, life suddenly changed for the man named Tri. He took a bus that very afternoon into Hue and wandered through the downtown commercial section. Somehow Tri discovered that a Chinese-owned shipping firm was hiring laborers, and he applied. The next day he found himself loading trucks with huge, heavy sacks of rice and other commodities. Tri earned a daily wage, the equivalent of about 30 U.S. cents, and he endured dehumanizing discomforts. To save money he often slept on the warehouse floor, and he worked six and sometimes seven days a week. But Tri claimed he grew to endure the hardships and even "like" the job. Working in the warehouse, he could at least maintain his family at a subsistence level, and for the first time in years feel relatively free of My Thuy Phuong's landlords and councilmen.

There were 10 or 20 other family heads like Tri in the village—driven off the land and into the city, separated from families by forces beyond their control. About 50 or 60 others remained in the village, also deprived of land but working as field laborers or wood gatherers. Most other villagers experienced the same intense economic and social pressures, and had to make many of the same financial sacrifices, but somehow managed to meet tax and rent payments and thus keep their land.

Like the tenant farmer Binh, Tri was involved in the slow process that brought many to the Viet Minh revolution. Beginning in the early 1950s, Tri was exposed to new ideas from several sources. First, in his warehouse work he met several covert Viet Minh agents long active in Hue. One of them, according to Tri, was an articulate and intelligent man who belonged to the I.C.P., and who took great interest in the political views of his fellow warehouse workers. According to Tri's son:

> My father kept telling us about the new ideas at the place he worked, and about his new friendship with a man he said was a Communist. My father began to talk

about how the French were using the people in the cities to get rich, and doing it by using the Chinese and small numbers of rich Vietnamese families.

In his weekly visits home, Tri was able to see the growing popularity and strength of the Viet Minh through conversations with two neighbors, his brother-in-law and nephew, who in about 1950 had become members of the local guerrilla force. Tri supported their struggle with occasional donations from his wife's small soup stand. His guerrilla relatives, according to Tri, did not directly pressure him to join or support their cause. "They only talked about the need for the people to unite to fight the Westerners," Tri said. Tri also recalled that he began to pay closer attention during those informal political conversations.

One day, neighbors invited Tri and his wife to attend a Viet Minh political study meeting in the village. They went with some trepidation. But later Tri told his son that the meeting was "interesting" and "full of good ideas." In 1952 or 1953, after many more conversations and a few more meetings, Tri decided to actively support the revolution. He occasionally carried small Viet Minh messages between Hue and My Thuy Phuong—small, crumpled pieces of paper, stuffed into the linings of cigarette packs. Tri also spread Viet Minh ideas in chats with fellow warehouse workers, and with neighbors. And he continued making contributions of food to local guerrillas. By the time of the 1954 Geneva Agreement, Tri was one of the village's most active Viet Minh followers. His son thought back and put it this way: "My father said the Viet Minh was the best thing for our country, and he said that we must all struggle hard to support the cause of independence."

6

Ebb Tide, Rising Tide

PILGRIMAGE OF REVOLUTION

Following the 1954 national partition, which ended the Indochina war for France, two regimes emerged in Vietnam. Ho Chi Minh headed one in the north, while in the south a regime led by Ngo Dinh Diem came into being.[1] Partition brought a definite ebb in revolutionary activity in My Thuy Phuong, as throughout the country. It ushered in a period of quiet waiting for most former Viet Minh followers, who expected their movement to gain power in the nationwide plebiscite promised for 1956 by the Geneva Agreement.

But a number of former Viet Minh left My Thuy Phuong and headed north across the seventeenth parallel line of partition. They took a long, roundabout route by jungle and mountain trails established during the anti-French struggle. At the time, according to Douglas Pike, 30,000 to 100,000 Viet Minh supporters from all parts of the south journeyed to the north, which they regarded as a safe haven.[2] It is unclear, however, precisely how many left the village. Most indicated only that "some" or "a few" made the journey, while others said that there were about six who made the pilgrimage of revolution to the north.

One of those who departed was the man Te, the former teacher who had become a local Viet Minh leader. He and his companions joined a political proselyting unit of the Vietnam People's Army. During the months of training, one event occurred that one of the trainees later described to his son as "the most thrilling moment of my life." That was when Ho Chi Minh visited the military unit and spoke briefly with each of the trainees. The son, now a peasant, stated:

> My father told us later that meeting Ho Chi Minh was an exciting time, and something he would never forget. In fact, he carried with him for most of his life a small photograph of Ho Chi Minh. He covered it with plastic so that it would not get wet, and sometimes he took it out for strength.

According to the man just quoted, many of his father's friends found similar strength and sustenance in vivid memories of that meeting with the bearded revolutionary, and many of them carried photographs of Ho.

More likely than not, Te and the others anticipated short stays in North Vietnam, perhaps a year or so, after which they would return home in time for the 1956 plebiscite. But the men most likely failed to anticipate Diem's cancellation of the electoral contest. Te stayed in North Vietnam for nearly five years. Some others from the village stayed as long, but most left after about two years.

North Vietnamese and exiled South Vietnamese "trainers" constantly showed Te and the others examples of leaders to emulate. A peasant who was close to the leaders explained:

> They [the trainers] wanted those men to turn into leaders just like Ho Chi Minh or General [Vo Nguyen] Giap. They wanted them to become very strong Communist Party members, and to understand everything about Communism. All of the men studied those things, even the low-level guerrillas.

A few of the men who journeyed north, especially those previously associated with the I.C.P., had long been conscious of Marxist-Leninist ideas. To strengthen the ideological grasp of those few and broaden the political consciousness of the others, individuals directing the training frequently organized political study sessions. One or two northern or exiled southern "political cadres" usually led such meetings, which consisted of lectures and discussions of pamphlets on political ideas. One of the men who returned from the north had these summarizing remarks about the training:

> It was a very interesting time for us in the northern part of Vietnam. We had always been very strong fighters for the Viet Minh, and we always admired Ho Chi Minh and the other Viet Minh leaders. The trip to North Vietnam was very difficult and very long, but we did not ever complain, because we knew the difficulties were for the revolution.
>
> Our training in North Vietnam was also difficult. Sometimes the food was not good. Sometimes we were very lonely and wanted to go home to see our families and friends. But we learned after a while not to be lonely, and learned to find strength in our revolutionary struggle. We learned not to think much about our families any more. We learned not to miss our families any more—like Ho Chi Minh.

Others similarly indicated that throughout the entire period of revolutionary activity in My Thuy Phuong, most insurgent leaders and guerrillas were more devoted to their cause than to families. However, they did not completely sever all family ties. For example, they made occasional covert visits to their families' homes, and often recruited or proselyted among relatives.

In summary, the northern journey made better revolutionaries of those who went—improving organizational and guerrilla techniques, strengthening their nationalistic feelings, thoroughly imbuing them with ideas of class struggle, and permitting their devotion to revolution to grow stronger than devotion to families. If not before, then certainly after the northern training, the men from My Thuy Phuong viewed north and south as explicit ideological as well as geographical entities. The northern experience, however, did not mean the men somehow surrendered their claims as local insurgent leaders to North Vietnamese or became involved in a North Vietnamese movement of conquest or subversion. As one peasant who knew the leaders remarked, "They were southern revolutionaries above all, not puppets of the North." The northern trip simply taught those who went to look for inspiration in Hanoi as they organized My Thuy Phuong's branch of a southern Vietnamese insurgency.

FAMILIAR ABUSES

For about its first year, the Diem Government offered some villagers the promise of a nationalistic regime that would somehow bring pride, prosperity, and peace to all of South Vietnam. But after the regime took shape, promise bore little relation to reality. "Mr. Diem's government began with much hope, and much nationalism and love of country," recalled a retired Diem-era soldier. "But later we understood that everything we wanted was not to be." An elderly peasant, who in 1975 was a member of the Cult Committee, had these words:

> My happiest day, the happiest day in my whole life, was when I saw two truckloads of French soldiers leaving Hue for the last time. They drove by my house, and they looked so sad. But I was happy. We were very happy to see the French go, and see a nationalist government take over.
>
> But then we saw that the government of Mr. Diem was sometimes very cruel and sometimes just like the French.

"Why did we support Mr. Diem?", asked a peasant woman. "At first he promised peace, and promised a government of honesty. But later we saw that there was no peace, and that the leaders were not honest. So how could we continue to support that man?"

What had happened to so drastically change attitudes? In short, the Diem Government, with heavy diplomatic and financial support from the

U.S., had become fiercely anti-Communist, and the Catholic Diem family suspicious of those who did not share its views. Under direction from the top, the Government attempted to "neutralize" dissenters—revolutionaries of all stripes, and many others, including anti-Communists, who opposed its policies.

In Thua Thien/Hue, the Government's programs were directed by a Diem family member, the autocratic Ngo Dinh Can. His word carried the force of law throughout the region, and under Can's direction Government rule meant regimentation and oppression—the pattern throughout South Vietnam. Can's most infamous program involved the so-called "strategic hamlets." These were heavily defended and highly organized groupings of families, established throughout the region, but never in My Thuy Phuong, ostensibly to "check" revolutionary influence. According to Hue residents who saw the hamlets, they resembled small concentration camps.

Under Diem, Government policies became unbearable for many individuals and groups of citizens in Thua Thien/Hue, and there were protests. Most notable were the several Struggle Movements of the early 1960s, led by Buddhist monks and lay leaders and widely supported. The early Struggle Movements are examined in the following chapter. Suffice it to say at this point that the Government's strong response to the movements earned it the bitter hatred of most Thua Thien/Hue residents, a hatred which extended to anyone viewed as a Government ally—including members of the favored Catholic minority, high Government administrators, and even officials in places like My Thuy Phuong.

In the village itself, most of the *same families* which had supported the French colonial cause constituted the pro-Government group. These were primarily the extended families of four or five large landholders, two large tradesmen, and several civil servants. Continuity within that group did not mean, however, that under the colonial and Diem regimes exactly the same individuals were sitting on the village council and dominating economic life in the village. Rather, between 1954 and 1963 it was often sons, brothers, or cousins of procolonial group members who assumed council positions and cooperated with each other and with Government authorities to gain wealth and influence for their extended families. Under both the colonial and the Diem regimes those families constituted no more than 3 to 5 percent of My Thuy Phuong's people—and largely *the same* 3 to 5 percent. In about 1958, for example, three of the village's four appointed councilmen were large landholders, and the fourth was a local large tradesman. All were prosperous, pro-Government, and had opposed the Viet Minh.

Another parallel with the colonial era was that during the Diem years the pro-Government group failed to attract many followers in the village. There were a dozen or so poorer people, retainers and clients of the group, who endorsed Government rule. But most of those forced to depend on the pro-Government group's largesse did so out of sheer economic or political necessity. There was little willing enthusiasm for the group, few or none of the strong traditional patron-client ties, and little or none of the security such relationships formerly offered clients. Instead, most villagers remembered the popularity of local Viet Minh leaders and programs, compared memories with the realities of the Diem period, and grew bitterly resentful. The reasons for that resentment are illustrated below.

During the Diem years a small number of pro-Government families controlled about 30 to 40 percent of My Thuy Phuong's land and many of the important local commercial activities—including rice purchasing and milling and sale of farm supplies. This was the same control pattern as in 1940–1954. Most families of the pro-Government group lived in substantial homes of cement and wood construction, unlike the majority of villagers, who lived in simple makeshift structures, often of roughly cut wood. In addition, most pro-Government families ate and dressed better than their neighbors, and often sent their children to private schools in Hue. That was an avenue of advancement effectively barred to poorer children.

Besides economic and other factors setting most pro-Government villagers apart, there were cultural divisions nearly identical to those that had divided the village during the colonial era. After 1954 many pro-Government individuals continued to consider France, and to a degree America, as sources of inspiration. They also preferred Western furniture designs and clothing as "modern" and "beautiful," and sometimes associated with Westernized Vietnamese in Hue. Furthermore, most such villagers—or about 4 percent of the local population—converted to Catholicism, since it had become the quasi-official state religion. Before that time there had been only one Catholic family in the village. The conversions occurred despite the strong anti-Government and by implication anti-Catholic identification of the village's active Buddhist groups. In about 1957, several pro-Government families built a small Catholic church in one of the ricefield hamlets, and with help from Hue Catholics, built a much larger one along Highway One. With the presence of these churches, and when a priest began regular visits to say mass, Catholicism strengthened. The converts' grasp of their new religion grew slowly, further widening the already wide cultural gap between themselves and the masses of villagers.

Between 1956 and 1963, Government district authorities appointed My Thuy Phuong's three to five village councilmen, the number of whom had earlier stood at six to eight.[3] The authorities took care to select politically loyal individuals for the council, including "village representatives," a "police councilor," and a "finance councilor." [4] The number of village representatives varied between one and three individuals during the course of the Diem regime. Authorities took similar care in selection of a village clerk, who assisted councilmen but who was not formally a council member.[5] The selection procedures, in short, did not significantly differ from those of the French colonialists in terms of their impact on the village council and the village. The procedures insured that the councilmen came from a wealthy and self-interested minority.

Under Diem the Government took a number of other measures to strengthen its influence in the village. First, there were local boundary changes. The Government expanded the physical area and population of council authority to include hamlets outside the central village area, and it gave the village the name Thuy Phuong—"Place of the Waters." Government presence was strengthened, second, by special public administration training courses for all village councilmen and other local officials. Most such courses were in Hue, and amounted to all-day meetings of several hundred civil servants from throughout the province to hear speeches by provincial and sometimes Saigon officials. To supplement these training programs, the Government assigned personnel from district headquarters for on-the-job training of My Thuy Phuong's civil servants.

Many abuses of council authority common in the village under the French regime became virtually routine during the Diem years. The abuses occurred as council authority expanded in several areas, including the execution of laws and regulations, tax collection, compilation of vital statistics, health, justice, public works, and so forth. As the council workload increased, there were continued inequities in tax and rent collection, continued unjust settlement of local disputes, and continued unfair distribution of communal lands.

Throughout the period, councilmen let it be known that such land, limited and in great demand, was available only to those willing to involve themselves in an informal "arrangement." This pattern was similar to that informally in effect during the colonial period. The council rented communal land only to those willing to pay slightly more than the amount officially set by local regulations. The village policemen collected rent payments. And the council simply ignored and forgot peasants in need of extra land but unwilling or unable to pay the extra rent—which went directly into councilmen's pockets. During the Diem years, councilmen had to compile population and other census data. This was another activity touched by corruption. A peasant spoke:

> When the police and council officials came around to our house to ask about our family, we knew why they were really coming. That information was for family taxes, and we knew the smaller the number of people reported for our family, the smaller would be the tax we had to pay. Everybody knew it. Everybody.
>
> So when they came, we knew it was best to cooperate. Sometimes we would give them a little bit of money, maybe just 100 piasters. Not much. We knew the money would go right into their pockets, and stay there. But we also knew that because of this corruption we would save money on taxes.

Villagers discovered that one form of corruption led to another, and corruption became so deep and widespread that it was virtually unavoidable. The case of the local dispensary is illustrative. In about 1959, the Government built a small district dispensary near the village's section of Highway One. It was supposed to be open to all district residents for first aid and inoculations, and even for maternity care. But these services were available only to those willing to meet the monetary demands of the nurse who worked at the facility. There was a schedule of small fees, to cover costs of services offered at the dispensary. But the fees people actually had to pay were considerably higher than those listed on the schedule. A peasant woman described the day in 1961 when her son fell from a tree he was climbing, and twisted and broke his arm. The woman rushed the boy to the dispensary and found there a nurse willing to help, but only at a price. The nurse demanded a small amount of money before tending to the boy.

Corruption also came to dispute-resolution. Law and local custom dictated that the village council fairly settle local disputes, but the alliance of local councilmen, large tradesmen, and large landholders brought departure from tradition and the letter of the law. Once a man who earned his living working as a laborer on others' land protested that he had been underpaid and overworked by a large landholder. The council heard the case and witnesses attested to the truth of the allegations, but the laborer lost.

There were many other instances of injustice in village dispute settlement. Looking back on the Diem years, people recalled that the council never resolved complaints against members of the pro-Government group in favor of complainants not from that minority. Two men who were councilmen during the Diem era actually confirmed this. There is also evidence that the majority of villagers over a course of years grew wise about their chances of obtaining fair hearings before the council, so brought fewer and fewer complaints. "Many bad things happened in this place," said a peasant, "and the council did nothing about them. The people lost faith in the council, and knew that it belonged to the big men."

In addition to expanding administrative responsibilities, the council assumed a more overt political role in local affairs after 1955. As Diem consolidated power, he established a quasi-official political party, the Personalist Labor Party, known as the Can Lao.[6] The party received heavy governmental support and became, in effect, an extension of the Government. Can Lao dedicated itself to Diem's philosophy of "Personalism." It directed members to serve the best interests of the people through enlightened, benevolent, and strong rule. In the village, councilmen became the most visible and locally influential Can Lao representatives. In that capacity councilmen endeavored, first of all, to attract members to the party. They saw to it that as many civil servants and soldiers as possible joined the Huong Thuy District Can Lao branch. However, few joined besides the soldiers and civil servants.

The councilmen's second major party task was to insure Can Lao success in the periodic elections for the National Assembly. There is evidence that this was reflected, first, in pressure on voters to support particular party candidates. Electoral control was rarely expressed as "instruction," but rather as "guidance." Councilmen simply spread the word in informal conversations that support for certain candidates was desirable. Villagers understood that if they did not vote as expected there could be deep trouble, even arrest. "Everybody knew that the elections were dishonest," recalled a peasant, "and everybody voted for the Government men because we had to." Another peasant said, "It would be much trouble for me if I voted the wrong way. I might be arrested, or get trouble with paperwork. So it was easiest to agree with the Government." Councilmen assured Can Lao electoral success, second, through outright ballot-box stuffing. "The province authorities in Hue told us this was alright," said a Diem-era councilman, "so we did it." The former councilman added that Can Lao candidates usually received upwards of 90 or 95 percent—and sometimes even 100 percent—of the votes cast in My Thuy Phuong.

Complementing the council's Can Lao support function was its involvement in numerous Government-sponsored associations and committees in the village, which involved a wide range of people. One such group was the Huong Thuy Farmers Association, which established a village branch in the late 1950s. Another committee, which attempted to assist and advise the village council in settlement of local and landlord-tenant disputes, was the Agricultural Affairs Committee. There was also a group called the Local Development Committee, designed to provide the council with assistance on economic development and public works projects in the village. Another local organization was the Parents of Students Association. Still another was Young Women of the Republic, inspired by Diem's sister-in-law, and aiming at involvement of women in support of various Government activities. And then there was Republican Youth, which emerged as an unofficial branch of Can Lao, and was a local paramilitary force.

Participation in these and other local "people's organizations" was coerced and hardly enthusiastic. For example, peasants understood that the Government expected them to belong to the Farmers' Association, so most grudgingly attended the occasional meetings. The Young Women of the Republic operated in similar fashion. Women had to join. Periodically, the Government organized and marched or trucked members from the village to sites of large rallies. There officials lined the women up, and told them to cheer at appropriate points during speeches by local, provincial, and sometimes national women's leaders.

Republican Youth organized nearly all of the young people over the age of about 15 for essentially the same sorts of events, and trained some in paramilitary functions. Again, membership was required. In the village, there were 20 or 30 of the paramilitary Combat Youth, part-time and poorly armed. Led by teachers, Government "youth and sports cadres," and local military officials, young people belonging to Republican Youth participated in rallies, sporting events, talent contests, and village cleanups, and assisted militiamen in static defense functions. Always these activities bore the mark of the Government, for Republican Youth leaders made clear to the young people that they expected attendance and enthusiasm at the special events, and that they would interpret noninvolvement and neglect of paramilitary duties as an anti-Government sign.

My Thuy Phuong's people had many other tales of manipulation and corruption by local councilmen, large landholders, tradesmen, and others. They are tales of a local pro-Government group that remained confident and powerful through the 1950s and into the 1960s. The group was confident because of the entire governmental system behind it, including the laws, regulations, and security forces which in general reinforced its domination of village life. And the group was powerful because for many years it and the Government succeeded in cowing political opponents—at least until the early 1960s, when a new revolutionary movement grew strong.

REFOCUSED MOVEMENT

During the early years of the Diem regime, many perceived the "remnants" of the Viet Minh village leadership in a new fashion. The "remnant" leaders began to seem indecisive, perhaps because some other local revolutionaries had departed for the north, or because of widespread bewilderment at the fate of the Viet Minh. One peasant recalled that the Diem years were frustrating ones for him:

> When our country was divided after the Geneva Agreement we all hoped that there would be a unified country very soon under the Viet Minh. But when that did not happen, we were sad that the Viet Minh seemed so weak. They seemed unable to do anything about that. They seemed to be very afraid of the Government. Many people here would have helped the Viet Minh if the Viet Minh had tried to continue struggling, but the Viet Minh was very quiet, and the national army and police operated very strongly.
>
> It was not until about 1960 or some year at about that time that the Liberation Front began to operate here. So before the Liberation began, it was a difficult time. Many of us did not know what to do.

Another peasant put it this way:

> Why did the Viet Minh do so much for us, and then stop? Why did they do so much to make our people into revolutionaries, and then leave us? The Com-

munists are very tricky. They did it because they knew that after a few years living under Mr. Diem and the Americans that we would be stronger revolutionaries than before. Ah, the Communists are very tricky!

This man's use of "tricky" was intended to convey respect, and bore no intended negative connotation. Still another peasant commented, "The 1950s were very difficult, and many people remembered the Viet Minh because it was something that we all supported. It made us proud. But when the Viet Minh no longer operated we had to wait for something new to take its place."

By the late 1950s or 1960–1961, the men who had journeyed north were back in My Thuy Phuong—or at least in the hills west of the village. "For so many years they had been away in North Vietnam," remembered a peasant, "and when they came back we couldn't believe it. Some of us thought that they had died. We were surprised to see them return, and we were very happy to hear them say that they wanted to organize the Liberation in the area."

On December 20, 1960, at a time of rising dissatisfaction in many parts of Vietnam, a variety of individuals, many of whom had been linked to the Viet Minh, founded the National Liberation Front of South Vietnam.[7] Its main objective, according to a Front publication, was to "overthrow the disguised colonial regime of the U.S. imperialists and the dictatorial Ngo Dinh Diem administration—lackey of the United States—and to form a national democratic coalition administration." [8] The Front began its activities with no nationwide organization of its own, but before long built one. In late 1961, the Front set up committees—at first just on paper—for Huong Thuy District, and then for My Thuy Phuong.[9] The village committee, called the Administrative Liberation Association, consisted of about seven to ten men, all of whom had been active in the Viet Minh. One or two of them belonged to the People's Revolutionary Party, which according to George Kahin and John Lewis was an "unconcealed communist element within the Front." [10] Kahin and Lewis also write that Communists dominated the Front from its inception, and imply that this came through the party.[11]

Village committee members named Te, the former teacher, and Minh, the large landholder's son, as chairman and vice-chairman respectively. The committee also placed the son of the peasant Truong in charge of Farmers' Affairs, and assigned others responsibility for Economy and Finance, Youth, and Security. In their new positions, Te, Minh, and many of their former Viet Minh colleagues began to build a new local political force. Their initial efforts were marked by essentially the same tactics that had been employed so successfully during the Viet Minh years. In the early years Front leaders moved through My Thuy Phuong mainly during hours of darkness. Sometimes carrying weapons, they made frequent visits to different parts of the village. The men approached families or small groups of family representatives, and talked with them about local conditions and the aims of the Front. A peasant recalled:

> I remember in the years right after Viet Cong became active—before Mr. Diem was overthrown—they came at night, usually just a few of them, and made our families listen to their propaganda. Those Viet Cong never threatened us. They never did anything bad to us, but we were a little bit afraid of them, because we did not know anything about them. So we all went, and listened, and usually did not say anything.
>
> Sometimes, also, people who were our friends and who were with the Viet Cong came to our house. Often they would tell us to join them. They said, "We are friends. You should join." They came to our house so often, and it happened to almost everybody here.

The Front's local leaders distributed flyers, leaflets, discussion sheets, posters, and occasionally newspapers. There were also Front radio programs, broadcast from clandestine stations in remote mountainous parts of South Vietnam.[12] While Front publications and broadcasts were technically unsophisticated compared with the Government's, their messages were imaginative and effective. There were a number of pamphlets issued by the Thua Thien/Hue Front organization which reached My Thuy Phuong. These addressed specific regional problems, citing specific incidents involving the Government and its opponents, and describing specific Front activities in specific places.

Front leaders began to portray their movement in all their conversations with villagers as the chief opponent of the Government, and as the chief hope for relief from the political oppression people increasingly associated with the Government. Those conversations concerned general national issues, dwelling at length on American aid to the Diem regime and the Government's pro-Catholic, anti-Buddhist orientation. Furthermore, local Front leaders and Front leaflets and broadcasts reported details of demonstrations and other anti-Diem activities in different parts of Vietnam.

After the first few months of Front activity, revolutionary messages began to flow once again in My Thuy Phuong. A peasant likened the village mood to the late 1940s, when the Viet Minh was taking root. "Then we had to be a little bit afraid of French police, and French spies," he said. "It was the same under Mr. Diem. We had to speak very carefully, and sometimes speak in strange ways, not really saying what we wanted to say, but only giving a little idea of the meaning we wanted." The peasant paused, thought for a moment, then flashed a quick smile. "What I mean to say," he concluded, "is that we were testing each other, testing new political ideas."

NOTES

1. Among the best of many books focusing on this period is George McT. Kahin & John W. Lewis, *The United States in Viet-Nam* (New York: Dial Press, 1967).

2. Pike, *Vietcong*, p. 53.

3. See Nguyen Thai, *Is South Vietnam Viable?* (Manila: Carmelo & Bauermann, 1962), pp. 68–70; available in East-West Resource Systems Institute Library, Honolulu, Hawaii. For a detailed discussion of the Diem-era civil service system, with qualifications for employment, salaries, etc. included, see Dale Rose, *The Vietnamese Civil Service System* (Saigon: Michigan State Advisory Group, 1961); available in East-West Resource Systems Institute Library, Honolulu.

4. *Cf.* Nghiem Dang, *Viet-Nam; Politics and Public Administration* (Honolulu: East-West Center Press, 1966), p. 154.

5. After May, 1963, the Government again slightly increased the number of council members, and it ordered councilmen chosen by members of hamlet administrative councils and by local voluntary group leaders. Because these hamlet and group leaders were themselves elected by the people, village councilmen were chosen, in effect, by indirect suffrage. Also see *ibid.*, p. 156.

6. This was short for *Can-Lao Nhan-Vi Dang*.

7. *The Pentagon Papers*, pp. 74–78.

8. *South Viet-Nam National Front for Liberation; Documents* (South Vietnam: Giai Phong Publishing House, 1966), p. 19; available in Cornell Library.

9. *Cf.* Vien, no. 23, p. 31.

10. Kahin & Lewis, *op. cit.*, p. 132; also see Pike, *op. cit.*, pp. 136–153.

11. Kahin & Lewis, *ibid.*

12. Some villagers said the broadcasts began as early as 1961. Others indicated they began in 1962.

7

Struggle

RENEWED BATTLE

Establishment of My Thuy Phuong's Front committee in 1961–1962 coincided with the beginning of local guerrilla warfare.[1] At the time, there were 15 or 20 guerrillas in the village, remnants of the earlier Viet Minh struggle, and officially members of the Liberation Army.[2] Local Front leaders organized guerrillas into three-man cells, and in 1962–1963 formed one or two squads.

The guerrillas needed no refresher course in military tactics, and suffered no particular lack of weapons. During those early years, in fact, guerrillas obtained weapons from a variety of sources, often fashioning their own. Knives, for example, were readily available, and guerrillas sharpened them into deadly weapons. They also manufactured hand grenades from a variety of available materials. Guerrillas had to obtain only explosive charges from outside the village. Front agents actually purchased some weapons, such as American carbines, from Government soldiers in need of pocket money. Among the most important of weapons were punji sticks, small sharpened stakes of bamboo used in traps. And the strangest guerrilla weapons of all were facsimile rifles, carved from wood.[3]

Several villagers commented that during the early 1960s—as during the Viet Minh period—they were frequently exposed to guerrillas, sometimes daily. They also noted that the guerrillas operating in My Thuy Phuong, like their Viet Minh predecessors, projected an image of simplicity. First, guerrillas dressed in the scantiest of clothes. They usually wore black shorts, along with shirts of heavy-duty material. Guerrillas avoided conspicuous colors and patterns or marks of rank. Occasionally they went barefoot, but more often than not wore sandals made of old tires, with soles of hard outer tire layers, and the supporting straps of inner tubes. These were the so-called Ho Chi Minh or Binh Tri Thien sandals, which had an added advantage when guerrillas strapped them on backwards. Worn in that fashion, the sandals left prints in mud or sand that misled trackers.

When guerrillas journeyed far from the village, each man carried, in addition to weapons and ammunition, a small plastic or metal rice bowl, a spoon, and chopsticks. In each squad or attack group one man carried a small pot and a cooking spoon. Guerrillas prepared and ate all of their food with these simple utensils. For sanitary reasons, they used an unusual eating method called "chopsticks two ends." The guerrillas served food to themselves with one end of the chopstick set and ate with the other.

Villagers' comments suggest, in summary, that the simple clothes and eating utensils not only identified guerrillas with the poor and enhanced their image as men making great sacrifices, but were highly practical, giving them greater tactical mobility than those they fought.

After 1954, a gradual Government military buildup occurred in the immediate vicinity of My Thuy Phuong. Army units occupied former colonial garrisons, and the Government constructed new Army camps in Thua Thien/Hue. It staffed the Huong Thuy District headquarters with about a company of soldiers, and used the headquarters as a command point for military activities throughout the district. Occasionally over the years between 1954 and 1963, larger numbers of troops from distant military installations came for operations to the village area. And soldiers from district headquarters paid frequent visits to the small building used by the village council and other civil servants.

Over the years, Army units organized operations to "neutralize" dissident influence in the village. Such operations came frequently, and they were more frequent and intense than local operations by French military units. The operations mainly involved Army troops from outside the district, along with a number of local military and paramilitary units. Here is a description of a typical operation, which people remembered primarily because it came at the time of the 1962 commemoration of Buddha's Birthday. As the description unfolds, it is important to remember that about 10 similar operations came to My Thuy Phuong between 1955 and 1963.

When several former Government soldiers who were actual participants in the operation looked back on it, they noted that it occurred about a week following a serious breach of security: local guerrillas had ambushed a military convoy moving through My Thuy Phuong. The operation also came at a time of mounting anti-Government agitation in the province. Buddhist leaders were becoming more vocal in their criticism of Diem's policies, and had focused attention on celebration of Buddha's Birthday. Hue's An Quang Buddhist leaders had requested Government permission to organize massive public prayer meetings and processions, but the Government had refused the request. Government suspicions of the Buddhists, and nervousness about increased guerrilla activity, led local Government authorities to organize military operations throughout Thua Thien/Hue at about the time of Buddha's Birthday. According to a Catholic priest from Huong Thuy District, "It was to show the V.C. that the Government was strong, and to make the opponents of the Government afraid."

The operation in My Thuy Phuong that day began quietly. In command was an Army major, who was assisted by a captain and several lieutenants, and who actually accompanied his troops. About one battalion of regular Army personnel was involved, and was augmented by a number of local units—one or two platoons of policemen, a platoon or two of local forces soldiers, and some village militiamen. While some villagers knew in advance about the operation, most did not. The sweep began about 5:00 A.M., when people were just beginning to stir. Men and older boys were preparing for a day in the fields and women were brewing tea and starting the day's rice pots. A peasant described how it all began: "We were just getting ready to go to work, as usual, when the soldiers came. There were so many of them, with guns and radios. They were in a line, like they were hunting wild pigs, and searched everywhere." The soldiers passed through the area of the peasant's house—searching, probing, questioning. "When the soldiers came to my house," the peasant remembered, "they divided in two. One group asked for our identification papers, and asked us many questions, and the other group searched the house." The soldiers detained any adult without complete identification, and anyone deemed suspicious met a similar fate. According to soldiers who were on the operation, Government forces detained 25 or 30, mostly adult males, and turned them over to Government district authorities for "processing." That usually meant detention of at least three or four days, interrogation, possibly torture, then release or imprisonment with or without trial.

There are indications that Government soldiers undertook the house searches with considerable energy. "They looked at everything," said a peasant woman. "They searched everything, and we did not dare complain." During the operation, soldiers engaged in widespread and systematic looting. The soldiers vied for the house-searching assignments, and seemed to prefer operations in densely populated, relatively prosperous villages like My Thuy Phuong, where they considered looting prospects better. People had many looting tales from that day's operation. Looting occurred during the course of house searches, and many types of loot interested the soldiers. One peasant woman claimed that three soldiers carried off six of her ducks. Another peasant woman said that a small stash of money disappeared during the search of her home—the equivalent of about US$10, which she had set aside for family emergencies.

Another peasant family lost a bicycle, while a tradesman's family saw its sewing machine carried off. A pattern emerged as the looting proceeded. Nearly all of the low-ranking soldiers in the search parties stole, favoring items that could be resold easily. And they looted most houses along the path of the sweep.

Many people, who may or may not have been associated with local guerrillas or other anti-Government groups, fled the searchers, and a static line of soldiers caught some who fled. The soldiers that day lined Highway One. Other soldiers moved toward the static line through the westward portion of the village. Several who wandered out toward the highway and the line of soldiers were detained. Three men who were members of the local guerrilla force fled from the advancing soldiers out toward the highway. The three carried carbines. As they approached the highway they probably sensed danger and grew cautious, for they began crawling through a small ricefield. It is unclear precisely what happened next, but the outcome is indisputable: the three guerrillas were killed.

Like the French operation described earlier, the 1962 Buddha's Birthday operation unsettled the rhythm of village life, inconvenienced and brought loss to many, and tarnished the Government's reputation. "Every time the Army came they made more friends for the V.C.," noted a peasant. Another peasant added, "Cruel like the French."

As the events of that 1962 operation unfolded, people were probably most aware of the role played by soldiers of the Army, for there were many of them, they were most heavily armed, and they did most of the looting. But police and other military units also assumed important roles that day—and many other days—in the village. During the Diem years, the police contingent in Huong Thuy District increased substantially, from a 1954 district-wide level of about seven men to a high in 1963, of fifteen to twenty. The Government assigned full-time policemen to My Thuy Phuong and other villages, and others to district headquarters, from which they could be drawn for operations and other special requirements. Police personnel received Government training in traditional police functions—levying of fines for petty infractions, settlement of local disputes, and the like—but also in several security functions even more sophisticated than those performed by district police under the French. While the colonialists had established intelligence nets of some complexity in the My Thuy Phuong area, the Government succeeded in duplicating that feat and improving on it.

Policemen also assumed other specialized tasks after 1954. They issued and later checked the required family and individual identification papers. As before, they collected taxes and sometimes rents, and enforced decisions of local authorities, including the village council. And as in the instance just described, policemen assisted in military actions which came to the village. Suffice it to add at this point that most Diem-era policemen in the area were corrupt. Their wide-ranging assignments, the lack of constant, honest supervision, and association with dishonest and opportunistic individuals in and out of the Government meant that corruption came almost inevitably.

But other units besides police supported the activities of Army regulars. There were the local forces, consisting in Huong Thuy District of one company of Civil Guard soldiers, most of whom were from local villages. And in each village of Huong Thuy, including My Thuy Phuong, there were part-time militiamen, who also performed security functions. The village had only about 20 or 25 militiamen, all of whom received some weapons training, and whose loyalties to the Government were generally strong.

The Civil Guard had a defensive mission. It guarded the Government district compound, important bridges within the district, and other important points in Huong Thuy. Militiamen guarded village offices, protected local councilmen, and patrolled village paths. Sometimes, as in the Buddha's Birthday operation, local-force soldiers and militiamen accompanied nonlocal Army units and policemen, and sometimes even participated in various aggressive thrusts into the villages. More often, however, local forces assisted in static or defensive phases of such operations. For example, they often served in blocking forces along perimeters of areas being searched.

Civil Guard soldiers, according to many sources, were not as well trained or as reliable as the Army regulars, and even less motivated to fight. And their desertion rate was high. "At least a third of my men were usually gone at any one time," said a former Civil Guard sergeant. "I should have punished them, but didn't like to," he added. Typically, soldiers deserted once every month or two. Desertion usually involved relatively short periods—five to seven days—and nearly everyone in local forces enlisted ranks practiced it. People considered local militiamen something of a joke. Their generally poor training and rag-tag appearance prompted one peasant to comment, "They could not even protect themselves, their training was so bad. How could they protect the people? What ridiculous representatives of Mr. Diem. Not cruel, just ridiculous."

It should be noted in passing that there were only about 50 men from My Thuy Phuong serving at any one time as Army regulars or Civil Guard members, meaning that during the Diem era military service did not take too many away from previous occupations or transform the village's work force. And desertions were actually minor economic stabilizing factors locally, as many who left units for short periods often aided relatives in the fields. Not helping much were the salaries paid Diem-era soldiers, which were so low that they added little to families' wealth and had almost no impact on the village economy.

The Diem years provided the people of My Thuy Phuong with ample and clear evidence that the Government's various security branches were strong in terms of weaponry and firepower, but weak in command, organization, and motivation. Many laid much of the blame for these weaknesses at the feet of about 10 Government military officers, who were widely known in the area. These soldiers, several of whom are briefly profiled here, held middle-echelon command positions, were chiefly responsible for Government security operations, and were indirectly responsible for administration in Huong Thuy of the entire Government program. They found themselves deeply involved with members of the village's pro-Government group in supporting Government programs for the village. In effect, these 10 officers and the pro-Government minority joined forces.

Few of these locally influential soldiers were from the area. Without exception, however, they were veterans of the French colonial armed forces, and in most cases were imbued with Western military strategies and cultural preferences. One of them was a man named Phuoc. From about 1958 to 1963, he was an Army lieutenant assigned to Huong Thuy District. To know Phuoc is to begin to understand how the apparatus for which he worked operated in My Thuy Phuong. So here is his story.

Lieutenant Phuoc was born and raised in a suburb of Hanoi. His father had been a tradesman, and he was brought up as a devout Catholic. When Phuoc was a young man, according to a relative, he volunteered for the French colonial armed forces and trained for a year or two in France itself before serving for about 10 years as a field artillery officer. When the Geneva Agreement partitioned Vietnam, Phuoc was among the thousands of refugees who journeyed from the northern to southern portions of the country. Phuoc voluntarily joined the Army in about 1956. "He wanted to fight the Communists again," said his relative. After being shifted around from unit to unit and from province to province, in about 1958 Phuoc was assigned to Huong Thuy District. He remained there until 1963, and in the course of a few years rose in rank to first lieutenant. Phuoc's advancement through the ranks was paralleled by an increase in his personal influence throughout the district, including My Thuy Phuong.

Phuoc was dedicated to suppressing anti-Government dissenters. Charged by the district chief with partial responsibility for security of the area, Phuoc became directly involved in military and police operations. He spent many hours every week organizing coordinated military and police antiguerrilla operations in the villages. In this connection, Phuoc spent much of his time setting up, supporting, and coordinating intelligence networks. People knew him best for this phase of his work.

There had been intelligence networks functioning in the area during the colonial era, but between 1954 and 1963, the Government gave such networks greater emphasis than ever before for suppression of dissent. Phuoc worked individually with the informers who constituted these networks, emphasizing in discussions his interest in several types of information. He wanted names of local guerrillas and information on people heard or suspected of criticizing the Government, including those *not* connected with the Front or, previously, with the Viet Minh. He also was interested in information on guerrilla activities, such as meetings, military plans, or taxation schedules.

There were about five informers working for Phuoc in My Thuy Phuong. Several who remembered him said that Phuoc grew elated when more detailed, "higher quality" intelligence came his way. This was information which was from reliable sources, and which concerned specific activities by specific individuals in the area. When he received such intelligence, Phuoc rarely delayed before acting. Once in 1961 or 1962, an informer presented Phuoc with a report that a particular peasant family in My Thuy Phuong had been assisting local guerrillas. Phuoc's immediate response was to arrest the whole family, except its youngest children. Phuoc held them as "Viet Cong suspects," despite their denials of guilt. While being held they were threatened and tortured, and Phuoc was in charge of the interrogation/torture sessions.

A peasant long active in Buddhist Family Association affairs offered another example of Phuoc's security function in the village. The peasant thought back to 1962–1963, when the An Quang Buddhist organization was rallying opposition to the Government's anti-Buddhist policies, and described Phuoc during that period as a "very busy man." According to the peasant and others, in early 1963, when nationwide anti-Government protests by Buddhists were intensifying, Phuoc learned that two local teachers, who were active in village Buddhist organizations but committed to neither Government nor Front, had gone to Hue for a meeting of Buddhist youth leaders. Phuoc ordered their immediate arrest. Police brought the two men to the Government district headquarters, and they appeared before Phuoc. According to one of them, Phuoc was at first deferential and polite, but soon his intentions became clearer. "He told us, very politely, that he had the authority to hold us indefinitely without charges," the teacher said, "and then he told us what he wanted." Phuoc was interested in obtaining the names of all those who had attended the meeting in Hue, and wanted a list of all Buddhist activists in the village. "They beat us and threatened our families with arrest," said the teacher, "but we decided to be strong and tell him nothing. We thought we were surely going to be killed." When the threats and beatings did not work, Lieutenant Phuoc sent the two teachers off to prison in Hue, where they remained until the fall of Diem.

These two vignettes demonstrate the role of one influential Government military officer in the village area. Phuoc's efficiency, loyalty, and enthusiasm in carrying out his security functions earned him the respect and favor of his superiors in the Government bureaucracy, and had a powerful effect in the village. That is, Phuoc's preoccupation with intelligence networks, and his involvement in more overt security operations meant inconvenience, arrest, jail, and in some cases even death to many of the village's anti-Government dissenters.

Lest his role be misunderstood, we should view Phuoc as only the most infamous of many influential Government soldiers assigned during 1954–1963 to the My Thuy Phuong area. In addition to Phuoc, there was a sergeant named Minh, who in 1962–1963 often led squads of soldiers into the village. According to a teacher, "Once in 1963 he helped beat up a group of Buddhist high school students. They were preparing for a demonstration in Hue." Another soldier was Hung, also a sergeant, whose job between about 1960 and 1963 was to train village officials in implementation of regulations and decrees. However, Hung's major involvement in My Thuy Phuong and elsewhere did not relate very directly to training. Rather, he was more interested in getting a share of the rents and taxes collected in the villages. "That man was so corrupt that he didn't even hide it," remembered a peasant. "He often took part of our rent money as he stood right in front of us."

And then there was Tu, the lieutenant from a devout Catholic family, who people remembered as "strongly anti-Communist." He was the officer under Phuoc who had direct responsibility for interrogation of detainees. Many heard that Tu displayed inhuman cruelty and sadism during the interrogation sessions, so gave him a special nickname: Tu the Dog.

As part of their general response to Government security forces, village guerrillas engaged in sniping and arranged ambushes along My Thuy Phuong's branch of Highway One. Just as Viet Minh guerrillas had done, Front snipers fired on military patrols moving through the area, and they occasionally targeted trucks in ambushes.[4]

A major guerrilla tactic practiced in My Thuy Phuong during the early 1960s involved the use of punji sticks. Here guerrillas depended upon support from the people for the tactic to succeed, for Front supporters, especially the relatives of guerrillas, were involved in punji stick production. In their free time, guerrillas and their supporters retreated to the hills west of the village or to "safe" homes, carrying with them a quantity of bamboo. The sticks were easy to make—sometimes even children helped cut them—and villagers produced them in huge quantities. After making the sticks, guerrillas and their supporters dug shallow trenches on either side of paths used by Government patrols in the village. They placed hundreds of punji sticks, sometimes tipped with human feces, in the trenches, pointed in toward the paths themselves. They then laid thin layers of grass and leaves on top of the sticks to conceal them. Guerrillas left the punji traps unattended, or retreated to sniping positions nearby.

In one instance, the snipers' wait was not long. In about 1962, a Civil Guard patrol approached along a village path. When the patrol reached the point of the punji traps, Front snipers opened fire, and several Government soldiers jumped to the sides of the path, immediately impaling themselves on the sticks. Seeing their success, the snipers faded away by tunnel, and the Government soldiers quickly retreated with their wounded. People recalled that particular punji incident because of the strong reaction it brought from the Government. A day after the incident, there was a company-size Civil Guard operation in the hamlet nearest the trap. Soldiers searched all homes in the area, arrested a few residents, and did some looting. A peasant who helped make punji sticks recalled:

When the Government military operation came, the Government soldiers behaved very badly, and were very cruel to the people. So people began to think to themselves that everything they had heard about the Government being bad was true. Maybe they supported the Communist side after that.

Others suggested that few felt anger with the Front after such Government retaliatory operations. There were three main reasons for that. First, many had actually been involved in or at least knew in advance of the Front actions. Second, Front guerrillas and local leaders conducted themselves in a generally polite and humble fashion. And third, those same leaders often warned and psychologically prepared people in advance of Government operations. The simple weapons of punji sticks were thus connected to the Front's political strategy, for not only did the tactic serve to undermine Government credibility and effectiveness, but the harsh Government response it elicited may have actually caused support for the Front to heighten.

During the first years of Front activity, guerrillas often brought pressure to bear against pro-Government villagers. A peasant recalled one instance:

There was a man on the village council who was very bad, and who everyone thought was taking money for himself. So one night the Communists began to put up papers all through the area near that man's house. The papers gave his name, and said that he must change his bad ways, or the people of the revolution would kill him. The papers were a warning.

There were other instances of such warnings by paper, but sometimes warnings took another form—destruction. A peasant commented on what happened to a corrupt policeman. "One night a very large bomb exploded in front of that man's house," he recalled. "It did not hurt anybody, but I think it made him very afraid." After the explosion, the policeman slightly changed his demeanor, becoming more cautious and not as blatantly corrupt.

Of more immediate importance to villagers were the attacks against some of the larger landholders. A peasant explained how Front personnel directed warnings against them:

When the rich landowners tried to collect rent, we let them know that we did not agree. We told the people to say, "No, we will not pay you so much. We will give you some, but not so much."

The landlords were afraid of us, so they had to agree. The people were so happy then, and they thanked us. We always said, "No, do not thank us. We were just doing our duty. We work for the people."

DEEPENING COMMITMENT

"There were so many people here who supported the Communists," a tradesman recalled, "that sometimes I had the idea everybody supported that side." He was speaking of the period 1962–1963. It was then that Government security activities intensified and resulted in the arrest or death of about 20 insurgents in My Thuy Phuong. And the Front met force with force. As guerrillas grew more active, there was a deepening of commitment to the Front in the village. Speaking of 1962–1963, a peasant had these words:

> It was an important weapon of the Liberation to organize as many people as possible. It did so because the Liberation depended on the people. Liberation means the support of as many people as possible, because if the people are not happy, then the military struggle can never be successful. The people are the most important, and at that time all the people here helped the Liberation.

Others said that at least 75 percent of My Thuy Phuong's people supported the Front, about 5 percent supported the Government, and the remaining 20 percent were uncommitted. About half the Front supporters were actively involved in assisting Front leaders and guerrillas, and the other half passively supported the insurgent cause. Speaking of the uncommitted, a small tradesman asserted, "They did not want to fight. They didn't care about politics." Others indicated that, as during the Viet Minh era, many of the uncommitted came under intense pressure from both Government and insurgent forces. And by the mid-1960s, many shifted to pro-Front stances—a phenomenon examined in Chapter 8.

People assisted Front guerrillas both directly and through an emerging network of runners and lookouts, and supplied reports concerning Government activities, some of which proved useful in planning attacks. As noted earlier, others helped guerrillas prepare punji traps, and still others volunteered to work digging the tunnels which honeycombed drier sections of the village. These manpower drafts, it should be emphasized, were entirely voluntary, though some volunteers may have helped due more to family or peer-group pressure than devotion to the Front cause. Drafts for the local guerrilla force are discussed below.

Finally, commitment to the Front was reflected in the willingness of many to give contributions to Front tax collectors. As during the Viet Minh period, there were no set "taxation schedules" for the village, nor tax-collection agents designated as such. The collectors usually identified themselves as members of the Finance/Economy Section of the local Front committee. Monetary contributions varied with the wealth of the families, and with the military activities of village guerrillas. In other words, collectors encouraged larger contributions from more prosperous families and during periods of heightened guerrilla attack. Many people who could afford no monetary donations, or who only gave token amounts of money, sometimes donated various types of food to the Front.

Most commonly they gave small stocks of uncooked rice. Occasionally men carried small amounts of rice and other food with them to the ricefields, ostensibly for their own consumption. Sometimes in broad daylight, they turned the food items over to local guerrillas—a fact which came to the attention of the Government, and which prompted it to prohibit the carrying of food to the ricefields.

A word on revolutionary organizations. In their recollections of early Front efforts in the village, people identified only the functional organizations mentioned above. They noted that only the Finance/Economy and Security sections were active. The functional liberation associations for peasants and youth did virtually nothing during 1961–1963. And with few exceptions local leaders did not use titles associated with the Front groups. They simply called themselves "cadres" or "older brothers."

There was little perceptible People's Revolutionary Party activity in the village during the early Front years. As noted earlier, only one or two local Front leaders were party members. There is no evidence that party membership gave those men special responsibilities in the village—only enhanced prestige among village leaders, who viewed party membership as very desirable. The party's covert organization for the province from time to time supplied its members in the village with political pamphlets, but during the early Front years the party formally had nothing to do with local Front organizations or policies.

The Front organization for Thua Thien Province most likely contained five sections, which were identified by Pike: (1) social movement organization and propaganda; (2) propaganda; (3) military proselyting; (4) training and indoctrination; and (5) Liberation Army provincial staff headquarters.[5] In Huong Thuy District, the Front's District Central Committee was similarly organized, and operated from the hills of Thua Thien Province under the close control of the Front provincial organization. The district committee, in turn, maintained touch with village committees. Some went so far as to suggest that local Front activities were totally controlled by district personnel, but most people with opinions on this subject suggested that control was loose. They said that Front district personnel simply passed along general policy guidelines to Front leaders in My Thuy Phuong, leaving most tactical decisions to those men.

By 1962–1963, the Front was extremely powerful throughout South Vietnam, mounting larger operations against Government troops, and utilizing more sophisticated weaponry. There was also considerable dissatisfaction with the Government and support for the Front in Thua Thien/Hue, despite—or perhaps in part because of—extensive Government military and police activities. And there are indications that in My Thuy Phuong the Front began to employ new methods. First, people who in 1962–1963 hesitated to support the Front began to feel pressure from an informal network of neighbors. Some of the more enthusiastic Front supporters did not hesitate to use ridicule and malicious rumors to persuade uncommitted neighbors. One villager, then a prosperous large tradesman, recalled what happened to him: [6]

> I hated the Viet Cong in those days, because the Viet Minh had killed my brother, and the Viet Cong and the Viet Minh were the same. So everyone knew that I would never join the Viet Cong. A few people came to me and told me that I should support them, and that if I did not support them I should be quiet, and not speak against the Viet Cong.
>
> Later, many people began to say bad things about me—that I was corrupt, and that I was a spy for the Government. But they knew that was not true. I was just selling things at my store.

Others indicated that rumors occasionally circulated, most likely originated by Front followers, to discredit people who were allied with the Government, or who were committed to neither side. The rumors against pro-Government individuals were sometimes vicious, but there are indications that rumors concerning the noncommitted were sometimes just as strong. There were instances when rumors spread that people hesitant to support the Front were, in fact, active Front members. Then to add credibility to the rumors, one or two local Front leaders or guerrillas sometimes made surprise nocturnal visits to the "targets." They made sure neighbors saw their visits, or later leaked word to them. After such visits, rumors of Front membership often became fact. Target villagers were isolated by pro-Government neighbors, and gradually Front followers won their friendship. Later, attendance at Front political meetings and conversations with new friends often led to complete transformations. Uncommitted or perhaps even hostile villagers became active, sometimes enthusiastic Front supporters.

Others in the village, especially able-bodied men, during 1962–1963 experienced mounting pressure to join the guerrilla force. Several people not aligned with the Government, but indifferent to the Front, were in early 1963 "invited" to join a Front military unit. The recruitment tactic here involved considerable pressure from family members and friends who might have already begun to support the Front. In a few cases where such tactics failed, Front personnel employed more direct methods. There are indications that a few were actually taken from their homes by armed parties of guerrillas, escorted to the hills west of the village, and told that they had joined Front forces. Government and American authorities usually reported such individuals as "kidnap victims." However, there are indications that many "victims" gradually overcame their initial indifference about the insurgency. They willingly remained with the guerrillas.

A word now on the Front's attitude toward religion—and especially toward Buddhism. As noted earlier, the An Quang Buddhist organization carried much weight throughout Thua Thien/Hue, including My Thuy Phuong. In the province there were many effective An Quang leaders, mostly monks, and in the village the Buddhist pagoda was active and had wide support. As the pro-Catholic Diem regime undertook its repression of the Buddhists in the early 1960s, there were many Buddhist-led demonstrations against Diem in Thua Thien/Hue. Many journeyed from the village to Hue for the marches, rallies, and prayer sessions, and there was minor Buddhist-led agitation within My Thuy Phuong itself—including circulation of anti-Government pamphlets and anti-Government prayer meetings at the pagoda.

The Buddhist movement attracted wide support in the village and throughout the region primarily because of the Government's anti-Buddhist policies. Another factor was the *uy tin* of movement leaders. These were the numerous Buddhist monks, nuns, and laymen in Hue and in many villages who assumed active, highly visible roles in organizing prayer meetings, and so forth. My Thuy Phuong's major movement leaders were two local pagoda elders, respected members of the Cult Committee.

The final major reason for the Buddhist protests' popularity in the village—and probably throughout the province—was the wide initial feeling that the Front was to some degree anti-Buddhist, that it had "missed" on an important, timely issue. This point and the Front's changing responses to the Buddhist movement are discussed below.

It should first be noted that in village meetings, Front leaders had words of harsh criticism for Catholics, because of close Government-Catholic Church ties. But always the leaders held out hope to local Catholics. Front messages urged those of all faiths, specifically including Catholics, to join the struggle against Diem. In response, a few Catholics joined the insurgency, but most remained firm Government supporters.

In 1961–1962, Front leaders in the village mildly criticized the provincial Buddhist movement, which then was beginning to gain strength. They accused the Buddhists of dividing the anti-Diem forces, which the leaders said consisted of people from all religions and most economic classes. Their special criticism focused on the Buddhist philosophy—which they described in meetings as passive rather than dynamic and not oriented to social change. A student put it this way: "At first, the V.C. thought the Buddhists were not strong enough revolutionaries." But as the Buddhists began to mount an effective, broadly based challenge to Diem, the Front leaders changed what they were saying. People began to hear from the leaders that the Buddhist movement was an important part of the anti-Diem struggle. However, they also heard the leaders characterize the Front as the "leading element" in that struggle, and as the only element with military forces to back up its demands. It is not clear whether this conciliatory attitude toward the Buddhist movement was an indication of Front policy for the region or nation, but in My Thuy Phuong it clearly represented a realistic reaching out by insurgent leaders for new supporters and an attempt to hold on to old ones.

Two men described the local Front shift in emphasis toward class warfare. First, a peasant remembered:

> The Front was very much against Mr. Diem, and explained why we should fight Mr. Diem using the same words that the Viet Minh had used before. But they also began propaganda about the power of the people, and how the people had to destroy the rich. This was the Communist idea, just like in North Vietnam or in Communist China. This was the type of idea they had for their struggle.

Another peasant said:

> During the Viet Minh movement the enemy was very clear. Everybody opposed the French and hated the French, but under Mr. Diem it was not as clear as before.
>
> In other words, the Liberation had to show the people why they had to fight. It had to show them why they as the poor class were being used by the upper class and by the Americans. . . .

In summary, despite setbacks caused by Government military and police pressure, and despite the rise of the Buddhist movement, the local Front leaders devoted the years 1961–1963 to building a strong revolutionary base. The general thrust of the movement at first differed little from that of the Viet Minh, for nationalism was the main rallying cry. But gradually ideas related to class struggle began to complement nationalistic appeals. Eventually, about 75 percent of the people joined the Front, in part because of patriotism, in part because they hoped the movement would work out answers to complicated problems of life in the village.

NOTES

1. People indicated that a "security cadre" on the Front committee coordinated guerrilla activities in the village, but did so with the help of the entire committee.
2. See Pike, *Vietcong,* pp. 232–252.
3. On one occasion, wooden facsimile rifles played an important part in a guerrilla operation: during a period when weapons were scarce, guerrillas carrying such rifles paid a nocturnal visit to a local civil servant. A peasant recalled, "When he saw so many guerrillas carrying so many [facsimile] guns, he was very afraid."
4. During 1945–1975, guerrillas often placed mines to interdict the railroad running north-south through Vietnam, but never along the section of track in the village.
5. Pike, *op. cit.,* p. 221, n.
6. The brother of that man quoted in the text had served the French colonial army as a low-ranking foot soldier. He died of gunshot wounds while on an operation against Viet Minh units in 1950.

8

Ascendancy

NEW CONDITIONS

My Thuy Phuong's guerrillas were inactive in the immediate aftermath of the coup d'etat that brought down Diem in 1963. There was no letup, however, in the Front's proselyting efforts. In broadcasts on the clandestine Liberation Radio and in meetings in the village, the Front claimed credit for the coup. A peasant had this comment:

> It was so happy after Mr. Diem was gone, because our country had been suffering for so long. Everyone was happy, and was sure that life would be better. We all supported the national government, and especially the Army. It was a new revolutionary government of the military, and we became very united behind the Army.

Another peasant recalled:

> The Communist propaganda was that the Front had led the fight against Mr. Diem, and they said they were the ones who killed him. This was on the Liberation Radio, and this was what some people who I knew liked the Communists said to me also. But we did not believe that, and we felt that the Communists had lost their strength.

Others made similar statements, suggesting that Front credibility suffered after Diem's death. And a few hinted that the coup caused some confusion within local Front ranks, and some indecision by local leaders. This was possibly because the leaders had no instructions about what to do or say under such suddenly changed circumstances, and their chief enemy was gone.

But these were short-run problems. In early 1964, the leaders began to reassert the nationalistic, anti-American ideas they found easiest to express. Through the informal network of Front supporters in the village, a message began to spread that the fight against the Americans had simply entered a new phase, and that the generals in control of the Government were no more representative of popular aspirations than any of the Diem-era leaders had been. Reflecting the views of many, a peasant described what happened:

> The Liberation Front had to begin speaking again about some of our old ideas. We had to talk to the people about the puppet army and puppet administrators in the cities and countryside. At first, the people were happy, and did not want to listen very much, but then they listened, and they agreed with everything we said. The people joined the revolution again.

PROSELYTING

During 1964–1967, the Front took advantage of its years of preparation, and weakness on the Government side to bid for total control of South Vietnam. With the Government crippled by instability in its top leadership and related paralysis of most security programs, 1964–1965 saw the Front nearly take over the country, mounting sustained attacks in hundreds of locations. According to the Pentagon Papers, in February 1965 American intelligence agencies reported the presence in South Vietnam of the first North Vietnamese troops.[1] And 1964–1965 also saw the arrival of the first large contingents of American combat troops.[2]

The arrival of U.S. Marines in Thua Thien/Hue meant increased pressure on the Front throughout the province. In My Thuy Phuong, Government and American forces killed and jailed a number of Front leaders and followers, and Front leaders faced some new problems—setbacks discussed in Chapter 9. However, 1964–1967 was generally a period of considerable local Front influence and Government weakness in the village.

In fact, My Thuy Phuong was in some ways close to being what the Marines called a "V.C. village." What kept it out of that classification was the fact that the pro-Government group remained in control of the land and other resources, and could call in police and soldiers. Those most closely linked to the Government apparatus were the *same individuals,* or from the *same families,* who had been active supporters of the Diem regime, and before that of the French. They constituted between 3 and 5 percent of the populace, mostly large landholders and prosperous tradesmen; half were Catholics. They found association with the Government personally profitable. Those who did not steal local funds or pressure people into paying bribes profited on imported goods sold locally. Or they benefited through favoritism (identical to that described in preceding chapters) in land distribution or dispute resolution.

But the Front had the people. A peasant commented, "The Liberation was the only political group that really loved the people. We learned that the Government did not." What could have been behind this comment? Perhaps in part it was recollection of the different political messages emphasized by Front leaders during their proselyting efforts in the village. These were the same types of meetings, training sessions, and conversations that had marked the 1960–1963 period of Front activity. Though the leaders deliberately intertwined many ideas in their proselyting, attention here focuses separately on each major message. Note that many villagers of all political stripes discussed the messages, which are presented below in no particular rank order.

With the arrival of American combat troops in Vietnam, the most important Front messages were those which *opposed the Americans*. A peasant recalled, "The Viet Cong during that period did nothing but talk to us about the Americans. All the time. They told us how the Americans were destroying our country, how they were controlling the Government." In discussing Front proselyting, many others similarly focused on the frequency of anti-American messages. And one of the most common Front slogans repeated in meetings, leaflets distributed in My Thuy Phuong, and in broadcasts, went like this: "Unite The People, Oppose The Americans, Save The Nation." [3] Reactions to these messages varied from outright rejection of them by most pro-Government villagers to enthusiastic agreement by many Front supporters. The majority, however, was generally receptive to and in agreement with them. A peasant's comment is illustrative:

> We often heard the Communists tell us about America. They said America was an imperialist country. They said America was destroying our fatherland. They said everyone must unite to fight the American army. Well, I'd say that almost everyone agreed with them. I did.
>
> Some may have disagreed about how to fight the Americans and not known whether to follow the Communists. But I think almost everyone agreed that the Americans had to go and that the Communists were the strongest ones to fight them.

Second, there were messages concerning the *history of the revolution in Vietnam and in the province*. Discussions in the village, leaflets, and broadcasts focused on ideas of revolt and resistance, with an emphasis on the recent Viet Minh struggle. Many of these 1964–1967 messages presented a class interpretation of Vietnamese history.[4] Complementing the historical messages were those focusing on *revolution and struggle in the world*. Front leaders often spoke of a world class struggle and of workers around the world uniting to oppose capitalist classes and imperialist nations. It is unclear how villagers reacted to the messages on revolution in Vietnam and elsewhere, but those messages no doubt widened horizons and perhaps changed world views of at least some.

Another Front focus was on the *history of the village revolution*. Here messages concerned the changes the French, Diem, and post-Diem regimes had brought to the village, on the impoverishment and loss of power by so many people, and on the local history of the Viet Minh and Front movements. Front leaders mentioned four revolutionary classes in discussions of local history—peasants who are landless, poor or proletarian, and middle class; workers; petite bourgeoisie of small tradesmen; and the national bourgeoisie of larger tradesmen. However, the leaders described peasants as the most important revolutionary force.

Despite some simplification on the question of Front origins, there are indications that messages on the local movement were far more understandable to large numbers of villagers than those focusing on the larger issues of Vietnamese and world struggle against class and national enemies. A peasant said:

> They kept talking about what it was like to live here, and they kept explaining to us what different things in our life meant in terms of Communist ideas. Some of us resisted those ideas, but they kept talking, and then people began to see that there were many things correct about Communist ideas. We could see, for example, that there were corrupt men in the area, and we could see them getting rich before our eyes.

Another peasant agreed, and added:

> The Liberation had answers for all of the most important problems that we all knew. They had an answer about land reform, which was that they would give land to the poor people. They had an answer about high taxes. They said that the Liberation would spend the taxes only for the people, and would collect them without corruption. They also said that they would help the poor, and this was something else that made them popular, because many people in the village were very poor.

Still another peasant said:

> At first very few people seemed to understand the revolutionary ideas, and did not understand some of the problems that were right in front of our faces.
>
> In the study sessions the comrades and the people talked about power. We said that the ones who had power in our society were ones who were puppets of the Americans, who were a rich class. The most important idea was that the poor class people listened to these ideas and agreed with them.

Next were those messages on *enemies of the revolution*. They directly and indirectly related to all the messages mentioned above. The chief enemies were the Americans and the "puppet" nations—such as South Korea and Thailand—which had sent military forces to Vietnam. But Front leaders also emphasized enemies much more visible to the people of the village. There were first the local puppets, or civil servants and soldiers serving in Government ranks. There was an element of compassion in discussions of the lower ranking of these individuals, for the leaders described them as unknowing—people who failed to understand the political implications of their Government service. But the Front reserved less compassion for those who served as police agents, Government informers, and some of the more infamous or corrupt local officials. Sometimes attacks on specific individuals marked Front political meetings. For example, there was the case of a Government village chief, a man noted for his corruption and incompetence. Front leaders characterized him as a "monster" in political sessions and repeatedly accused him of being exploitative.

As part of the Front effort to develop the people's class consciousness, the proselyting effort focused on the most successful local landholders, and on their manipulation of land, including communal land. Again Front leaders singled out specific individuals in the meetings and attacked them by name. Similarly, the leaders attacked tradesmen who overcharged for goods and moneylenders who profited "excessively." Local reactions to the messages naturally varied. Many members of the pro-Government minority grew fearful as they, their friends, and families were the very enemies the Front had singled out. But most people were quite excited with what they heard. For example, a peasant noted:

> We began to agree that all the rich men in the area were doing nothing to help the people. We saw, for example, that the landlords were very close to the local authorities, and got richer under the protection of the local authorities. Sometimes, for example, they had policemen help them collect rent.
>
> So we began to think of all these men as enemies, and we became very brave and very strong. We did things we had always been afraid to do before. We talked about these men as enemies and said their names. They had to change their ways.

Many very general Front messages touched on the *promise of a better life*. The movement leaders, broadcasts, and leaflets simply repeated that defeating the Americans and the Government would bring improvements in life. There were few specific ideas on Front plans for that better life. Instead villagers heard only general statements concerning rights to land, the wider sharing of political power, the Front's responsiveness to "people's problems," and other general benefits of Vietnam "at peace." When that peace came, the Front messages suggested, all the people would live happier, more productive, secure lives. It is unclear how villagers received these general promises. Certainly they heard similar messages from the Government, which promised a better life for the people after defeating the Front. However, a peasant noted:

> The Communists kept saying, "If you fight for the revolution you will have a good life." They said that to always be struggling would bring more prosperity and happiness to all the people. We thought that the Communist policy would be

good, that new social policies would be good, because that would mean everyone would share more in the economic development.

And another peasant stated, "The Liberation men said that all the people had to fight the Americans and the puppets because when we did that there would be peace, and it would be a happy time again. We knew that everyone would not be rich under the Liberation policy, but we hoped that life would be better."

Next were messages concerning the *People's Revolutionary Party,* which the Front presented to villagers as the "vanguard" of the movement. Only two or three in the village actually belonged to the party, but Front messages characterized an invitation to join as a high honor. The party accepted people as members only on the recommendation of one or two long-term members, and only after the prospective members had demonstrated dedication to the movement by supporting guerrilla activities, proselyting in the village, or taking other actions to assist the Front. Front messages described the party as receiving moral encouragement and inspiration from the Labor Party of North Vietnam, and presented it as the purest expression of the people's will—the soul of the Front. Most villagers held the party in high regard because of these messages, though few thought they would ever be permitted to join. But for local Front leaders, it was different: the ideal of party membership served as an extra incentive to work hard. A leader commented, "The cadres were always very proud. They always worked hard, and they knew that the best of them, those who worked hardest for the revolution and are most intelligent, could become party members. It was one of the things that made them struggle so hard."

An eighth major message focused on *sacrifice and struggle* to support the movement. This was related to the messages on world, Vietnamese, and local history, which emphasized the elements of class struggle. A peasant recalled a Front meeting that focused explicitly on sacrifice and struggle:

> The meeting was of about 10 people, and the comrade was a member of the Liberation Front. He asked us all to talk about our own work for the revolution. One man got up and said he had given some money to the revolution. Another man said that he had helped the guerrillas in an attack. A few others said that they were giving valuable information to the Front. I said that I had told the Front about an Army operation that might be coming.
>
> So the cadre listened to all these things and said, "Well, these things are good, but they are not enough. You must all sacrifice more and struggle harder for the revolution." He said that we are letting others sacrifice for us, and he said that the people's struggle would never be finished until all the people united together to struggle against the Americans and puppet government.

These admonitions were well received in My Thuy Phuong, but it is difficult to evaluate their effectiveness. It is clear only that many made risky sacrifices and struggled persistently to aid the Front.

Ninth of the major messages concerned *heroes of the revolution.* The printed and spoken Front messages contained a set of role models for people to emulate—men, women, and even children who contributed significantly to the movement, and in their contributions revealed heroic personal characteristics. The most shining hero mentioned repeatedly was Ho Chi Minh, whose life, accomplishments, and ideas Front leaders, leaflets, and broadcasts described and analyzed for villagers. In the messages special emphasis focused on Ho's closeness to the peasant masses, and on Ho as a wise, guiding uncle. Two villagers recalled the discussion of Ho as fatherly leader and fighter. A peasant said:

> Many of the [Front] cadres respected and loved Ho Chi Minh very much. A few of them said they had met Ho, and some of them carried his photograph with them. They all said they admired Ho Chi Minh for leading the struggle, and liked him because of his bravery, and because he was in the highest position in the Communist organization. They all tried to tell the people these things, and to make Ho the leader of all the people.

And a student discussed Ho:

> Ho Chi Minh was always our leader. He always was in our minds, and always was the most important person in all the Liberation propaganda. He was very high. But we were told that we could be as good and as strong as Ho Chi Minh by dedication, sacrifice, and by hard study. All of those ways we could fight imperialist America just like Uncle Ho.

A minority of villagers, mostly pro-Government individuals, did not share the student's respect for Ho Chi Minh. They feared and often despised him. But the majority reacted quite positively to the Front messages about Ho. They venerated him and said they wanted to be like him.

Ho Chi Minh was certainly the loftiest of the heroes discussed in the village. However, people heard about a few other heroes of national stature. One of these was Nguyen van Troi, the young Front sympathizer who in 1964 tried to assassinate Robert McNamara, then Secretary of Defense, during an official visit to Saigon. Troi's attempt failed, and Government forces captured and later executed him. Many Front messages eulogized Troi and hailed his act, deeply impressing at least several young people. But most of the Front heroes were from backgrounds similar to those of ordinary villagers, and Front leaders, documents, and broadcasts pictured them as heroic because of small revolutionary acts that anyone could conceivably have performed. In other words, they were model heroic followers.

For example, there were the "American-killing" heroes. The Front heavily complimented individuals and guerrilla units able to kill Americans. In fact, it established a schedule of awards for "American-killing units" and individual "American-killers." Similarly, the Front honored units and individuals that performed effectively in military engagements.

Stories of such units from other parts of Vietnam and from the province were important parts of the hero messages. But the most important heroes of all were ordinary men, women, and children who were neither full-time guerrillas nor leaders in their local communities. Several recalled hearing about the following supposedly real heroes:

> Two young women who tempted some U.S. soldiers to lay down their weapons with promises of sex, who then killed the Americans.
>
> An old woman who assisted guerrillas in setting up an ambush against American soldiers.
>
> A young boy who befriended some U.S. soldiers, and then led them into a Front ambush.
>
> An old man who led his village in resistance to a powerful landlord.
>
> A Government soldier who deserted his unit for the Front, carrying with him several weapons and stolen documents, and who encouraged two or three of his fellow soldiers to go with him.
>
> A schoolboy who secretly spread the teachings of Ho Chi Minh among his classmates.

The Front usually presented these heroic vignettes in clandestine radio broadcasts, in small meetings of Front leaders and guerrillas in the hills west of the village, or in periodic small gatherings throughout My Thuy Phuong. In addition, Front pamphlets carried such heroic follower images. None of the Front pamphlets definitely read in the village is presently available, but a few pamphlets containing probably similar heroic descriptions are available from other areas. For example, one pamphlet dated 1964 contains the story of three women from a Thua Thien hamlet called Duc. The women distracted three Government soldiers long enough for other Front members to kill them. Later they supposedly poisoned to death 30 more soldiers.[5] Finally, several students mentioned a foreigner they most admired, an American "hero" and "friend of Vietnam" they heard of in Front broadcasts. This was a man named Norman Morrison, who on November 2, 1965, sat on the Pentagon steps and burned himself to death to protest American policy in Vietnam.

There were widely varying reactions to the hero messages. Members of the pro-Government minority rejected them *in toto*. As noted earlier, most people responded well to the Ho Chi Minh messages. But they selectively received the other hero messages. For example, women responded well to the messages about heroic women, and children drew inspiration from the vignette about the schoolboy spreading Ho Chi Minh's teachings. In general villagers often identified with and tried to emulate the model heroic followers from backgrounds most like their own.

Intertwined with the above messages on revolution, class enemies, struggle, and heroes is a tenth and final major message, the *role of the people in the movement.* Front proselyting efforts, especially the informal contacts between leaders, guerrillas, and ordinary villagers, made people aware of the many ways they could assist the Front's difficult struggle to achieve power through a General Uprising.[6] First, there was emphasis on cooperation with the local guerrilla force as the most important way in which they could assist the revolution. A peasant remembered:

> This was the most important part of the Front propaganda. All of the other things were important, because the people had to agree with the Communist political beliefs, but it was most important for the people to cooperate. The people had to give the guerrillas support, or they [the guerrillas] would be dead.

Front leaders told people how to assist as lookouts, runners, and spies within the Government apparatus, and urged them to hide guerrillas, donate labor to dig tunnels, transport supplies for the guerrilla force, and directly assist attacks. The Front also encouraged villagers to join the guerrilla force. Here the Front closely tied appeals for struggle and heroism to a specific appeal for able-bodied men to take up arms with the Front. For most people, the most impressive bearers of the recruitment messages were guerrillas, who, in effect, presented themselves as living examples of dedication and sacrifice. The recollection of one peasant is illustrative:

> One time Viet Cong [guerrillas] came to my house. At first, we were all very afraid, but the Viet Cong told us that we should not be afraid. They said that they came only to visit us, to talk with us about the village and the war. They said that all the people had to join the revolution, and that the men of our family should be first. They talked about what a difficult life it was, but they did not mind the danger and the difficulties, because they knew they were fighting for the freedom of Vietnam.

The Front also encouraged people to support guerrillas in other ways. A peasant remembered:

> They told us that to give money and food to the Viet Cong was a way of supporting the revolution. They told us that everyone had to sacrifice, by giving a little bit of money or rice to the Viet Cong guerrillas, and money to the Viet Cong tax cadre.

Many responded by contributing money and rice to the Front. Such contributions during 1964–1967 were quite similar to those of the early Front years, coming as they did at the request of local guerrillas or of men known as tax collectors, and varying with wealth of families and needs of the Front organization. In retrospect, it is clear that during 1964–1967 the Front succeeded in its proselyting to secure support for guerrilla activities, as many villagers aided the local attack—the subject of Chapter 9. The proselyting even affected those who supported the Government or remained politically uncommitted, for it left all with strong impressions of a guerrilla force close to the people, dependent on local support for its very survival.

The Front also discouraged people from cooperating with the Government. Again tied to the Front's emphasis on enemies and a history of revolutionary struggle in the area, the Front described noncooperation as an effective way of fighting the Government. It should be noted, however, that the Front generally took care to maintain "legal" status vis-à-vis the Government for as many of its followers as possible, so urged noncooperation when feasible and minimal cooperation at all other times. When the Government organized elections, for example, the Front urged people to either sabotage or boycott the balloting, if they could do so without arrest. The Front treated the Government's few and ineffective development programs in similar fashion. And those who assisted Government security branches in any but token and begrudging fashions earned the title "betrayer of the revolution."

FRONT COMMUNITY

The Front brought significant changes to village life during 1964–1967. These came because of the movement's own strengths, because of weakness on the Government side, and *despite* occasional setbacks brought mainly by the U.S. Marines—a subject of Chapter 9. A peasant commented on one change:

> The Liberation taught us that everyone had to cooperate, and that we were all struggling for freedom and independence. The Liberation idea is that all people must cooperate. For example, if one family is very poor, or has something that is bad luck happen to it, then we will all cooperate to help that family.
>
> Also, we all cooperate, without ever asking for money, in the planting and harvesting of rice. Those are just a few examples of the people helping each other. Before the Liberation, the people were very divided and suspicious, and always trying to get money from each other.

A Government village official stated:

> The Communists had the idea that everyone must work together for revolution, to fight together, to help even the poorest people in the area. This is the greatest strength of that side. You know, they really do work closely with the people. They are close to the people, and encourage the people to cooperate, which is something that gives them great strength. And it is something that our republican government cannot do too well.

There were many manifestations of this cooperation among Front followers. Villagers noted that people began to cooperate in time of need, such as after family tragedies or during harvest and planting times. A student from a peasant family gave an example of such cooperation:

> There was a woman whose husband had been in the [Government] Army and was killed. This widow had four little children, and she was very poor. The only land she had was a small piece of land for vegetables. Her children needed food and sometimes needed medicine when they were sick. All of the people began to help her in different ways. We gave her small amounts of money. A few people gave her rice. One family gave her a small piece of land to grow more vegetables, and some of the men fixed the roof of her house.

As the Front's proselyting efforts began to focus explicitly on class issues and point out local class enemies, people occasionally cooperated to solve common economic problems. For example, in about 1965, a tradesman who operated a small shop in the village became the target of a boycott. People knew the man, who was closely aligned with the village council, for his high prices and links with local moneylenders. Most villagers simply stopped buying at his shop. A peasant recalled:

> It was a very happy matter, because everyone was united opposing that man. After a few weeks of no one buying from him, he began to lower his prices, and influenced the moneylenders to lower their interest rates a bit. The people were very happy, and they understood that they had won because they had united.

A minority of civil servants and people strongly committed to the Government asserted that cooperation among villagers during the mid-1960s grew out of widespread fear of the Front—assertions which such individuals possibly based on their own fears. However, most who commented on the years 1964–1967 echoed the notion of widespread and enthusiastic cooperation among those aligned with the Front. As cooperative bonds among the people strengthened, many became involved in a wide variety of Front activities, including formal study meetings and other gatherings, and the informal discussions and conversations sparked by Front members. All of this brought out the 10 intertwining messages already discussed. Normally no more than 40 or 50 came to political study meetings at a time. A peasant described his neighbors' reactions to the meetings:

> It started as a very slow thing, you know. The Communists came to us and said that we had to support them by going to meetings. Well, at first nobody wanted to, but we all went when our neighbors encouraged us to go. At first many of us did not understand the meetings, and there were ideas that we did not really understand. But after some time the political ideas of the Viet Cong seemed clear, and many people began to agree with those ideas.

Another peasant described people's attitudes in these words:

> The people liked to go to study. We did it because everyone went, and because we knew that not to go was to hurt the revolution. Many people had strong ideas of their own, and some of them gave those ideas at the meetings.

> The meetings were interesting, and people liked to go. It was just like the old days in Vietnam, when people went to the *dinh*. . . . You know, the *dinh* is very important, and just like at the *dinh* the spirit of the people is very high at the Viet Cong meetings. . . .

When people occasionally spoke up at the meetings, it was usually to comment on corruption by local civil servants, on high rents, or on police repression.

During the mid-1960s, My Thuy Phuong's Front leaders, like their Viet Minh predecessors, were men of very special qualities. Those qualities drew many to the movement. The leaders numbered about 10 in all, and were the same men who led the insurgency during 1961–1963. All had served with the Viet Minh, two as local leaders. The other Viet Minh leaders were dead, in jail, or too physically weak to fight.

For local leaders as well as guerrillas, important opportunities to strengthen revolutionary resolve were the "self-criticism" sessions, which often occurred in the village during 1965–1967. The leaders often organized such sessions at meetings of the local Front committee, and also at many gatherings of guerrillas.[8] A guerrilla recalled:

> The self-criticism meetings for cadres were about once a month. One of the leaders was in charge, like a chairman. At some of the sessions, just about everyone stood up and told about their backgrounds, and about their ideas of revolution, and then they told what they had done to help the revolution in their work. . . .
>
> Then they would tell about their mistakes and weaknesses. For example, if a man had treated a woman badly, if he had thought of himself for only one minute and forgotten the people's revolution, then he would tell that, and he would have to explain why he had a minute of weakness.

The self-criticism sessions were rarely forums for accusation or rumor-mongering. Front leaders encouraged all present to participate in discussions, and most did so. They told those who said nothing to think about themselves, and be prepared to speak about personal strengths and weaknesses at future sessions. And the meetings were sometimes deep emotional experiences for those in attendance. They served to reinforce the bonds of commitment to the movement of both leaders and guerrillas.

Beginning in about 1964, a number of changes in the local Front organization also reinforced those bonds, and the bonds of many others to the movement. First, the Front extended its formal committee structure to My Thuy Phuong's hamlets. Local leaders and followers chose four or five individuals per hamlet through a series of small meetings in each hamlet. There was no balloting for the selections, only recommendations from the leaders, some discussion, and "agreement" from Front followers. The hamlet committees performed many of the same types of functions as the village committee—collection of money and food, proselyting, support of guerrilla attacks, and so forth—and were closely controlled by the village leaders. Note that those leaders retained their flexibility in local implementation of Front policies set at higher levels, which usually came to them in the forms of general directives. And the People's Revolutionary Party had some indirect influence through a few local leaders, the only party members in My Thuy Phuong. The members devoured the pamphlets they occasionally received from party contacts and incorporated ideas from the pamphlets in local proselyting. The only other evidence of significant party influence in the village was noted above—Front leaders' tendency to work harder in the hope of someday gaining party membership.

In about 1964, the Front began to expand what Pike characterizes as the "all-important" Front organizational units below village and hamlet levels, the liberation association cells.[9] A peasant said:

> The cells usually had three to five people. The Liberation let the people join them, and did not force anyone. They were important, because every time there was a political message from the leaders, or an announcement of some political activity, we learned about it through the cells. It was a good method, because if one person in a cell was told something he would surely tell the other people. A very strong method.

The cell structure, in other words, was a formalization of the long-existent covert insurgent network. It permitted people to better share Front ideas and share in Front activities, including the guerrilla attack. It also enabled local insurgent leaders to more effectively influence their followers. The Front also tried to promote its most important functional organization, the Farmers' Liberation Association. But no more than 20 peasants ever joined this group's one or two cells, and its only activity consisted of passing class-related political messages among peasants. It should also be noted that there were no local Front organizations for women, children, or other functional categories of people. Most villagers were formally tied to the Front only through the cell structure just described.[10]

During the informal Front gatherings and conversations, including contacts among cell members, most everyone felt relaxed—a contrast with the formal gatherings, where few talked without prompting. A university student said:

> When the people were talking to each other in families or with their friends, they were never afraid of anything. They talked about a lot of ideas, and they could never give good speeches. But they talked using common words about many ideas. Very often many people would take an idea that they had heard from the Communists and talk about it with their friends. They would talk a little while about that idea, then talk about something else, tell a story or a joke or some-

The village under rocket attack, March 1975.

Sea evacuation from Danang, March 1975.

Government election day, February 1975.

A guerrilla dead by Highway One, March 1975.

Washing clothes in a stream.

A traditional dance.

Repairing a shrine.

An irrigation device.

A typical home.

A Buddhist pagoda.

The government office.

Camp Eagle view. (U.S. Army photo)

Camp Eagle view. (U.S. Army photo)

Miss Black America at Camp Eagle. (U.S. Army photo)

101st soldiers display enemy weapons, captured in 1968. (Pacific Stars & Stripes photo)

A government militia member.

Guerrillas eat at a Thua Thien base camp. (N.L.F. photo captured by U.S. Army)

U.S. soldiers waiting to depart from Camp Eagle, 1972. (U.S. Army photo)

Front propaganda for U.S. troops near the village. (Photo by Dick Hughes)

A guerrilla meeting in Thua Thien. Weapons hang left rear. (N.L.F. photo captured by U.S. Army)

A typical village path.

An ammunition truck passing; a peasant returns from the fields.

The rice fields.

The railway through the village.

> thing like that. But they would often return to that first idea and try to understand it.

As people discussed Front ideas throughout My Thuy Phuong, they applied some of them to the realities of life in the village. For example, a peasant observed:

> The people would always talk, eat, and drink together. They talked about some of the new ideas. Some of them [the people] came from the Communist side, and they talked and talked a lot about how these ideas could change their lives.
>
> For example, if they had heard something about the Communist land reform policy, they would talk about how the Communists' policy might affect their land, or how they might get more land from the policy.

It should be noted, incidentally, that of all Front policies, land policy was most popular in the village, most likely owing to the local land abuses by members of the pro-Government minority. Front leaders never spelled out their land policy in detail, but the people understood that the Front, in general, stood for fairness in land distribution.

Although fear of informers caused some to hold back during the informal contacts with friends, neighbors, and relatives, most people were able to relax, speak their minds, and take the risk of argument. According to a peasant:

> Of course Vietnamese like to talk to other Vietnamese. They talk about everything. They talk about family, friends, the problems of the world, and the problems of the nation. So when the Liberation Front's ideas about revolution and fighting the Americans and the puppet government were brought to this area by the cadres, the people began to talk about them.
>
> And, you know, the people really enjoyed talking, because when they talked they became loyal to the Communists. They also saw with their eyes that the Communist cadres were trying to be close to them. They saw that the cadres came to them, and talked to them, listened to them, and asked questions of them. So they knew that the cadres cared.

Many others stated that local Front leaders indeed seemed sincerely interested in the welfare of the common man, and tried hard to be "close to the people."

As formal and informal proselyting efforts continued in My Thuy Phuong, the Front leaders' challenge was to overcome some people's deep-seated feeling that commitment to revolution could become inconvenient and lead to danger and family tragedy. This was partly simple reluctance to form political commitments of any kind, and partly many people's desire to hedge their bets—two related tendencies which of course also affected Government programs. By making commitments to neither combatant side, many hoped to avoid the costs of commitment, the main cost being vulnerability to attack as one side's enemy.

The hedging of bets meant giving both sides indications of support, such as payment of taxes to both Government and Front, or having sons join one army or another. Such moves usually placated both sides, especially if neither found out about the help to the other, and bought time for the uncommitted. But as might be expected, all too often these villagers were unable to conceal their hedging of bets, and came under general suspicion and pressure from both sides.

Over the years, these tendencies were in evidence during the extended periods of political uncertainty about local balance of power, but when that balance clearly shifted in favor of one side, there were corresponding shifts among the uncommitted—and sometimes among the committed, too. Many began to support the side which appeared stronger, sometimes abandoning support for the seemingly weaker side. As noted earlier, one such shift occurred during the years when the Viet Minh in effect ran the village. Another occurred during the early Diem years, and still another during the period under consideration here, 1964–1967. As noted in Chapter 7, villagers classified about 20 percent of My Thuy Phuong's people in the uncommitted group for 1962–1963. During 1964–1967, the uncommitted dropped to 10 to 15 percent. To win them over, Front leaders endeavored during 1964–1967 to create the sense of a fast-approaching General Uprising and sure victory. They urged everyone to support the revolution—immediately and totally. A few commented in general on the effectiveness of these Front efforts. For example, a peasant noted:

> Many people were at first afraid to do much to help the Liberation Front. But after a while they saw how strong the Liberation was in the whole area. They felt, "Now we must help. They are going to win. We are going to help."

Another man, who worked as a Government civil servant, had these words:

> The Vietnamese people are very quiet, and don't like to talk much about politics [with foreigners], and so probably very few would tell you this. You know that the people in this area were very strong supporters of the Communists for a few years around 1965. Almost the whole area was a Communist area, and Communists controlled Gia Le, especially at night.
>
> The people thought that the Communists were going to win, and so they supported them very strongly, and accepted all the Communist ideas because they felt that the Communists had the best future for them.
>
> So it was a challenge for the Government to give the people an answer to the Communists. In those years, the Government gave no answer, so almost everyone followed the Communists. The people were waiting for the Government to become strong, and then they would support the Government.

What happened to one peasant family, to which we shall give the name Hung, illustrates what it was like to be politically uncommitted during 1964–1965. The Hung's had actively assisted the Viet Minh struggle but remained politically inactive during the Diem years. To maintain that neutrality, beginning in 1962, Hung and his wife gave small sums of money and some rice to Front cadres and guerrillas, but also paid Government taxes and fees. In 1964–1965, Hung and his eldest son helped Front guerrillas dig holes for rice caches, and that son joined the Government provincial forces. Hung commented, "When my son entered the military, the Government had less reason to suspect us, but some other families who supported the Liberation side did not like us for that. They spoke badly about us." Such criticism came especially from the families of local guerrillas.

Finally in late 1965, the Hung family tilted toward full support of the Front. It increased contributions to guerrillas and local cadres, almost eliminated contributions to the Government, and began actively assisting the local struggle. Two sons assisted guerrilla operations, and the son in the provincial forces helped out when he could by providing the Front with intelligence reports. Hung noted that his family's shift in 1965 to an actively pro-Front stance came because by that year the movement was overwhelmingly influential in the village. He added, "When my family began to help the Liberation more and more, we did not worry so much. The Liberation guaranteed our lives."

A small minority of villagers, most of whom were members of the pro-Government group, had different explanations for insurgent strength. A representative statement is this one, by a local councilman:

> The Viet Cong often had meetings and study sessions concerning political matters to which they forced the people to go. They told them that if they did not go they would be killed or given fines, and they said very bad things about people who did not go. To make people afraid and force them to go, the Viet Cong sometimes denounced people to their faces.

As noted earlier, many who argued that Front strength was based on fear were themselves fearful of the insurgents, perhaps due to the widely known label they bore—"enemies of the people."

Despite the minority emphasis on fear, most villagers suggested, in summary, that during 1964–1967 the Front's meetings and self-criticism sessions and the informal chats and other contacts among neighbors brought most everyone into the movement. That included about half of the previously uncommitted. The Front imbued its followers with ideas of antiimperialism, class struggle, nationalism, and mutual cooperation. By 1964–1965, about 80 to 85 percent of the local populace supported the Front, and about 5 percent the Government. The remaining 10 to 15 percent attempted to stay politically uncommitted, sometimes experiencing intense pressure from both sides. And about 60 percent of the Front supporters regularly helped Front leaders and guerrillas. The others were passive supporters of revolution. In other words, most villagers were at least as deeply committed to the Front during 1964–1967 as they had earlier been to the Viet Minh.

THE TWO FAMILIES

Among those who supported the Front during the mid-1960s were the Binh and Tri families introduced in Chapter 5. Through the early 1960s, the two families experienced many of the difficulties and frustrations that had caused widespread dissatisfaction with the Government. And both families drifted, seemingly naturally, into affiliations with the Front.

Binh, the tenant farmer who had served as a lookout and general supporter of the Viet Minh guerrillas, became one of the more active Front members. He did not join the guerrilla force, but often participated in small military actions which the Front classified as self-defense operations. Binh said he participated most enthusiastically in the actions directed against large landholders, especially the man who in 1950 had forced him to sell his land. He helped scatter leaflets and place explosives near the home of another large landholder, and commented, "The man was very bad. He got rich from many of us, and took our land when we were very poor. So it made me very happy to help struggle against him." On his affiliation with the Front, Binh said:

> Supporting the Liberation was difficult for me, but I felt I had to do it. I think probably I did not make much money during the years I was supporting the Front, but the important thing is that I was helping in the revolution, and that made me very happy.

Binh and many others were enthusiastic about assisting guerrilla operations, and many used the word "happy" to describe feelings about such help.

During the 1960s, the warehouseman Tri also supported the revolution. He participated in local Front meetings, occasionally gave donations of food to Front guerrillas, and emerged as an important member of the network of local Front supporters. Tri commented on his political conversations: "I always liked to talk to other people, my friends and relatives, about political questions, and I always would give them a position that opposed the Government and supported the Liberation." Tri's exposure to urban working conditions and numerous friendships with people from other villages meant that he was a man of wider experience than many of his neighbors. In conversations many looked to him for insight and guidance. Tri recalled:

> The talks we had were very interesting. People would ask me what the workers felt, and whether the Liberation was having success in other villages and the city.
>
> The people had heard many things about other places—a lot of propaganda and ideas. But often the people were not sure. These were people, you must remember, who always stayed in one village, and did not know much about the outside. Sometimes I tried to explain things to them, and it made me happy to do that.

Both Binh and Tri involved other members of their families in the insurgency. Their wives and some of their older children began to help the movement in small ways. They passed messages, contributed food, and spread pro-Front ideas among friends and schoolmates. By the mid-1960s, Binh and Tri were active, enthusiastic Front supporters. They were products of a long evolutionary process—from apolitical, reasonably happy subsistence existences; through a period of economic loss, psychological upset, groping, and initial receptivity to new political ideas; to full involvement in the Viet Minh and then Front movements.

During 1964–1967, the vast majority of villagers joined the Binh and Tri families in supporting the cause of revolution.[11] Most did so from the heart. "Support" had many meanings for many people—ranging from active involvement in the local Front network to sympathy for but not assistance to the cause. To summarize, the Front repeated the Viet Minh accomplishment. It built a revolutionary movement in My Thuy Phuong. The movement had leaders who cared, institutions tied to the people, and messages which held promise for the future. It united 80 percent or more of the villagers in a community of sharing and sacrifice.

NOTES

1. *The Pentagon Papers*, p. 409.
2. *Ibid.*, pp. 382–509.
3. *Cf.* Robert Shaplen, *The Road From War; Vietnam 1965–1970* (New York: Harper & Row, 1970), p. 23; FitzGerald, *Fire In The Lake*, pp. 169–172.
4. See, for example, Liberation Radio Broadcast, December 10, 1970, in "Daily Report; Asia & Pacific" (Springfield, Virginia: National Technical Information Service, Foreign Broadcast Information Service, U.S. Department of Commerce, December 11, 1970), p. L2; hereafter referred to as "Daily Report."
5. "Ten Years Battle Against the United States" (South Vietnam: National Liberation Front of South Vietnam, 1964), pp. 53–54, in Douglas Pike, ed., "Documents on the National Liberation Front of South Vietnam, 1959–1966," item 710, Wason microfilm 1562, Cornell University Library.
6. For background on "General Uprising," see Pike, *Vietcong*, pp. 76–77.

7. *Cf.* Alexander Woodside, *Community and Revolution in Modern Vietnam* (Boston: Houghton Mifflin, 1976).

8. See FitzGerald, *op. cit.*, pp. 203–208.

9. Pike, *Vietcong*, pp. 229–230.

10. Some indicated, however, that the Front organized a "Youth Liberation Association" in Thua Thien, and some village youngsters joined, especially during 1964–1967. This group's only activity in the village was an occasional leaflet distribution.

11. Possible indications of the loyalty of Front followers in the province to the movement are the relatively small numbers of people who deserted North Vietnamese Army units and Front civil and military organizations. During 1963–1965, only 406 deserted those ranks, in 1966 there were 206, and during the first eight months of 1967 there were 236. Complete figures for later years are not available, but Thua Thien/Hue Government officials told the author that there were never large numbers of so-called *hoi/chanh* deserters. See "Province Report, Department of the Army, Thua Thien Province, I CTZ, MACV Advisory Team 18, APO 96258," September 3, 1967, p. 7; available in the U.S. Army Center for Military History, Washington, D.C.; this is the monthly advisory report, which was filed under that title from 1967 to 1973. Before 1967, the reports were called "Report For Month Ending. . .", and were filed by the U.S.A.I.D. Reports Officer, Thua Thien Province; the entire 1966 record is available in "Thua Thien Papers, 1966," folder 10, box 10, Center for Military History. Hereafter, all these documents are referred to as "Thua Thien Report."

9

Attack!

TAKING ON THE MARINES

The first Americans came to the village in 1965. That was when President Lyndon Johnson sent a combat unit of the U.S. Marine Corps to Thua Thien/Hue, part of America's efforts to shore up the Government and defeat the Front.[1] The Marines initially based themselves at a place called Phu Bai, which is about four miles south of My Thuy Phuong. From their new base, Marine units began extensive operations throughout Thua Thien and in Quang Tri, to the north.[2] Battles raged all around My Thuy Phuong during the Marine years, 1965–1967. Here are highlights of a few major operations:

> On February 27, 1966, a Government regiment alerted the Marines that it needed help in Phu Thu District, which lies very close to the village, to the east. In response a large number of Marine assault helicopters departed Phu Bai—the beginning of Operation New York. The Marines attacked and continued to do so for four days with wave after wave of helicopters, artillery, and soldiers on the ground. According to Marine statistics the final tally for the four-day period was 122 Vietnamese killed.[3]
>
> In the area immediately west of My Thuy Phuong, a three-battalion operation called Fremont ranged over the countryside between July 10 and October 31, 1967. When it ended the Marines reported 17 American and 123 Vietnamese fatalities, with 260 American soldiers wounded.[4]
>
> Throughout much of the period of Marine activity in the area, a special composite military group, Task Force X-Ray, had the mission of protecting the Phu Bai base, screening the western approaches to Hue, and keeping open Highway One.[5] X-Ray operations, which varied in size, almost certainly came directly to My Thuy Phuong.

These operation summaries and statistics reflect the mounting war near the village.[6] And in My Thuy Phuong itself there was a mounting war, too, with one side clearly taking the initiative. A peasant spoke of the years 1964–1965:

> The Communists were very strong during that time. Communist guerrillas freely attacked Government soldiers, in places where the Government had checkpoints and outposts. Many of the people supported them. The people told them where the soldiers were, told them what time to attack, and helped them to escape. The Communists were very strong. There were also many attacks against American and Government vehicles on Highway One, and against the police and Army operations.

Another peasant recalled:

> It seemed that everybody supported the Liberation during that time. This was the time that the American army was just coming to fight in Vietnam. Everybody liked the Liberation Front, and supported all of the policies of the Liberation. The most important policy they supported was the revolutionary war. The people had learned about the struggle, and knew that the guerrillas needed their support. So everyone sacrificed and struggled along with the guerrillas.

Despite these and other people's comments that many supported guerrilla operations during 1964–1965, there are indications that during those years only five or six actually joined the local full-time guerrilla force, which consisted of about twenty men and few if any women. People implied that family obligations discouraged most from becoming full-time guerrillas, for to do so meant giving up farming or other occupations. It also meant exposing family members to pressures from Government security agencies, and increasing the chances of untimely death, which would mean family difficulties. Most local guerrillas were thus without pressing family obligations—including holdovers from the Viet Minh era whose families had adjusted to their absence, and young unmarried men whose families could survive without them. During the entire period of Front activity, 1961–1975, there was variation in the support guerrillas received locally, but little change in guerrilla recruitment patterns.

There were many small guerrilla operations in My Thuy Phuong during 1964–1965, most of which involved unarmed men, women, and children assisting in various ways. A peasant commented:

> Everyone liked to help the revolutionary struggle in every way possible. Some of us did simple things like giving information to the Front on the Government Army, or on police activities. Other people gave guerrillas food and money. Other people helped guerrillas hide. Some other people helped guerrillas make traps and guns. Everyone liked to do it. We were happy to help.

A low-ranking Government soldier looked back on the mid-1960s, when he was still in high school:

> Oh, yes, the Viet Cong was very strong at that time. That was when everyone was tricked by the Viet Cong, and supported what they called the "people's revolution." Everybody took large dangerous chances to help the Viet Cong, even when there were attacks against the nationalist soldiers in this area. I can remember once when I was a little boy I helped the Viet Cong carry a message.

Finally, a local civil servant summarized the period 1964–1965: "At that time this was a Viet Cong village, controlled by day through all areas all the way up to both sides of the road. At night even the road was controlled by the Viet Cong." Many others described insurgent influence as extensive and several also spoke of that influence in geographic terms.

Most operations conducted by the U.S. Marines during 1964–1967 were in the lowlands and mountain areas outside of My Thuy Phuong. But the Marines came near enough that villagers felt a disruptive ripple effect of war. For example, convoys of Marine trucks traveled My Thuy Phuong's branch of Highway One and made it dangerous for those on foot, bicycle, or motorcycle. A peasant woman tearfully recalled what one convoy brought her:

> I was walking along the road with my son, who was wearing a hat. There was a string to hold the hat to his chin. One of the American soldiers grabbed the hat, and pulled my son up and under the wheels of the truck. The truck stopped, but it was too late.

Seeing her son grabbed away and crushed before her eyes shattered the woman's life. She said, "He was my only son, and my sadness is so deep that it will never end."

A peasant described another problem along Highway One:

> The American soldiers went by in their trucks and shot as many water buffalo as they could. They liked to see the animals fall, I think. They killed so many that after a few years we felt to have water buffalo was very dangerous. One time a boy was hit in the leg when an American soldier tried to kill the water buffalo he was sitting on.

Several thought of the convoys and spoke of C-rations, the small green cans of meat and other foods distributed to American combat soldiers on operations. In the village C-rations became dangerous weapons in the hands of U.S. Marines, who often threw them from passing convoys at buildings and people. "The American soldiers threw the cans very hard, and very fast," remembered a high school student. A healed gash on the boy's forehead was his reminder of the Marines and of the day a hail of little green cans stopped a group of students bicycling to school.

As they launched their offensive operations in Thua Thien/Hue, the Marines not only passed along the highway through the village, but literally passed overhead as well. My Thuy Phuong's airspace bustled with

Marine helicopters ferrying soldiers into battle, hauling equipment, or rushing out casualties or prisoners of war. The choppers brought noise and swirling, choking dust storms to the village. But there were sometimes other problems connected with the choppers. A peasant recalled an encounter he had:

> One day I was walking back home from the ricefield, carrying tools on my shoulder. Then behind me I heard a large, loud noise. A very bad noise. I looked back and saw an American helicopter following me, shooting down the path toward me. I was very scared, so jumped into the water by the side. Just one moment later, the bullets went right by. So scary.

During those years, no large-scale Marine activities, with the likely exception of X-Ray operations, came directly to the village. However, many grew concerned. A peasant's comment on the Marines was typical of many others: "When the American Marines came everyone began to worry more and more. We could see the war getting bigger and bigger. And we worried about heavy fighting coming here." [7]

Shortly after the Marine Corps began military operations in Thua Thien/Hue it launched a program called Combined Action. The Marines presented this as a new and innovative approach to the military requirements of Vietnam.[8] It came to My Thuy Phuong in the form of a Combined Action Platoon, or C.A.P. In theory, the C.A.P. integrated a Government platoon of local Popular Forces soldiers with a squad of American Marines.[9] In August of 1965, the C.A.P. began its operations in the village.[10] It consisted of about 30 Vietnamese soldiers and 15 Marines. They lived in a U.S.-constructed building along Highway One, near the center of the village. The compound bore an American stamp, for Marine supply personnel had thoroughly equipped it. Even the food was "Made in U.S.A."

A retired Vietnamese C.A.P. soldier said that most of the Marines stayed very close to the compound—except when ambushes or patrols called.[11] Those operations came nearly every night, and sometimes during daylight hours as well. A peasant commented on a C.A.P. ambush:

> One time I was going out to the ricefields early in the morning, about 5 o'clock, walking with my son. Just when we were crossing into the ricefields someone shouted, "Don't move!" They fired their guns once or twice to scare us. And then the soldiers, and two Americans following them, asked us for our papers, asked us why we were out so early, and asked us where we were going. We were very afraid that they were going to arrest us, but finally they let us go.

Others remembered the C.A.P. and spoke of death. A village councilman said:

> One night there was frightful shooting, so much of it, out in the ricefields. They were shooting back and forth for about 20 minutes. When we got up the next

> day, we saw the Americans and the soldiers bringing in two bodies, carrying them in a raincoat. We knew the dead men. But the soldiers said they were V.C.

Some familiar problems cropped up during C.A.P. operations. For example, once in 1967 a daytime C.A.P. patrol moved through the western portion of the village. The soldiers converged slowly on a small home, completely surrounded it, then entered. The owner, a peasant, recalled that Vietnamese soldiers on the C.A.P. stole some money during their house search. Another vignette illustrates the type of on-the-job training the Marines brought their allies through the C.A.P. A retired Vietnamese C.A.P. member said that once in 1966, C.A.P. officers organized a night patrol near the ricefield hamlets. About five Marines and a squad of Vietnamese soldiers proceeded into the ricefields along narrow paths, heading toward the hamlets. Suddenly heavy fire from two or three directions blanketed them. Two C.A.P. soldiers were hit. A Vietnamese died instantly when a bullet ripped through his head, and an American was lightly wounded in the shoulder. During the cross fire Vietnamese soldiers helped call in artillery and air support. Casualties during the contact were very one-sided. C.A.P. soldiers found no evidence the next morning that any members of the ambushing guerrilla force had been wounded or killed. There were no bodies or blood trails. But the operation was not a total waste of time, according to the retired Vietnamese soldier: "Operations like that made us better soldiers. The Americans were so brave that we became brave, too. We learned to call for support from headquarters."

The C.A.P. remained until March or April of 1970.[12] It brought the village frequent small unit operations, in some ways probably helped improve fighting abilities of Government soldiers, and had an undetermined effect on My Thuy Phuong's insurgent force. But like the large Marine operations, the C.A.P. also brought disruption and fear to village life.

By 1965–1966, American military activity throughout the province was causing the Front some problems. Illustrative are several captured documents from the area, which include admissions of problems. In one of them a Front commander writes, "the enemy has implemented the policy of terrorism and the demagogical policy." He asserts that Government information efforts "created dissention among our forces and various religious sects, [and] aroused nostalgia among our soldiers and cadres. . . ."[13] The commander also reports:[14]

> Generally speaking, the reason why shortcomings rose to a high degree was because of the enemy's stepped-up activities in various fields and because our cadres were not deeply concerned with the welfare of the people in the liberated area. Because of the above shortcomings our cadres were incapable of controlling the people and restoring security in the liberated area. . . .

Another document is an "absolute secret" resolution of the First Conference of the Tri Thien Hue Military Region Party Committee, held on September 15–19, 1966. In part, it reads: [15]

> The guerrilla warfare development is not homogeneous, not strong enough. The guerrilla strength is still low (not even 1 percent of the population). Women are still disregarded and are not recruited by the guerrilla force. The military and political training of the personnel is low. Many Party members have not yet joined the guerrilla force. The ratio of covert guerrillas is fairly high (47 percent), but their activities are few. Many liberated hamlets have no guerrillas. The basic militia corps has not been established.
>
> Generally speaking, guerrillas are still weak in fighting. Their forms of activity are limited. They are still weak in counter-sweep operations and in communication warfare. Their political struggles have not been satisfactorily combined with military and enemy proselyting. They have not satisfactorily performed fighting, protection of the villages, people and agricultural production. They have not carried out the role of being a backbone of the people's political struggle and of the resupply of concentrated units. Full-time agricultural production members are still too numerous. There is an acute shortage of cadre (there are only 276 hamlet unit cadres in 475 liberated hamlets).

In My Thuy Phuong the establishment of the C.A.P. and some Government security activities brought the death of two or three Front leaders. Police arrested and jailed for varying terms one or two other leaders, along with twenty or thirty Front supporters. In addition Government and American forces killed and captured about five of the village's estimated twenty guerrillas, while causing a few pro-Front families, fearful of arrest and heightened danger, to begin withholding support from guerrilla operations.

Despite the new problems there are indications that throughout the province during the mid-1960s the Front began to resist heightening Government and American military pressure. For example, on July 7, 1966, a district committee of the Thua Thien People's Revolutionary Party adopted a resolution calling for indoctrination and reindoctrination. Part of it reads: [16]

> All Party committee members must improve their ideology in order to understand the general situation of the various battlefields, clearly understand the guidelines and policy of the Party, and also correct the wrong, rightist ideology.

And during 1965–1967, My Thuy Phuong's Front leaders attended meetings organized by the Front branch in Huong Thuy District. The sessions focused on ideology, and on specific tactics to meet heightened military and police pressure. In turn the leaders organized meetings of village guerrillas to discuss political goals and tactics, and held conversations with residents to pass on the messages. They also explicitly urged all cell members to be alert for informers and if arrested not to reveal Front members' names. In other words, Front leaders tried to strengthen their ties to the people. And the people's comments, included in the preceding chapter, suggest that the leaders succeeded, for the ties became strong indeed.

But the Front had another response to heightened military pressure: upgrading of its armed forces. In about 1964–1965, it began a nationwide shift toward "mobile warfare," which involved buildup of main and local force maneuver units.[17] In the special military zone called Tri Thien Hue, which included Quang Tri and Thua Thien/Hue, the Front built up battalions and regiments of its main forces.[18] There was also a buildup of the Thua Thien local forces, the battalions and companies controlled by the provincial and district structures.[19] According to Front followers, when the insurgency organized main and local force military units for the shift toward mobile warfare a number of men long active in the local guerrilla force joined those units. Ten men, about half of the village's most experienced guerrillas, departed for training at Front base camps, and for future combat throughout Tri Thien Hue.[20] Their departure required another upgrading response. Local leaders recruited about 10 people serving in the so-called self-defense force of guerrilla supporters—loosely organized and usually unarmed individuals who assisted the Front in various ways, such as spreading leaflets or serving as lookouts—as replacement members of the local guerrilla force. Two of the recruits were women.[21] Veteran guerrillas personally trained the former self-defense members, trying to pass on the lessons of many years' experience.

As a further response to heightened military pressure, snipers became more active along the highway.[22] The Front also organized more ambushes, placed more booby traps, and directed more attacks against Government troops. Local guerrillas, like their predecessors of the Viet Minh period and early anti-Diem years, enjoyed almost unhampered movement and control through most sections of the village. Government soldiers were generally safe only in their compounds and by other heavily guarded points, and had only some daytime control in other sections of the village.[23]

Beginning at about the same time the Front provided guerrillas with better weapons, including Chinese AK-47 rifles, grenades, and explosives, many of which likely came through North Vietnamese Army channels. There is even one indication, not mentioned by villagers, that guerrillas received special uniforms. An American report from 1966 includes this passage: [24]

> The V.C. have organized in the Huong Thuy District, a V.C. "sapper" squad comprised of twelve persons and at present they are believed to be active in the Thuy Phuong village. Of increased concern, is the fact that this group is known to operate in uniforms similar to those worn by the National Police. It may be the white shirt and grey trousers or jungle uniforms similar to the police field forces. All are armed with carbines and/or sub-machine guns. Limited identities and descriptions are known to the National Police.

Also in about 1966, guerrillas and some of their supporters improved the complex of tunnels dug in 1962–1963. Most of the improved tunnels stretched over huge areas, had two or three entrances, and consisted of interconnected passages of many shapes and functions. Guerrillas hid themselves, their weapons, and rice stocks in the underground maze, and used tunnels, as in previous years, for escape after attacks. A student put it this way: "I've heard that in America there are very big subway systems in the cities. Well, the guerrillas had their own subway system, too!"

There were occasional attacks during the mid-1960s against American trucks moving along the highway through the village, and American military patrols, possibly part of the Marines' Task Force X-Ray, also came under attack. A peasant discussed the Front's strategy:

> Let me tell you how we fought the Americans. We knew that we did not have the weapons to fight them in the open, so we had to fight another way. We used tunnels to move in the areas where there were American soldiers on operations. That would let us escape quickly.
>
> So we would put many pieces of sharp bamboo in the ground near the paths they walked on. Very many pieces! Then we would shoot at the Americans when they were on the paths. They jumped on the bamboo and got very hurt!
>
> When that happened, the Americans always did the same thing. They would be very angry, and might kill some people, or shoot up some houses, or have a big operation in the area. They never found us, but made many enemies when they did those things. This is the way to fight Americans.

On October 19, 1966, there was an incident on Highway One that caught the attention of American advisors, and which several villagers remembered. That evening Front snipers took up positions along the highway. A small truck approached the center of the village, guerrillas opened fire, and the truck came to a halt. A peasant remembered, "Right away the guerrillas saw that it was not an American vehicle, but a vehicle driven by a Frenchman who worked for the [French-contracted] power company." The peasant would have concurred with the U.S. Government telegram on the incident: [25]

> SNIPER ATTACKED VEHICLE ON ROUTE 1 GIA LE AREA HUONG THUY DISTRICT DRIVEN BY MANAGER OF HUE ELECTRIC COMPANY, GEORGE TANVILLE FRENCH CITIZEN. VICTIM SHOT IN STOMACH AND HANDS, AFTER ATTACK V.C. GAVE VICTIM FIRST AID WHO IS NOW IN HUE HOSPITAL.

According to an American advisory file, between July and December of 1967 there was extensive Front military activity throughout Thua Thien/Hue.[26] Front activity for Huong Thuy District is summarized in Table 9.1.[27] Included in the file for the same period are these My Thuy Phuong incidents: [28]

TABLE 9.1. Front Activity in Huong Thuy District, July–December, 1967 *

Type Incident	Number Incidents	Number Killed	Number Wounded	Number Missing	Structures Damaged
Assassination	5	6	—	—	—
Abduction	7	—	—	26	—
Mortar Attack	3	1	7	—	—
Road Mining	2	2	2	—	—
Demolition	2	1	2	—	bridge, house
Small Arms Attack	—	—	—	—	—
Leaflets	—	—	—	—	—
Booby Traps	—	—	—	—	—
Totals	19	10	11	26	2

* *See* "Thua Thien Terrorist Activity, 1967–1968" (U.S.A.I.D./Viet Nam, Public Safety Division), folder 60, Box 19, 19/66:23–7, Center of Military History.

> August 14, 1:00 A.M.—One V.C. squad infiltrated into Dong Tam hamlet, Thuy Phuong village, Huong Thuy District and shot to death one civilian. . . .
>
> September 5, 5:50 A.M.—Unknown strength of V.C. blew out a bridge within Thuy Phuong village, Huong Thuy District. The bridge damaged 80%, one P.F. [Popular Forces soldier] and one civilian wounded.
>
> September 9, 3:30 P.M.—Unknown strength of V.C. entered Dong Tam hamlet, Thuy Phuong village, Huong Thuy District and blew up a civilian house. One three-year-old child killed.
>
> October 24, 8:00 P.M.—Military jeep running between Phu Bai and Hue detonated a V.C. mine within Thuy Phuong village Huong Thuy District. ARVN [Government Army] KIA [killed in action] one captain one soldier and one civilian WIA [wounded in action].

In about 1967, the Combined Action Platoon came under attack. Nearly all local guerrillas were involved in the C.A.P. attack, together with guerrillas from other parts of Huong Thuy District. A guerrilla described it:

> One time, before Tet Mau Than [Tet of 1968], we attacked that Marine base, the house. There was about a company of us. We snuck in at night, and fired on them very heavily. We fired and fired all night, and they tried to shoot back. They called in helicopters to try to kill us, but that didn't help much. I don't know how many we killed, but I heard there were many. Only two or three of us died.

This incident, which was one of the largest guerrilla attacks ever conducted in My Thuy Phuong, left a strong impression on many. A student contended, "The people were very happy after they saw how brave the

Liberation Front guerrillas could be in such an attack against the Americans. Many of us thought to ourselves, secretly, that we must support the Liberation Front." And a retired Government soldier who fought alongside the Americans during the C.A.P. attack, said, "That attack scared everybody for years. From then, we could not be sure about the defenses of the army. I will never forget it." This man was frequently reminded of the Front's display of strength during the C.A.P. confrontation. He wore a plastic leg, a replacement for one blown off during the attack.

In addition to its sniping, ambushes, and other military attacks against American and Government security activities, the Front also launched a fierce attack against a wide range of local pro-Government individuals, including civil servants, prominent military officers, large landholders, moneylenders, and some tradesmen. Attacks against such people came after small Front meetings in My Thuy Phuong and surrounding villages, where people discussed "class enemies" and possible actions to oppose them.[29] As during the Viet Minh period and early 1960s, Front followers directed various types of warnings at enemies—including leaflets, rumors, and sometimes harmless bomb blasts. These were the first part of the attack.

People did not agree on how many such attacks there were over the years. Some suggested that there were four or five incidents, and others said there were more. Most concurred that the majority of the attacks occurred between 1965 and 1967, and that many Government allies during those years lived in constant fear, daring not to sleep in the village.[30] To illustrate, people described the killing of a Government village chief, who many regarded as corrupt. In 1967, the Front circulated leaflets addressed to the village chief, stating that if he did not improve his behavior he would be "punished by the people." Eventually, Front leaders decided to have him killed. A small number of people began to observe his comings and goings over a period of several weeks, to find out what time he went home, whether he traveled alone or with others, and whether he was armed. When a complete picture of the man's activities was ready, the guerrillas moved. They shot the village chief dead.[31]

When people discovered Government informers, local insurgent leaders chose from a variety of responses. They usually decided to kill those intelligence agents deemed most dangerous, often in ambushes or late-night visits to the agents' homes. Usually warnings preceded the killings—leaflets, rumors, or explosions timed to go off near the informers' homes or places of business. If the warnings failed to deter, then killings often followed. And sometimes when the leaders learned of Government agents in or near the village they tried to use them against the Government itself! That is, Front supporters passed false information to the agents to drain Government resources and destroy the informers' credibility. Several recalled one incident with amusement and even fondness. That was the time Front supporters passed a piece of information that appeared important to an informer. The false information concerned reorganization of the Front committee for Huong Thuy District, and included names of supposed Front agents in the area. A peasant described what happened:

> They gave the information to that man they knew was a spy, and he took it to the Government intelligence agency. The information was the names of important cadres in this area. They were real names, but none of them was a member of the Liberation. The names were those of Government men. These were men who had always been against the Front.
>
> So when the Government received this information a few days later, they arrested some of those men. Everybody was very happy, because we knew they had the wrong people, and we knew that maybe even those men would begin to hate the Government.

As the Front attack intensified during 1965–1967, many in the province, including My Thuy Phuong villagers, became involved in large anti-Government demonstrations called Struggle Movements. Led mainly by An Quang Buddhist activists and students, these movements aimed at changing certain Government policies to improve democracy and freedom. The demonstrations also had strong anti-American overtones, and in 1966 caused most Americans to evacuate Hue. Demonstrators also sacked and burned Hue's American Cultural Center.[32]

Some villagers, especially students, went to Hue to join the main demonstrations. But the most dramatic local contribution to the movement involved people placing family altars on Highway One. Many carried altars out to the highway, and placed burning incense, fruit, and other offerings on them—all to slow Government troop movements. Eventually the Government, with American advisory help, crushed the 1966 Struggle Movement.[33] Troops removed the altars from the highway, soldiers who had deserted returned to their units, and the Government reestablished a semblance of control.[34]

During the Struggle period, the Front conducted few military activities. Its strategy was to win converts among those angered by Government suppression of the demonstrations. Insurgent leaders in the village and clandestine radio broadcasts characterized the 1966 movement as but the latest expression of revolutionary struggle, and tried to identify the Front as a leading anti-Government struggling force. There were few indications of how people received these claims. One man, a Government soldier, stated:

> Everybody was opposing the Government. It was as if all the people were united against the Government policy, and everybody demanded that the Americans do something to change the Government, to make democracy real in Vietnam. When the Struggle Movement did not succeed, everyone was angry at the Government. I don't think that anybody supported the Government. Maybe the people liked the Communists more after that. Who knows?

A man who thought he *did* know was a peasant, a part-time guerrilla. He recalled:

> The Struggle Movement was very good for our side. It made the people think about the most important struggle—the one against the Americans. Many of the people who supported the revolution grew very strong during that period, and I think some new people began to follow the Liberation.

This and many other comments suggest, in summary, that Government suppression of the Struggle Movement brought heightened anti-Government feelings and perhaps made easier the Front's intensified attack. And the Government's tough responses to later demonstrations, especially those that opposed the elections of 1967, had similar effects upon attitudes.

TET OFFENSIVE

The Front and North Vietnamese attacks of February, 1968, brought extensive fighting to nearly every section of South Vietnam, including the village of My Thuy Phuong.[35] The Front began careful preparations in the region for the Tet Offensive during the days before January 31, 1968.[36] The lineup of military forces committed to battle by the North Vietnamese in the province included an operational staff, two assault infantry regiments, and two reinforcing infantry regiments.[37] Closely supporting the North Vietnamese main forces was the entire Front provincial organization. According to a U.S. Army study, the Front "created an extremely favorable environment for the Offensive by collecting intelligence, planning routes, storing food, and controlling the populace in the lowlands around Hue."[38]

During the last days of January, 1968, North Vietnamese and Front units were moving rapidly through the region. On the night of January 28, 1968, two days before Tet, a number of heavily armed sapper groups in battalion strength infiltrated Hue. In a published report, Government analysts suggest that part of the infiltration route was very close to, if not through, My Thuy Phuong.[39]

As the North Vietnamese forces moved into position around Hue, and as the sappers began infiltrating the city, Front guerrillas began their preparations for attack. In the village, word of the coming offensive reached Front leaders a few weeks before it occurred. A guerrilla commented:

> I remember that the comrades told us that something very big and very important was going to happen soon. They told us that soon there would be a General Uprising to drive the Americans out of Vietnam, and to destroy the puppet government. They told us all to get ready for a hard struggle, and for much sacrifice.

The Front directed its attacks in the village at many of the old targets. Beginning on January 31, coinciding with the coordinated North Vietnamese assault on the Hue Citadel and actions by local guerrillas and sympathizers throughout Hue and other parts of the province, insurgents launched a variety of attacks in the village. These aimed primarily at weakening local Government and American forces. The attacks brought the temporary collapse of the local Government apparatus, for civil servants and soldiers deserted nearly *en masse*. When the offensive began, soldiers and civil servants serving in and around the village simply disappeared, and did not reappear for a week or 10 days. During the offensive, there was sniping along Highway One directed at Government and U.S. troops, and Government installations in the village came under intermittent small arms fire. Guerrillas targeted nearly every military vehicle moving through the village. Snipers hit a jeep carrying a group of Government officers, killing one of them, and they wounded an American sitting in an open U.S. Army truck.

The guerrillas also stepped up terrorist actions against Government officials and other enemies in the immediate village area. They threw at least two satchel charges at homes of Government civil servants, and there were two or three direct confrontations with old enemies. A low-ranking Government soldier recalled what happened to his neighbors: "The Viet Cong came on the first day of Tet, and came to the house of the man living next to me. He was Catholic, and had been a supporter of the Government. They took him away. He was captured, and his family never saw him again." [40] Others confirmed this incident and related it to a concerted Front effort to attack long-time enemies. Five others disappeared from their homes during the first two days of the offensive, and only two returned.

There were no other major guerrilla military activities in the village, and only one significant Front proselyting activity: Front followers distributed a large number of leaflets. The message of the leaflets was that a General Uprising had come, and that it was time for all the people to unite in a fight against the Americans and the Government. The Government radio station, the most important source of Government information for the province, carried a few news reports during most of the offensive, but much patriotic music. Some people listened to Front broadcasts. For example, the insurgency broadcast the following message in the province on February 12, 1968: [41]

> The golden opportunity to completely triumph over the U.S. aggressors has come. We have won and are winning. Let the army and people of Thua-Thien-Hue rush forward on the impetus of victories, resolutely smash the puppet army, overthrow the puppet administration, crush the American bandits' aggressive designs, and together with the army and people of South Vietnam advance to achieve final victory.

Within a few days of the beginning of the offensive, Government and U.S. military units began to respond. The Government's First Infantry Division, which had been surprised by the attacks, reorganized some of its forces, recaptured parts of Hue, and reasserted Government influence in the countryside.[42] The First Division was heavily buttressed in this attempt by American units, which directed very intensive air and ground operations against North Vietnamese and Front forces. Some U.S. bombs and artillery fire fell in the areas west, southwest, and northwest of the village. Because there had been Front military activity in the villages of Phu Thu District, east of My Thuy Phuong, there was some shelling and bombing there as well, but none in My Thuy Phuong itself.

On about February 6 or 7, 1968, the first American and Government patrols reappeared in the village. Guerrillas did not attempt to directly confront any of them, although sniping and punji stick traps continued to hamper the operations. Instead, guerrillas and their supporters simply retreated into homes, tunnels, and the hills. The Tet Offensive in the province did not lead to the General Uprising that the Front had predicted.[43] However, it did bring about the total but temporary collapse of the Government apparatus in both city and countryside—at a high cost in casualties and property destruction.[44] An American advisor reported on post-Tet conditions in the province: "The Tet offensive in late January disrupted all efforts in the countryside, and effectively destroyed all semblance of G.V.N. rule until late February."[45] Without a doubt, that is precisely what happened in My Thuy Phuong.

An Army captain assigned to the village reflected the most common reaction of the pro-Government group to the Tet Offensive:

> The Viet Cong had a big loss during Tet Mau Than. The people all clearly saw how cruel the Viet Cong were in Hue, and the Viet Cong had to retreat because the people did not join their attack and instead were afraid of them and ran away from them.

A peasant said:

> The Government side was at first very weak. The soldiers ran away, and the Communists walked right in. In this area, the Viet Cong was very strong, and was free to move anywhere through the area. They had always been strong here, but during Tet Mau Than they were very much in the open.

A civil servant stated:

> We began to worry about the Americans, and wondered how determined the Americans were to help us. Did you know that not one American base was attacked by the Viet Cong? They attacked only Vietnamese bases. Now why was that? I think, and many people think, that it was because the Americans had made a secret arrangement with the Communists.

Several other pro-Government individuals expressed similar beliefs about American foreknowledge of the Tet attacks.

A peasant summed up what many politically uncommitted people were thinking during the offensive:

> There are many people in Vietnam who stand in the middle. During Tet Mau Than the people in the middle had a difficult time. On the one hand we saw the Communist side being very strong. They killed many people. But we saw that the Government side was very weak, and needed to have the Americans to support them.
>
> I think everyone respected the Communist side more because so many of the guerrillas died in the attacks. The important thing about Tet Mau Than is that the Communists made the Government very weak.

And the numerous local Front supporters hoped for a Front victory during the offensive. A peasant described the period in these words:

> There were many people who liked the Liberation Front who were worried, and who didn't know what was going to happen after Tet Mau Than. They were afraid that the revolution might have been lost, because the Americans and the Government Army seemed very strong.
>
> But I think they knew that the Liberation Front was even stronger, and that it had pulled back from the cities and the villages to the mountains. The people knew that if the American planes had not been there, and if the American Army had not come to hit very strongly, the Front would have won.
>
> So I think many of them looked on Tet Mau Than and were sad about all the dead and all the trouble. But I think they thought it was a victory for the revolutionary movement.

A student who often spread leaflets for the Front recalled:

> Yes, Tet Mau Than was a very important time for the Liberation. It was a great struggle against the Americans, and I think it was a victory for the Liberation, even though the Liberation had to retreat from Hue. It was a very strong victory. It showed the people that the Americans could be defeated.

In retrospect, we must conclude that the scope of the Tet attacks in the province, and the harshness of attacks in the village itself left an indelible mark on minds in My Thuy Phuong: the offensive reminded everyone of the Front's power.[46] For the estimated 5 percent of the people who were Government supporters, Tet of 1968 intensified hatred of the Front, and for some planted seeds of doubt concerning American dependability as an ally. The 10 to 15 percent who were politically uncommitted remained so, but were deeply impressed by the Front's strength. And My Thuy Phuong's Front supporters, an estimated 80 to 85 percent of the people, were left with proud memories of the boldest strikes yet against the Government and its ally.

NOTES

1. See "U.S. Marine Corps Civic Action Effort in Vietnam; March 1965–March 1966" (Washington, D.C.: Historical Branch, Headquarters, U.S. Marine Corps, 1968), p. 17.

2. See *The Marines in Vietnam; 1954–1973*, p. 47.

3. *Ibid.*, p. 53.

4. *Ibid.*, pp. 85, 97.

5. *Ibid.*, p. 97.

6. Also see Appendix IV, item 1, "Agricultural Production for the Support of VC/NVA Troops in MR V," dated 1965, cited in "Viet Cong Loss of Population Control; Evidence From Captured Documents," in Douglas Pike, ed., *Captured Documents* (Saigon: U.S. Mission, circa 1968–1969), vol. 5, p. 6; Vietnamese original not cited; available in Cornell University Library.

7. In light of such comments by villagers, a statement in a Marine publication seems curious. When the Corps transferred a Marine unit from the My Thuy Phuong area in 1965, Marines reported that "people were sad and heartbroken," and they "lined the road for 300 meters watching . . . the Marines leave. The Marines noted that *many* of the people were crying . . . ." [See "U.S. Marine Corps Civic Action" p. 58; emphasis in original.]

8. *Ibid.*, p. 39; also see "U.S. Marine Corps Civic Action Effort in Vietnam; April 1966–April 1967" (Washington, D.C.: Historical Branch, Headquarters, U.S. Marine Corps, 1970), p. 10.

9. See "Fact Sheet on the Combined Action Force" (Danang: III Marine Amphibious Force, March 31, 1970), p. 1; available in Histories and Museums Division, Headquarters, U.S. Marine Corps, Washington, D.C.

10. "U.S. Marine Corps Civic Action (1968)," p. 39.

11. The only mention of My Thuy Phuong's C.A.P. in available records is in "Thua Thien Report," December 5, 1967, p. 11.

12. The departure date is according to Col. Charles W. Dyke, who was assigned to the 101st Airborne's Camp Eagle from September 26, 1968 to June 2, 1970. He served in a variety of assignments, ranging from battalion commander to officer in charge of plans, training, and personnel functions at Eagle. He likely served in the village longer than any other American. (Interviewed at Fort Campbell, Ky., September 25, 1975.)

13. "Summary Communique on the Enemy and Friendly Situation During the First Six Months of 1966," document captured in November, 1966 by the 101st Airborne Division, cited in Pike, *Captured Documents*, p. 4.

14. *Ibid.*, p. 5.

15. "Viet Cong Recruitment; Data From Captured Documents," dated December, 1967, in *ibid.*, pp. 7, 8; Vietnamese original not cited.

16. "Indoctrination and Reindoctrination," dated January, 1968, in *ibid.*, p. 1; Vietnamese original not cited.

17. These were the Regional Forces (*Bo-Doi Dia-Phuong*) and Main Force (*Quan-Doi Chu-Luc*). Also see Pike, *Vietcong*, pp. 236–240.

18. See "Thua Thien Report," September 3, 1967, p. 4. Also see "The Viet Cong Infrastructure; A Background Paper" (Saigon: U.S. Mission, 1970), pp. 3, 8; available in Cornell University Library.

19. See "Viet Cong Recruitment; Data From Captured Documents," pp. 2, 10.

20. See "Thua Thien Report," August 3, 1967, p. 2.

21. Prior to the recruitment of these women, few local guerrillas were women, although numerous women aided guerrilla operations in various ways. According to villagers, Front leaders rarely tried to recruit women for the guerrilla force.

22. American advisors reported, "Occasional V.C. sniper activity still exists in the Gia Le area (Huong Thuy District) constituting a hazard while traveling on route #1 between Hue and Phu Bai." ["Thua Thien Report," October 4, 1966, p. 18a.]

23. Government compounds sometimes came under Front attack. People said that sniper fire and mortar rounds "sometimes" fell on the compounds. U.S advisors reported that a polling place in My Thuy Phuong came under mortar attack during the September, 1966 Constituent Assembly election. ["Thua Thien Report," October 4, 1966, p. 18a.]

24. "Thua Thien Report," December 31, 1966, p. 18a.

25. U.S.A.I.D./Hue telegram to Public Safety, U.S.A.I.D./Danang, in "Thua Thien Weekly and Monthly Report, 1966," folder 35, box 17, no. 71A5365, Center of Military History.

26. An earlier mention of Front strength in Thua Thien/Hue is a document dated July, 1966: U.S. advisors reported that the insurgency controlled 70 percent of Thua Thien by day, and 73 percent by night, versus Government control by day 11 percent and 8 percent by night; in terms of population, however, the Front was said to control 7 percent by day and 56 percent by night, and the Government 53 percent by day and 25 percent by night. [See "G.V.N. and V.C. Control of Area" (Hue: U.S.A.I.D., July, 1966), one page, in *ibid.* Also see "Thua Thien Report," January 25, 1966, p. 2b; Vien, no. 20, p. 117; Shaplen, *The Road From War,* pp. 90–120; Vien, no. 8, pp. 156, 168.]

27. See "Thua Thien—Terrorist Activity, 1967–1968" (Public Safety Division, U.S.A.I.D.), folder 60, Box 19, 19/66:23–7, 71A5365, Center of Military History.

28. Excerpts of August 17, September 6, September 12, and October 27, 1966 reports in *ibid.,* with military time notations converted to conventional times.

29. Some suggested that the Front's provincial organization had to approve all such attacks.

30. Many took refuge at night with friends and relatives in Hue.

31. Villagers did not agree on where the village chief was shot, at home or on the road. There is, however, confirmation of the killing: anthropologist Gerald Hickey learned that the village chief died the day after Hickey's visit to My Thuy Phuong in 1967. [From a conversation May 29, 1975 at Cornell University.]

32. See Shaplen, *op. cit.,* pp. 48–73; FitzGerald, *Fire In The Lake,* pp. 276–291; "Civil Unrest in Thua Thien and Quang Tri 10 March thru 30 April 1966"

(U.S.A.I.D./Hue, May 3, 1966), enclosure 5, in "Thua Thien, Weekly and Monthly Report, 1966."

33. See the June 24, 1966 monthly Public Safety report for Thua Thien, in "Thua Thien, Weekly and Monthly Report, 1966."

34. According to several, the 1967 Struggle Movement brought no such demonstrations to My Thuy Phuong.

35. For a good account of the Tet Offensive nationwide, see Don Oberdorfer, *Tet* (Garden City: Doubleday, 1971). An interesting analysis of news coverage of the offensive can be found in Peter Braestrup, *Big Story; How the American Press and Television Reported and Interpreted the Crisis of Tet 1968 in Vietnam and Washington* (Boulder, Colorado: Westview Press, 1977).

36. See Douglas Pike, *War, Peace, and the Viet Cong* (Cambridge: M.I.T. Press, 1969), pp. 126–131.

37. See Pham Van Son et al, ed., *The Viet Cong "Tet" Offensive (1968)* (Saigon: Printing and Publications Center, Republic of Vietnam Armed Forces, 1968), p. 284; "Special Intelligence Study NR 33–68 on the Hue Tet Offensive . . ." (Camp Eagle: 101st Airborne Division, December 29, 1968), pp. 1, 5, available in the 101st Airborne Division Museum.

38. "Special Intelligence Study," p. 6.

39. See Son et al, *op. cit.*, pp. 252, 285, 288.

40. Most villagers assumed that the man was dead, and in 1974–1975 his remains had not yet been found.

41. Liberation Radio broadcast, February 12, 1968, in "Daily Report," February 13, 1968, p. KKK3.

42. See "Synopsis of the Battle of Hue" (Camp Eagle: 101st Airborne Division, January 10, 1969), p. 2; available in 101st Airborne Museum.

43. Front confidence was so great during the offensive that on February 14, 1968, it established a People's Revolutionary Committee for the province. (See Vien, no. 22, pp. 43–44.) That committee issued a lengthy analysis of the Tet Offensive in April, 1968. (See "Daily Report," April 18, 1968, pp. L1–L3.) See also "Information on the Victory of our Armed Forces in Hue From 31 January to 23 March 1968," translation of a captured document, the authenticity of which was never confirmed, made available to the press in April, 1969, by the U.S. Mission/Saigon.

44. There are widely varying estimates of the number of casualties during the offensive. See "Synopsis of the Battle," p. 2; "One Year Later . . . The Rebirth of Hue" (Saigon: U.S. Information Service, Vietnam Feature Service, TCB–037, circa 1969), p. 1, available in the 101st Airborne Museum; Douglas Pike, "The Viet Cong Strategy of Terror" (Saigon: U.S. Mission, 1970), pp. 41–64; Vien, no. 37, pp. 122, 126; Gareth Porter, "The 1968 'Hue Massacre,' " *Indochina Chronicle*, June 24, 1974, no. 33, pp. 2–13; Alje Vennema, *The Viet Cong Massacre at Hue* (New York: Vantage Press, 1976).

45. "Thua Thien Report," April 4, 1968, p. 1.

46. Official analysts on both sides of the conflict shared villagers' fixation on the power of the offensive. See, for example, Son et al, *op. cit.*, p. 248, and *Hue Anh-Dung*, pp. 54, 57, 61.

10

Fighting the Eagle

THE CAMP

A major turning point for My Thuy Phuong's people came in early 1968: the landing of Camp Eagle. With that event, American disruption of village life began to accelerate. As part of the U.S. Army buildup in the province, about two companies of American soldiers came to the village on January 28 and 29, 1968.[1] The companies belonged to the 101st Airborne Division (Airmobile)—the "Screaming Eagles." The 101st came to share major combat responsibilities in Thua Thien/Hue with the Marine Corps.[2] There is no available information on just why the village was selected for Camp Eagle, nor is it clear who made the selection. It is clear, however, that the camp literally changed the face of My Thuy Phuong, and at its peak supported more Americans—10,000 at a time—than there were Vietnamese in the village.[3]

Personnel from the 101st constructed Camp Eagle in a section of My Thuy Phuong called Gia Le 5, a sparsely inhabited area of rolling, sandy hills in the western part of the village. Before the camp, Gia Le 5 had a few homes, many acres of vegetable gardens, and numerous graves. The first people directly affected by Eagle were the two or three families who lived in Gia Le 5. Government officials ordered them to relocate, and gave them one month to do so.

People spoke with resignation about relocation of the families, and loss of the garden area to Camp Eagle, but anger replaced resignation when they discussed another subject—the graves of Gia Le 5. Before construction began on the camp, bulldozers destroyed many of the graves. Neither

101st nor Government officials gave notice of what was about to happen, so people had no chance to relocate graves or to protest. Colonel Charles Dyke, who spent nearly two years at Eagle, denied that his unit damaged any graves, but the consensus of many villagers was that the bulldozers destroyed between twenty-five and thirty graves.[4] The 101st left other graves standing, and simply constructed buildings over and around them.[5]

After breaking ground, about two companies of U.S. soldiers brought Camp Eagle to life with a frenzy of construction activity.[6] The first objective was to secure Eagle's boundaries. Tons of barbed wire arrived, and soldiers strung it around the camp. They also constructed metal reconnaissance towers, and dug bunkers, fortifying them with sandbags. And construction began on Camp Eagle's most dominant and important feature, a massive helicopter takeoff and landing zone. The next stage involved construction of more durable buildings and other facilities around Eagle's 3,150 acres. Soldiers laid roads and walkways throughout the camp, built barracks, mess halls, a chapel, a command headquarters, put up an elaborate gate at the camp entrance, and placed small signs around the camp. One sign over a wooden walkway leading from the helicopter landing zone read, "If You Want It Done, Ask The 101." [7]

Camp Eagle presented an image of bustling activity. U.S. soldiers provided ammunition, equipment, men, food, and artillery support for a string of 101st firebases throughout the province—like Firebase Bastogne and Firebase Birmingham—and for ground operations organized from Eagle and other major installations. A stream of trucks and helicopters transported requested supplies to the firebases.[8]

Incidents along the highway became virtually daily occurrences. With convoys moving more regularly than ever before, the bullets and C-rations continued to fly, and water buffalo to fall. Air transport of equipment and men, which with the 101st Airborne meant choppers, greatly raised the noise level in the village. An average of 45,000 to 50,000 takeoffs and landings occurred every month under the supervision of Eagle Tower.[9]

Another important Eagle function involved training. American soldiers instructed both 101st and Vietnamese soldiers within the boundaries of Eagle, and at nearby Firebase Birmingham. These were refresher courses for American soldiers recently arrived from the U.S., and first-time training courses for Vietnamese soldiers.[10]

Although most of Eagle's soldiers kept busy at duty assignments, many had low morale. Several Americans formerly based at Eagle asserted that the morale problem was mainly related to antiwar sentiment and homesickness, and its most dangerous expression involved alcohol and drug abuse.[11] To their credit, Eagle's commanders did not allow prostitutes on base—a "solution" to the morale problem adopted at many other U.S. installations. But there were quite a few other "morale boosters." The doors of many Eagle hootches—buildings for 20 or 30 men each—had illustrations of a gun-toting Screaming Eagle soldier and the gently prodding words, "What Have You Done For Him Today?"[12] The 101st also created eight clubs for its different units, and for the different ranks of American soldiers on base.

There were films every night at Eagle, and frequent steak and chicken barbecues. Intramural sports involved many men. A television station broadcast from a trailer in Hue.[13] And occasionally the 101st brought stage productions to the outdoor "Eagle Entertainment Bowl." On Christmas Day, 1969, for example, the Bob Hope Show arrived. Connie Stevens, astronaut Neil Armstrong, Miss World, Les Brown and the Band of Renown, and "a Chinook-full of great looking girls" appeared before an enthusiastic audience estimated at 18,500.[14] On the camp, Hope joked, "In my honor, they changed it to Camp Chicken. I'm under the command of Colonel Sanders. Hope the enemy doesn't find out I'm finger-lickin' good."[15]

One Vietnamese, a Government officer, was unimpressed with Camp Eagle's activities: "America is a very rich country, and came to Vietnam to support the Vietnamese, so of course it must use everything it has to support us." But others in the village were not so blasé. A peasant recalled, "When I heard about and saw the activities on that camp, I couldn't believe it. It was like another world to us."

The images of American superabundance and movement, Americans at work, and Americans at play baffled many others. But some, though perhaps baffled, sought jobs at the base. Very little information is available on the number of Vietnamese hired to work at Eagle.[16] It is clear only that in 1970 the three major installations in the province—Camp Evans, the Phu Bai base, and Camp Eagle—employed about 4,700 Vietnamese to support different branches of the 101st Airborne. The 101st paid Vietnamese employees an average monthly wage equivalent in 1970 to about U.S.$23, which is about what blue collar workers earned in Hue in civilian jobs.[17]

In My Thuy Phuong, relatively few—between 50 and 75—sought jobs on the base. This was partly due to Front pressure to steer clear of the Americans, and also because of a conscious effort by the 101st to discourage job-seekers from the immediate vicinity. According to Colonel Dyke, residents of the village were in a better position, because of proximity to the camp, to assist guerrillas in reconnaissance, stake-outs, and attacks. So the 101st considered them security risks and therefore undesirable employees.[18]

Every morning hundreds of Vietnamese men and women, some from the village, waited outside the main gate. Eagle headquarters set daily hiring requirements, and U.S. soldiers had to choose from among the crowds of waiting, anxious laborers. All of the jobs were menial, and some even demeaning, but the Vietnamese were anxious to work. A small number of them, including some from the villlage, worked in the camp laundry, a Korean contract operation, or in the mess halls or post exchange. Others worked picking up papers and garbage. Still others dug ditches and performed other maintenance tasks. Finally, there were men and women American soldiers called "shit-burners," whose job it was to dispose of feces from Camp Eagle's latrines.[19]

Others profited from the camp but did not work there. Although the 101st declared the village off limits to American soldiers, violations of the ban were frequent enough to permit off-base "services" to emerge. Some small shops opened on the road leading into Eagle, selling soft drinks and beer. Most of these shops were also black market currency exchange points, and they sold marijuana and other drugs. Others along the road specialized in same-day laundry service, so some houses were literally covered with drying American uniforms and undergarments. Several profited handsomely from illicit contacts with 101st soldiers. One man, at the time a Government soldier, lived along the road, and tried to cultivate friendships with U.S. soldiers. Through such friendships, he bought soft drinks and beer from the post exchange, and sold those items on the local market, splitting profits with the Americans. Another man, a Government soldier, worked as a pimp.

And then there was Tony. The case of the young boy who took an American name illustrates how exposure to Camp Eagle changed a dozen or so young men and boys in the village. At about age 12, Tony left his impoverished mother, wandered onto Camp Eagle, and simply stayed. There U.S. soldiers informally adopted him, and for about two years he rarely left Eagle's boundaries. The boy picked up military slang, and learned the heavily accented English language of the southern U.S. He grew to love American food and appreciate American rock musical groups, especially the Creedence Clearwater Revival. After two years at Eagle someone then decided to put Tony to work. The boy began travelling with a 101st military police unit. "They would drive me into the village," Tony remembered, "and when I saw anybody selling things on the black market I would get out of the jeep, give a signal, and they would have a Vietnamese policeman arrest that person."

At age 15, Tony for some reason turned on his American benefactors. He recruited two or three others his age from the village and nearby Phu Bai, and began to steal from open-top U.S. trucks. Typically, the boys waited near the intersection in My Thuy Phuong where the trucks had to stop. One of the boys would climb up onto the trucks and toss boxes to friends waiting below. Later, when the trucks slowed, the boys tossing boxes would climb down and escape by waiting motorcycle. Periodically, Americans driving the trucks caught Tony. But usually the boy's "tender" age worked in his favor, as did his command of English. The Americans never jailed him.

Many other children and some village women became Camp Eagle's garbage-pickers. South of the camp, just across the village border, there was a garbage dump, which served Eagle and other nearby installations. Open trucks hauled garbage to this spot and dumped it. The dump was a veritable gold mine of abundance for the garbage-pickers. They found numerous usable or resalable items there, including packing materials, office supplies, uneaten food, and castoffs from individual soldiers. Every day about 12 children and women from the area could be seen at the dump. Sometimes their eagerness for "good" garbage was so great that they climbed unloading trucks, and sometimes there were tragedies: a few children were buried under avalanches of dumped garbage.

Then there were Camp Eagle's combat activities. These did far more than heighten tensions and bring social and economic changes to the village, for they caused significant physical damage as well.

First, there was perimeter defense. As part of the defensive arrangement, throughout Eagle there were various types of bunkers, partly underground structures of metal and sandbags for use in event of attack. The perimeter itself consisted of a maze of tanglefoot and concertina wire surrounding the camp. Throughout the perimeter area, 101st soldiers scattered claymore mines and gas cannisters, set with trip fuses.[20] The entire area, it should be noted, was completely devoid of vegetation, a result of chemical defoliation.[21]

But the bunkers, the wire, the claymores, and the gas were not enough, in the estimation of 101st commanders. Every night, and often during daylight hours as well, fifteen or sixteen patrols of four to twenty men each moved outside the perimeter. They ranged as far as about two miles from the camp, crisscrossing My Thuy Phuong and surrounding villages.[22] In addition, Eagle commanders sent small groups of five to nine soldiers armed with M-16 rifles, grenade launchers, and various types of mines on nightly ambush missions.[23] Sometimes with faces greased black for concealment, the soldiers proceeded two to three hundred yards in all directions from the perimeter. Ambush parties waited low and patiently for Vietnamese to wander near the camp.

Many in the village, especially those who lived in sections closer to Eagle, had numerous stories of the perimeter. Most felt that to approach the camp from any direction, day or night, was risky, for patrols and ambushes seemed to be everywhere, and bunker guards were alert and always looking for targets. A peasant described what happened once when he tried to visit his family cemetery plot, in an area within sight of Camp Eagle:

> I came during the day, and was carrying a few tools with me. My son came up behind me with a wheelbarrow, to carry dirt. But when we got to the graves, there was much firing coming from the American camp. And I heard one or two bullets hit around us.

Many others spoke of the foot patrols and ambushes, and still others described a gas which from time to time filled the air around Eagle and drifted into the village. This was C.S. tear gas, which the Army used for riot control and other military purposes. A 101st document describes the gas, which has a nauseating effect when inhaled, as effective for "areas where the enemy is intermingled with the civilian population." [24] According to a peasant woman, "I can remember so many times when the gas would come out from the American camp. And I can remember choking and not being able to see because of the gas."

Bullets from Eagle's defenders frequently rained on the village. "The Americans were always shooting up flares to illuminate the ground, and they fired at nothing at all," remembered a tradesman. "You would think that the American camp was always under attack." Others concurred in this, and suggested that it was a rare night indeed when the crackle of small arms fire did not sound at Camp Eagle. Adding to the racket were the tremendous, piercing concussions of artillery pieces, fired from Eagle to support military operations in the province.[25]

Several contended that sometimes there was a veritable frenzy of firing around the camp. A former 101st soldier called such episodes "mad minutes." He described them: [26]

> Our mad minutes . . . were at the perimeter fence. Every once in a while at Camp Eagle, every two months or so, the order would just come down, "Okay guys go to it." You got a mad minute. And everybody picks up a weapon with both hands, both feet, and they shoot. They don't care what they shoot at, just as long as it's away from the base area. That's a lot of fun too. All those sickies.

A peasant recalled that on several occasions he observed a "wall of fire" around the camp. The American explained this phenomenon: [27]

> On our perimeter we had . . . what's known as Fugas. . . . It's flammable, and they put it in barrels. What they do to it is they explode the barrel over an area and this flaming jell-like substance lands on everything, if it's people or animals or whatever. And you can't get it off. It just burns, and you rub it and it sticks on. You just spread it all around.

From the standpoint of the 101st commanders, Eagle's perimeter defense was far from the most important American military activity in the village. And from the standpoint of the people, it was far from the most disruptive. Over the years, patrols of U.S. soldiers crisscrossed the village, sometimes in combination with Vietnamese soldiers. The patrols usually came every day, day and night, and often involved house-to-house searches for suspects or weapons. Choppers sometimes ferried men out to village ricefields, and American air strikes and artillery occasionally supported ground operations.

There was also continued dislocation of village residents by the camp. Sometime in 1969, Government officials, at the request of 101st commanders, ordered several families living along the camp access road to move their houses back several yards from the road. They cited security requirements, and promised restitution payments. The families complied with the request, despite great reluctance to do so and some futile protests to American and Government authorities.

The 101st employed nearly every tactic in the book in My Thuy Phuong, and there were some tactical aberrations. The recollections of many people permit reconstruction of three illustrative incidents involving 101st soldiers:

1. In early 1968, just after establishment of Camp Eagle, 20 or 30 choppers raced to the village ricefields, hovered low over the swirling, rippling rice stalks and unloaded their passengers, about 150 fully equipped U.S. soldiers. The troops quickly proceeded to round up three or four peasants, who had no time to flee. The Americans tied the peasants' hands behind their backs and looped ropes around their necks and between them. When the Americans pushed or pulled one among their prisoners, all the tied men suffered. The 101st soldiers led the peasants to a small bridge over a canal, where five or six Americans forced them to sit. The captors then took turns punching and kicking the captives, and swore and spat at them. According to one of the peasants held that day, "They were so insane and angry that we were certain they were going to kill us." One American urinated on two of his captives. Later, after the beatings and humiliations had reduced the men to semiconsciousness, the Americans wandered off, leaving their tied captives on the bridge.

2. Another day in 1968, so-called "death on call" Cobra choppers and spotter planes circled low over My Thuy Phuong.[28] "We had never seen so many at one time before," said a peasant. "There was a big operation, and lots of gunfire." The Americans apparently felt threatened by something that day, for they called in an air strike. Two or three bombs fell from a fighter plane on one run over the village. "It was frightful," said a peasant woman. "I shook all over, and was very afraid." The bombs landed in the ricefields, and damaged the walls of an irrigation canal. A spark or shrapnel from the explosions touched off a fire in a nearby house, and the flames consumed three peasants. Two of the victims were children.

3. One night sometime in 1969, a squad of U.S. soldiers patrolled the hamlet closest to Camp Eagle. The soldiers were armed with M-16 automatic rifles, pistols, knives, and grenades. They moved cautiously along a sandy, winding footpath, lined on either side by vegetable plots and shade trees. They entered a peasant house, a small wooden structure. One soldier remained in front and another moved behind it to stand guard. The others entered the door and saw a small family group huddled fearfully in front of them. There was an old man, his wife, a 14-year-old boy, and two high school age daughters. In pidgin Vietnamese, but mostly in English, one of the 101st soldiers ordered the Vietnamese to stand. The soldiers searched the old man and the boy, and pushed them to a corner, where an American stood over them with a threatening M-16. Clearly the villagers were prisoners in their own home. Choking with emotion as she spoke, the mother recalled what happened next: "They pushed us around and attacked my daughters. They pushed them to the ground, and raped them again and again."

Although many spoke of American patrols, bombing, and artillery strikes as if they occurred daily, it is uncertain how often the air strikes, choppers, artillery strikes, and American patrols came to the village.

However, one phase of the 101st Airborne's activity stands out. People pointed to 1968–1970 as the years of heaviest direct American involvement in their midst. No one seemed aware of the name 101st commanders gave their increased military actions during part of this period—Operation Nevada Eagle.

Nevada Eagle occurred in 1968–1969, and was a 288-day series of military operations throughout Thua Thien's lowlands, and later its mountains and valleys. It came again and again to the village. Details of numerous specific military incidents from the Nevada Eagle period were clear in many individual villagers' minds, but no one had an overall view of all local Nevada Eagle operations. There remains, however, a detailed record of Nevada Eagle in the 101st Airborne archives. That document shows that the operation involved extensive daily fighting, with large numbers of casualties.

Nevada Eagle activities in the village were primarily by company-sized 101st units. The operations, according to the official battle record, came frequently, and they took a high toll. American soldiers killed, wounded, and detained many villagers, including some local insurgents. They also seized rice and guerrilla supplies, and destroyed guerrilla tunnels. Operations were particularly intense in the area of the ricefield hamlets, which had long been Front strongholds. Nevada Eagle and other operations of early 1968 prompted people living in those hamlets to abandon homes and move into more central parts of the village, where they remained until 1972.

The exact frequency of Nevada Eagle operations in the village cannot be determined from the battle record, for the 101st only reported operations with "contacts." The probably large number of uneventful, "routine" operations went unrecorded. It is impossible to determine whether the 101st exaggerated battle statistics, or whether it failed to report tactical aberrations, such as summary executions of prisoners. Even if flawed by exaggeration or underreporting, the battle record nevertheless verifies villagers' statements about frequent, intense, and destructive U.S. military operations near their homes. That record is summarized in Table 10.1.[29]

There was one other significant American military effort in My Thuy Phuong—the programs called Civic Action. U.S. Marines had the first Civic Action program, which they said aimed at helping the Vietnamese people. Marine medical aid teams occasionally paid visits to the village for treatment of minor ailments, and one or two Marines taught English in a local elementary school.[30] Marines also distributed C-rations to families they considered needy, clothes to village children, and soap to people of all ages.[31] And in one reported instance, Marines helped clear rubble from an area of the village that had been bombed, presumably by American aircraft.[32]

While the Marine program was fairly modest, the 101st Airborne ap-

TABLE 10.1 Operation Nevada Eagle, 1968–1969, in My Thuy Phuong *

	May	June	July	Aug.	Sept.	Oct.	Nov.	Dec.	Jan.	Feb.	Totals
No. Company-sized Operations with "Contact"	12	10	8	1	2	2	5	6	4	2	52
No. Reports of Misc. Action	0	3	2	0	1	0	0	3	2	1	12
No. Vietnamese Killed	20	4	0	2	1	1	2	2	4	0	36
No. Americans Killed	0	2	0	0	0	0	0	0	0	0	2
No. Americans Wounded	18	25	3	0	0	0	0	0	1	0	47
No. Vietnamese Detained	20	8	46	0	4	20	23	16	3	0	140
No. Guns Seized	4	4	0	0	2	2	1	3	2	0	18
Tons of Rice Seized	3+	34+	0	0	0	0	0	8+	0	0	45+
No. Seizures of Ammo., Equip.	3	2	2	1	2	1	1	2	2	0	16
No. Tunnels Destroyed	200+	2	0	0	0	0	0	1+	1	0	204+
No. Traps Destroyed	6	11	0	0	0	0	0	0	0	1	18
No. Reports of Misc. Damage	2	0	1	0	0	0	0	1	0	0	4

* *See* "Combat Operations After Action Report" (Camp Eagle: 1st Battalion, 501st Airborne Infantry, 101st Airborne Division, March 1, 1969), pp. 142–190; available in 101st Airborne Museum.

proached Civic Action in a big way. Its projects in the village included four classrooms and numerous wells.[33] Camp Eagle personnel occasionally distributed different foodstuffs, clothing, and presents, often to commemorate Christmas or Vietnamese holidays. In addition, the 101st organized medical visits to the village.

But Civic Action also had an outright political side. First, American soldiers became involved in information activities to support the Government. The 101st sometimes sent ground loudspeaker and audiovisual teams to the village, to publicize intelligence programs and a program called *Chieu Hoi,* which aimed at encouraging desertion from insurgent ranks. Second, Civic Action personnel became heavily involved in direct support of Government intelligence and police activities. In December of 1969, the 101st command approved construction of a police station for My Thuy Phuong.[34] The Civic Action group became involved in extensive leaflet drops throughout the province, including the village. It also undertook local operations called "ground nostalgia/fear campaigns," involving assignment of ground loudspeaker teams to combat units.[35]

When asked, most villagers were unaware of the Civic Action efforts. As one peasant put it, "How can I remember anything good about the Americans when they did so much bad?" The peasant and nearly all his neighbors associated the U.S. Marines and 101st Airborne only with military operations in and around the village. In a publication, the 101st claimed that Civic Action led to "the closest and best rapport with Vietnamese officials and citizens of any military region in South Vietnam." [36] However, villagers' ignorance of Civic Action suggests that the efforts did little if anything to help people or to create rapport. In fact, the evidence from official records just presented suggests that in many instances Civic Action directly supported the very activities which brought greatest disruption to village life.

STRATEGIC WITHDRAWAL

The coming of Camp Eagle marked a major turning point for the Front in My Thuy Phuong. Not even the Tet Offensive had brought such changes.[37] A peasant recalled what happened. "The Liberation Army had to take its guerrillas and its cadres out of the village," he said, "because they would have been killed if they had remained behind. Many people who supported the revolution were sad at that, and the Liberation cells became weak." Several confirmed this contention about the cells, and noted that between 1968 and 1972, the People's Revolutionary Party had no influence in the village, and the Front functional groups no activities. Party and functional group messages, which in earlier years had never reached many, simply stopped flowing, a function of intensified American military pressure throughout the region on party and Front organizations.

A guerrilla said that what had long been a friendly environment for insurgents began to change after the establishment of Camp Eagle:

> When the Americans came to Gia Le with their base, many people became very afraid, and did not help the revolutionary side as much as before.

> Most of the revolutionary cells died, and the people became divided. They were afraid to tell us much about the American or puppet troops, and they were a little bit afraid to talk to the cadres who were still in the local area.

Villagers estimated that after establishment of Eagle through 1972, Front support decreased to roughly 50 percent of all villagers, about 30 percent of whom assisted guerrillas and remained active in the local insurgent network. The remaining 70 percent were passive Front supporters. Villagers also suggested that the number of Government supporters, passive and active, increased to about 10 or 15 percent of the people, and the remaining 35 to 40 percent were politically uncommitted.

These shifts from the 1964–1967 support patterns were expressions of the widely shared tendency, mentioned earlier, to tilt toward support of overwhelmingly strong political forces. However, note that during 1968–1972 the shifts were mainly from the Front to the politically uncommitted group—from which shifts back to the Front could be made with relative ease. There was only a slight increase in number of Government supporters, due mainly to people's dislike of Government and American security activities. And there is no evidence of improved perceptions of the local pro-Government group. Most villagers continued to resent what they felt as the group's oppression.

It is interesting to compare villagers' perceptions of political loyalties and trends with those of American advisors. The computerized U.S. evaluation system rated each of Vietnam's hamlets as to its overall degree of security. "A" was the highest rating, meaning a virtual Government bastion, while "E" meant a place with strong Front influence; "B", "C", and "D" were hamlets somewhere in between. The worst possible rating was "V", meaning complete Front control—a "V.C. hamlet." Here is how My Thuy Phuong looked to the Americans during 1968–1972: [38]

Date	**Dong Tam** (Thanh Lam, Tho Vuc)	**Dong Tien** (Gia Le 1, 2)	**Dong Luc** (Gia Le 3, 4, Lang Xa)	**Dong Loi** (6 Gia Le Thuong, Loi Nam Gia Le Ha)
Jan. 1968	B	C	D	unsafe at night
Jun. 1968	D	E	E	unsafe at night
Dec. 1968	C	C	C	unsafe at night
Jun. 1969	B	B	B	unsafe at night
Dec. 1969	B	B	B	unsafe at night
Jun. 1970	B	B	B	unsafe at night
Jan. 1972	B	C	C	C
Dec. 1972	C	C	C	C

Note that in American eyes the village was for the most part a "B" or "C" area. Such ratings meant "secure" or "relatively secure"—a generally favorable environment for the Government, with only some insurgent influence. Interestingly, the only month which came reasonably close to villagers' own assessments of political tendencies for the *entire* period 1968–1972 was June of 1968, when My Thuy Phuong averaged out at "E."

Although Front popularity dipped during 1968–1972, the insurgent military attack persisted and constituted the major Front activity in the village. There were ambushes, sniping incidents, attacks against Government soldiers, such as those guarding bridges, and occasionally pressure against local pro-Government villagers. However, because of American and Government military pressure, guerrillas had to launch most of their attacks from the hills west of My Thuy Phuong. They had less local help in the attacks, and many attackers were killed or captured, especially during Operation Nevada Eagle. In fact, between 1968 and 1972 over half of the village's guerrillas died or were jailed. And the Front replaced few of them—for most people saw the heightened military pressure and hesitated to join the guerrilla force.

Continued Front guerrilla pressure in the village against the Government and its foreign ally must be viewed as but part of the pressure brought by insurgent forces throughout the province.[39] For Huong Thuy District, an American advisory report includes information found in Table 10.2 on insurgent activity during April–December, 1968.[40]

TABLE 10.2. Front Activity in Huong Thuy District, April–December 1968 *

Type Incident	Number Incidents	Number Killed	Number Wounded	Number Missing
Assassination	4	4	—	—
Abduction	5	—	—	19
Mortar Attack	6	3	9	—
Small Arms Attack	2	3	8	—
Taxation	2	—	—	—
Totals:	19	10	17	19

* *See* "Thua Thien—Terrorist Activity, 1967–1968."

And a 101st Airborne study of Front activity in Huong Thuy District during 1970 gives another and later indication of the context of continued guerrilla activity in the village. According to the study, there were 36 Front-initiated incidents in the district, representing 9 percent of all incidents reported for the province during 1970. The incidents in Huong Thuy consisted mainly of collections of rice and money and attacks against Government installations. There was an average of three incidents per month that year.[41]

Guerrillas focused squarely on Camp Eagle. U.S. Army combat records contain many references to attacks against the base.[42] And villagers described numerous instances of sniping, mortaring, and sapper attacks against Eagle, all involving small numbers of guerrillas. However, Colonel Charles Dyke recalled an attack that involved many guerrillas, the time in May of 1968 when a sapper force attacked the Eagle perimeter.[43] According to Dyke, the sappers were North Vietnamese soldiers, most of whom wore shorts and had blackened their faces and greased their bodies. Villagers contended that about half of the sappers were North Vietnamese, and the rest were nonlocal Front guerrillas. "They were fanatics," Dyke commented. He stated that American soldiers killed about 100 sappers "inside the wire" of the base. Four U.S. soldiers were killed in the action, and fifteen wounded. Another man who served at Eagle, Sergeant Major Michael Collins, noted that one of the sappers was somehow able to hide for several days within the camp before being discovered and shot.[44]

As American and Government security efforts intensified in the village and throughout the region during 1969–1971, Front and North Vietnamese forces gradually reduced the scope and frequency of their operations.[45] A peasant commented on the period:

> Many people had supported the Front for so many years, and then the Americans came and killed many of them and made them [i.e., Front leaders] leave. So then we had to follow the Government, and we thought the Government side was not as good.

Another peasant recalled:

> Life became very difficult under the Government. They began to take more and more people into the Army. . . . We were all sad, and many of us thought that under the Liberation, when the Government was weak and the Liberation was strong, then it was a better life for the people.

There are indications that during the years 1968–1972 insurgent leaders were not often seen in the village. The men lived in the jungle, and only occasionally returned to My Thuy Phuong. They spent considerable time simply moving around, to avoid military blows like Operation Nevada Eagle. But despite great difficulties, the leaders continued to carefully plan and coordinate guerrilla attacks, allowing for the harsh new reality of fewer active supporters.

About six of the estimated ten local leaders were killed or captured during 1968–1972. They were replaced by younger, less experienced, less popular men. People claimed little knowledge of this "new generation" of leaders, possibly a reflection of the leaders' withdrawal to the jungle. However, many did claim that the newest leaders were intelligent and highly dedicated, aware of insurgent strategy and local history. Most of them had in effect served low-profile apprenticeships to early Front leaders, helping out and learning all the time. Several were actually related to the deceased leaders. All had been close to them, often sitting in on important meetings and in some cases helping organize leafletings and other small local actions. In general, the 1968–1972 leaders, like the movement they represented, had ties to the village and a revolutionary past. Camp Eagle did not break the ties, only strained them.

Despite military and leadership changes on the insurgent side, weakening of the cell structure, and less involvement of people in Front activities, revolutionary messages continued to reach My Thuy Phuong. During 1968–1972, there was some Front use of the old tactics of spreading rumors and periodically distributing leaflets. And Front messages continued to reach people by word of mouth and clandestine radio broadcasts. Throughout that period the messages remained timely and to the point. For example, a 1970 broadcast included a message from the Tri Thien Hue Liberation Front Committee, part of which reads:[46]

> Our people and people throughout the world continue to condemn the U.S. imperialists for their war acts against the Democratic Republic of Vietnam. Upon hearing that the U.S. aggressors have again bombed the north and have committed towering crimes against our people, the Tri Thien Hue Liberation Front Committee sent a message to the sworn brotherhood Quang Binh-Vinh Linh Fatherland Front Committee exposing the Nixon clique's bellicosity and stubbornness. . . .

Other Front messages accused the American military of damaging fruit trees through defoliation. This was actually a valid charge, since defoliation damage in Huong Thuy District was "widespread," according to a U.S. Government report.[47] People indicated that they were "very much interested" in this message, which came in leaflets, conversations, and broadcasts. And then there was a Front leaflet directed at children. It urged them to befriend American and Government soldiers and assist the Front by gathering information on military activities, by overcharging for soft drinks and turning profits over to the Front, and by stealing weapons and military supplies.[48] This message also came from some local insurgents. However, there is no evidence that children actually heeded it.

Front messages calling for noncooperation began to focus on Camp Eagle. According to a peasant, "The Viet Cong warned everyone not to work there. They said to work there would help the Americans and hurt the revolution." Many confirmed this assertion and indicated that mainly due to Front pressure, relatively few from the village worked at Eagle. And some who did were actually Front agents, assigned to gather information on the Americans. The 101st was thus partly correct in regarding My Thuy Phuong residents as security risks!

Finally, there was continued Front emphasis on heroes, the most important of whom remained Ho Chi Minh. Several recalled that when Ho died in 1969, Liberation Radio carried a message from the provincial Front organization, including this passage:[49]

With respect to the Tri Thien Hue people, President Ho had closely followed and guided us in every phase of struggle, and advised and encouraged us in our victories as well as in our difficulties. In the most recent letter addressed to cadres, people, and armed forces of Tri Thien Hue, he asked us not to be proud of our victories, not to be discouraged faced with difficulties, and to firmly hold to the class standpoint. He advised us to constantly resort to criticism and to continuously improve our revolutionary virtues.

To his soul, the cadres, combatants, and compatriots of Tri Thien Hue pledge to develop their victories, to overcome all difficulties, to correct shortcomings, to develop strong points, to unite closely to dash forward to fulfill their task, and to strictly carry out his advice.

In summary, Camp Eagle brought a dramatic shift for the Front in My Thuy Phuong. Through the camp's entire range of disruptive and often destructive activities, it forced Front leaders and guerrillas into retreat, killed some of them, and caused some Front followers to drift away. As noted earlier, Front support fell from over 80 to about 50 percent of the populace. But the insurgents made tactical changes, kept up their military pressure, and continued to circulate word of their struggle. In effect, the Front adjusted to the Eagle.

NOTES

1. The arrival date was provided by Command Sergeant Major Michael Collins, a 101st Airborne soldier who served at Camp Eagle. [Interviewed at Fort Campbell, Ky., September 26, 1975.]
2. For data on unit deployment in Thua Thien/Hue, see Commander in Chief, Pacific, *Report On War In Viet-Nam* (Washington, D.C.: Government Printing Office, 1968).
3. *Screaming Eagle,* March-April, 1972, p. 21; a publication of the 101st Airborne Division Association, Greenville, Texas, available at the Public Affairs Office, Ft. Campbell, Ky.
4. See note 12, Chapter 9.
5. See Vietnam Veterans Against the War, *The Winter Soldier Investigation: An Inquiry Into American War Crimes* (Boston: Beacon Press, 1972), p. 79.
6. See note 1.
7. The sign appears in a photograph provided by the Public Affairs Office, 101st Airborne Division, Ft. Campbell, Ky.
8. 101st Airborne Press Release, no. 10–58–71, Camp Eagle; all press releases cited are available in the 101st Airborne Museum, Fort Campbell, Ky. Hereafter they are cited as "Press Release."
9. *Screaming Eagle,* September-October, 1970, p. 21.
10. Press Release, no. 10–3–71.

11. See Richard Boyle, *Flower of the Dragon; The Breakdown of the U.S. Army in Vietnam* (San Francisco: Ramparts Press, 1972).

12. See note 1.

13. *Screaming Eagle,* February 1, 1972, p. 8.

14. *Screaming Eagle,* March-April, 1970, p. 3.

15. *Ibid.*

16. Col. Charles Dyke remembered only that "between one and six or seven thousand" Vietnamese worked on the base, with a hiring peak in 1969. (See note 12, Chapter 9.)

17. "Economic Impact of 101st Abn Div (Ambl)" (Camp Eagle: 101st Airborne, October 14, 1970); available at 101st Airborne Museum.

18. See note 12, Chapter 9.

19. A pattern found on other American military bases did not emerge at Eagle. There were no "hootch maids," women who worked for individual U.S. soldiers cleaning clothes, shining shoes, and cleaning up. The soldiers performed these tasks themselves. Col. Charles Dyke asserted that the bans on maids and on prostitutes were strictly enforced, and people in My Thuy Phuong corroborated the claim. (See note 12, Chapter 9.)

20. See note 12, Chapter 9, and note 1, this chapter.

21. "Senior Officer's Debriefing Report" (Camp Eagle: 101st Airborne, May 11, 1970), p. 13; available in 101st Airborne Museum. Also see Frank Browning & Dorothy Forman, eds., *The Wasted Nations* (New York: Harper & Row, 1972), p. 275.

22. See note 12, Chapter 9, and note 1, this chapter. For an excellent account of what it was like to serve in the U.S. military in Vietnam, see Philip Caputo, *A Rumor of War* (New York: Holt, Rinehart & Winston, 1977).

23. See "Combat Notes Number 10" (Camp Eagle: 101st Airborne, March 5, 1968), pp. 3, 5; "Operational Notes Number 7" (Camp Eagle: 101st Airborne, November 10, 1969). Both documents available at 101st Airborne Museum.

24. "Senior Officer's Debriefing Report," p. 13.

25. See "Operations Note Number 10—Field Expedient Target Locator" (Camp Eagle: 101st Airborne, April 1, 1970); available in 101st Airborne Museum. Also see Vietnam Veterans, *op. cit.,* pp. 79–80.

26. Vietnam Veterans, *op. cit.,* p. 80.

27. *Ibid.*

28. *Rendezvous With Destiny,* Summer-Fall, 1971, p. 4; 101st Airborne publication available at Public Affairs Office, Ft. Campbell, Ky.

29. "Combat Operations After Action Report" (Camp Eagle: 1st Battalion, 501st Airborne Infantry, 101st Airborne Division, March 1, 1969), pp. 142–190 [entries listed chronologically]; see also "After Action Report (Offensive Operations 17 May–28 February 1969)" (Camp Eagle: 2nd Brigade, 101st Airborne, March 5, 1969). Both these documents, reports from different units, are available in the 101st Airborne Museum.

30. "U.S. Marine Corps Civic Action" (1968), attached map.

31. *Ibid.,* p. 27.

32. "Thua Thien Report," December 31, 1966, p. 12a.

33. AC of S, G–5, "G–5 Activities" (Camp Eagle: 101st Airborne, November 5, 1969), p. 5; available in 101st Airborne Museum.

34. AC of S, G–5, "Civic Action Priority List" (Camp Eagle: 101st Airborne, December 14, 1969), p. 8; available in 101st Airborne Museum.

35. See AC of S, G–5, "G–5 Activities" (Camp Eagle: 101st Airborne, December 25, 1970), p. 2; available in 101st Airborne Museum.

36. *Rendezvous With Destiny,* Summer-Fall, 1971, p. 9.

37. The intensity of the post-Tet military attack against the North Vietnamese and Front forces was such that even some of the main force North Vietnamese units operating in the Tri Thien Hue zone apparently began to experience problems of morale. See "Press Release" (Saigon: U.S. Mission, no. 197–68, October 12, 1968), pp. 1–2, in Pike, ed., *Captured Documents.*
 In 1969, American advisors wrote of the Front's "many problems and frustrations." (See "Thua Thien Report," August 3, 1969, p. 4.) Note that in late 1968 or early 1969 the local Front committee's name was changed to "Revolutionary People's Committee." It consisted of several of the same men who led the local Front movement through the early 1960s, minus several who were dead or in jail, plus several younger leaders, most of whom were related to the older leaders.

38. Information provided by Robert Jones III.

39. See Vien, no. 22, p. 286.

40. This data was gleaned by the author from the file "Thua Thien—Terrorist Activity, 1967–1968;" see note 27, Chapter 9.

41. "Analysis of V.C./V.C.I. Related Activity in Thua Thien—1970" (Camp Eagle: 101st Airborne, February 21, 1971), p. 3; available in 101st Airborne Museum.

42. See "Significant Activity Since January 1970" (Camp Eagle: 101st Airborne); chronological file (no page numbers); available in 101st Airborne Museum.

43. See note 12, Chapter 9; "Thua Thien Report," June 4, 1968, p. 4; Vien, no. 37, p. 125.

44. See note 1.

45. North Vietnamese and Front forces, however, continued to claim great success on the Tri Thien Hue battlefields. (See Vien, no. 33, p. 165.)

46. Liberation Radio, December 5, 1970, in "Daily Report," December 7, 1970, p. L–2.

47. Huong Thuy District report, one page, attached to "Thua Thien Report," September 4, 1968.

48. See also "Thua Thien Report," July 3, 1968, pp. 5–6.

49. Liberation Radio, September 18, 1969, in "Daily Report," September 19, 1969, p. L–2.

11

Quiet War

BUILDING RESENTMENT

"Revolution does not originate with peasants with a high standard of living and full stomachs."[1] These words, in a report by an American advisor in Thua Thien/Hue, perfectly sum up the philosophy behind the most important civil programs initiated by the Government in My Thuy Phuong—those related to economic development.

There were other programs in the civil realm, too. These involved a process called political development. Here the Government aimed at fostering political loyalty to its leaders and institutions, and undermining such loyalties on the insurgent side. A colonel of the U.S. Marine Corps, who served as a high-ranking advisor in the province, perhaps unintentionally illustrated the sort of thinking associated with Government political development efforts: [2]

> If you build a schoolhouse in a village, what have you done? You've built a schoolhouse, right? Why'd you build a schoolhouse? Just so you'd have a schoolhouse? Hell, no!
>
> You build a schoolhouse because, hopefully, the Vietnamese people of this little hamlet will say, "What a wonderful government we have. Let us fight for our government." This is what you're trying to get across to them—this is why you build a schoolhouse. To win this war, you've got to get the people behind their government. . . .

These quotes from American officials reveal one side of the civil programs. Let us now briefly examine the *other* side—people's reactions to the programs in My Thuy Phuong. In discussing the programs, most villagers dwelt but superficially on the nuts and bolts of program operations. They emphasized instead the general manner in which programs were controlled by the local pro-Government minority and the widespread resentment they engendered. The discussion here follows that lead.

There were, first, the economic programs.[3] The most important of them aimed at increasing agricultural production and agricultural mechanization. To achieve the first of these objectives, the Government introduced what peasants locally called "I.R." rice varieties. I.R. rice, which was developed in the Philippines, provides higher yields than indigenous Vietnamese rice if properly fertilized, irrigated, and treated with pesticides.[4] In the early 1970s, the Government clerk in charge of agricultural matters in the village persuaded about 30 local peasants to plant the new variety. The I.R. seeds, fertilizer, and pesticides were at first available through local retailers, and at reasonable prices. Peasants planted about sixty-two acres with the new variety, and had about two years of reasonable yields. But then there came a change.

"Suddenly everything doubled or tripled in price," stated a peasant. "The retailers were making huge profits, especially on the pesticides, which only a few places sold, and which we needed most of all." To make matters worse, the peasants began to get lower prices for their products. "There was an arrangement between the buyers and the fertilizer and pesticide retailers," the man added. "They divided the profits. They were making so much, and we made less than before." The Government agricultural cadre in the village office had set these conditions. People suspected that the cadre had made a deal with local retailers and rice wholesalers to share in the profits from supply purchases and resale of I.R. harvests. The arrangement brought high profits to the retailers and wholesalers, and probably money to the cadre. People were uncertain about amounts of money involved. It also created an illusion of change and progress in the village, and the agricultural cadre probably reported that his efforts had brought "agricultural development." A peasant who was involved in the I.R. program said:

> Many people here did not care much about politics. We only wanted to plant rice and live happily. I am an example of that. But when we saw the cadre and the businessmen getting rich on that program we became angry at the Government. We saw clearly how corrupt the Government was, and we began to support the Liberation.

Another peasant, himself not a cultivator of I.R. rice, recalled, "We watched that program carefully and saw the rich men get richer and the poor men just stay the same. It was a very bad situation." And a university student said, "The program made people hate the Government." Others made similar statements, indicating that they saw the I.R. program as an attempt to exploit the desperation and poverty of a few, and they grew resentful of the Government for promoting it.

Another agricultural program encouraged vegetable and fruit production for American military units in the province. In March of 1969, peasants from Thua Thien/Hae were selling produce to U.S. forces at three major installations, including Camp Eagle, at the rate of U.S.$42,000 per week. At that time, military demands still exceeded supply, so the American military and the Government began a coordinated effort to increase supplies of corn, lettuce, tomatoes, watermelon, pineapples, and other items. In a report, an American aid official wrote that such buying "places badly needed development funds into the hands of the farmers who will now be able to buy pigs, chickens and cement to improve their living standards." [5] In My Thuy Phuong, however, the reality of agricultural production for American units did not exactly fit this description. A peasant commented on the program:

> I began producing lettuce and tomatoes to sell to the Americans. But I had to give to one rich man, and he was the one who actually gave it to the Americans and got money. He gave me some, of course, and it was a higher profit than I could get in the Vietnamese market. But most of the profit went to that man. Many other people here have had the same thing happen.

This comment and others suggest that middlemen began operating in the village, buying produce from peasants and turning it directly over to American supply channels. But due to language, cultural, and legal barriers, the peasants could not deal directly with the American soldiers, and most profits went to the middlemen. While exact figures on profit margins are unavailable, it is clear that many had strong negative opinions about the program. This peasant's comment is typical:

> Many people here got angry about this program. We saw a few people get rich from the program, but most did not earn that much more money. The people were angry at the Government and at the Americans for having that program. Maybe some joined the V.C. because of it.

There was another agricultural program that had a similar effect on attitudes. As noted earlier, many of the village's poorest residents—about 100 in all—had long made extra money through work as agricultural laborers, often for large landholders, each of whom controlled between 15 and 30 *mau*. Usually such work involved harvesting, cultivating, or irrigating the fields. In 1970, a Government agricultural mechanization program touched the lives of these laborers. Two years earlier the American aid program had begun importing mechanical cultivators and pumps, and it distributed over 200 small tractors free to villages in Thua Thien.[6] In 1970, American officials presented a tractor to the village council in My Thuy Phuong, which on the day of the turnover organized a ceremony and demonstration of the machine. The council decided that one of its members, a large landholder, would be caretaker of the machine, a decision which almost immediately meant lost jobs for five men working as cultivators on the councilman's land. The tractor thus enabled the councilman to save most of the money he usually spent on salaries for laborers. It should also be noted that the councilman occasionally lent the tractor to two or three fellow large landholders, with similar consequences for a few other laborers. And since all local land was under cultivation, the tractor did nothing to increase agricultural production.

While the tractor directly affected very few, many were aware of its impact, perhaps because of the fanfare with which it came to the village. A peasant had this comment, typical of many others:

> The Americans bring their machinery over here, and sell it to the Vietnamese at a profit. Then an American company comes and sells us gas. Then another American company comes and sells us parts and tools to repair the tractor. All this does is make the American companies richer, and make people like us, who have to work with their hands, poorer.

A number of Japanese water pumps had a similar impact. In this instance, the pumps did not come as direct U.S. aid. Rather, in the late 1960s, large landholders and a few village tradesmen purchased about 10 of them from Hue businesses cooperating with another American aid effort—the Commodity Import Program, discussed below. Some of the landholders and tradesmen rented their pumps to peasants, unquestionably saving the peasants time and money they might otherwise have spent irrigating their ricefields. They would have paid that money to many of the village's agricultural laborers, who used traditional wooden pedal devices of the sort described in Chapter 1 to irrigate fields. "At first we saw them and thought they were very nice," commented one of the laborers. "But then we realized that those machines were going to take our jobs and make us poor." Others indicated that the arrival of the water pumps affected between 10 and 20 laborers, many of whom lost income to the machines. There is no sign that the pumps in any way increased agricultural production. And as with the tractor, the economic impact of the pumps, albeit small, brought resentment of Government programs and personnel.

The Commodity Import Program was a U.S.-supported attempt to stimulate the retail sector of the South Vietnamese economy through complicated foreign exchange guarantees, keeping money flowing to Vietnamese tradesmen.[7] Although none of the village's tradesmen directly participated in this program, many indirectly did so. Hue businesses imported the subsidized goods, and sometimes resold them to the tradesmen. Many villagers bought imported goods in Hue or in local shops. During the years after 1963, there was an increase in the number and range of imported goods owned by My Thuy Phuong residents. Many bought Japanese motorcycles, radios, bicycles, cloth for clothing, and agricultural supplies. While everyone enjoyed having these imported goods, and few understood that the U.S. had subsidized the imports, many noticed Hue and local tradesmen growing prosperous. Exact income figures for the tradesmen are unavailable, but people noticed that many of them built nice homes, acquired ricefields, and sent their children to private schools. A student had this comment: "The Vietnamese people like all of these [material] things. But we hate the men who sell them to us, and we oppose the Government for protecting them."

A final Government economic activity was the Village Self-Development Program, which emphasized small construction projects in villages.[8] Under this program, the Government formed local "people's organizations" to make specific recommendations for and plan projects, and granted the organizations money to complete the projects. District and village authorities monitored construction progress, which usually involved labor donated free by the people.

Under the program, villagers dug several wells, but all the wells were located near homes of councilmen. In 1966, they reexcavated two irrigation canals, but noticed that the canals brought water mainly to ricefields owned by two wealthy councilmen.[9] A peasant spoke of local reactions to the irrigation project:

> When the Government made us work on projects like this one, it did not know that many people were angry, but afraid to say anything against the Government. If we said anything, they would arrest us and say, "Viet Cong."
>
> Many of us, while we were digging, talked and said that the Government men and the rich men should come to dig too. When we finished the project many of us felt angry. And we were more united to oppose projects like this one.

There were other Self-Development projects, including repair of the market and a small bridge, construction of a culvert/dam, and improvements on the local Government office and on the district dispensary within village boundaries.[10] As these projects proceeded, people noticed several abuses, including favoritism and corruption by councilmen, and suggested that councilmen's profits were heaviest on the projects involving construction or repair of public structures like the market or dispensary. Villagers could not estimate how high those profits were, but were nevertheless certain they were substantial.

On the program as a whole, a tradesman said, "It was very badly administered. The people could see the men in charge being corrupt, and they thought that the Government was protecting the corrupt men." A student noted, "Very bad. Ridiculous. The only ones helped by the Self-Development program were the Government followers, not the people." These and other remarks suggest, in summary, that the Self-Development program brought My Thuy Phuong a few physical improvements, including new and repaired community facilities. But like the other economic programs mentioned above, Self-Development activities brought few benefits to the people. Such benefits as there were accrued mainly to corrupt officials and others of the pro-Government minority. The majority saw the inequities of all the economic efforts, and grew bitter about the programs—and about the Government.

The Front sometimes tried to benefit from the bitterness. It waged a sort of "quiet war" against the programs. A peasant recalled this instance from the 1960s:

> The Government cadre wanted to build irrigation ditches to carry water to the fields, and came to us to try to get the people to give their labor free for the project. But then everybody heard from the Communists that the program was bad, that it would help only the rich men, and that we should not do it.
>
> Of course we saw that, and we also thought the same thing. We thought it was ridiculous to work with that program, but the Government made us help the project, and we had to do it. So the new water ditches were dug, but many people were angry with the Government.

A student from a peasant family had this comment:

> The Front sometimes told us about the economic programs [at political study sessions], but there was very little that we did not already know about those programs. The [Front] cadres directed us in speaking about those programs. We talked about them as programs that hurt the poor people, and we all agreed. The only question was on the best way to save money and not have to worry about the programs.

Concurring with this was a peasant, who added:

> The Government program for rural development was bad. It had always been bad, but it was worst during the years after Ngo Dinh Diem was killed. We all knew that we had to escape from those programs.
>
> The V.C. were very clever. They showed the people how to unite, and to escape from the programs by uniting with the Viet Cong.

Another reaction was this one, by a low-ranking Government soldier from a peasant family. "It was very happy. The people were united, and we were fighting together against something we did not like. It was like when we were all opposing the French." There were similar reactions to other Government activities. For example, several spoke of a mid-1960s immunization campaign for water buffalo, organized by the Government's Agricultural Service to fight an outbreak of some livestock disease. Government immunization teams began touring the villages of Thua Thien Province, giving free injections to all water buffalo. The Front response was to promote a rumor that the inoculations would kill the cattle, and that the Government was trying to hurt the peasants because of their support for the cause of revolution. Insurgent leaders urged peasants not to permit inoculations, and to ignore the warnings about livestock disease. As a result, villagers did not permit inoculation of even one water buffalo in My Thuy Phuong, and the agricultural cadres left in frustration.[11]

A local school administrator told a similar story. Also in the mid-1960s, Public Health Service personnel tried to inoculate children in a village school to protect them from some disease. But a rumor began to circulate that the inoculations would render the children infertile 50 years hence—a "punishment" for local support of the Front. After hearing the rumor, very few parents agreed to have their children inoculated, and their suspicions of Government intentions and sincerity heightened. A peasant commented on the incident: "Sometimes we fought the Government in very clever ways. The health program to give the children shots was destroyed by our rumor. It was part of the struggle against the puppet government."

Another part of the "quiet war" involved the Government's political development efforts. The most important of these programs were designed to create a national electoral system. At the lowest level, this meant election of hamlet and village officials. Between 1963 and 1975, Government district authorities administered such elections, held a veto power in nomination of candidates, and dominated the elections themselves. Nominees for all local positions had to pass security checks. That is, district authorities barred candidates they viewed as anti-Government or "pro-Communist." Domination of the elections, many asserted, came through ballot box-stuffing or outright fraud in vote-counting.

A village council election in February of 1975 typified many that had preceded it. For that contest, district authorities had approved fifteen candidates for the eight four-year council positions, including six incumbent councilmen, one local policeman, one soldier, five Army veterans, and two civil servants. These individuals came from a variety of backgrounds, but all were strong Government supporters. Most owned or rented at least three to five *mau* of riceland, an above-average amount, and in a few cases twenty or more *mau*. Some were prosperous tradesmen or corrupt officials.

The district chief, an Army major, repeatedly visited the village during the balloting that day. He commented:

> We want to make sure that we have at least 90 percent of the voters voting, and to do that each voter is approached by the inter-family heads in the village, and is urged to come. In the afternoon, when closing time at the polls is coming near, and if anyone has not voted, we will send the inter-family heads around again to urge him to come.

So inter-family chiefs got out the vote. They were the lowest-level Government officials, all appointed and unsalaried, and responsible for keeping census and voting records on all families in small sections of the village. There were 102 such individuals.

Over 90 percent of the eligible voters came to the polls that day in 1975. An elderly peasant commented, "We know we have to vote, because they mark our papers, and if they know we have not voted, later on they cause us trouble." The election results surprised no one. Although it is uncertain how honest the ballot count was, only the incumbent council chairman lost, reportedly because he had fallen out of favor with the district chief. In other words, all but one of the incumbents were reelected.

Over the years, the Government organized many village and hamlet elections in My Thuy Phuong, most of which were like that just described. A small number of people, mostly Government officials who organized the elections, described them as successes. These remarks by a village councilman are illustrative of such minority views:

> The people always supported the elections very strongly. They were proud and happy to see that our Government was supporting democracy like that. And so on election day they went with happy hearts to vote, and they were very interested in getting the [election] results. The people were very happy to be able to elect representatives to the village council, and they supported the Government very strongly.

But a peasant said, "It was the same for years. Everyone had to vote, and we had to vote for Government men. If we did not, we knew there would be trouble." Many others had similar recollections, reflecting what was certainly the majority view.

There were other elections in the village. In 1967, the Government drafted a constitution, which provided for a two-house legislature, a president and vice president, and a provincial-level council. Over the years, My Thuy Phuong voters helped elect people to all these positions. Elections came and went, leaving many villagers with suspicions about electoral honesty and fairness. In all the elections, Government officials kept the pressure on to vote, and to vote "correctly"—for pro-Government candidates. There were many voting irregularities connected with village council elections, and pro-Government slates always won. There was some rigging of provincial council and national legislative elections, but not in all cases. For example, during the upper house elections of 1970, and in the lower house elections the following year, anti-Government An Quang Buddhist-endorsed candidates carried My Thuy Phuong and all of the province, possible indications of at least honest vote counts.[12]

Several were able to remember details of one clear instance of electoral irregularity in the village. That came in October of 1971, during the one-man election-referendum, when the Government asked voters to say yes or no on President Nguyen van Thieu and his policies. Before that election, villagers experienced intense pressure to vote from council members, other civil servants, and the inter-family heads. Several commented that on election day clerks assigned to the polling station instructed them to mark ballots for Thieu—and to do so in the clerks' presence. Others contended that they witnessed soldiers and civil servants voting repeatedly, and a few said they saw policemen destroying ballots before counting began. Thieu received more than 90 percent of the votes cast in the village, according to the village chief. "It was an honest election," he said. "The people here support our President almost 100 percent."

There were other comments, mostly by Government officials and stridently anti-Communist individuals, that the elections were fair and popular, and reflected strong support for the Government. There were many, however, who disagreed. For example, a peasant said, "The elections are just trouble for us. The Government forces us to vote, and the candidates are usually men who the Government approves. But the people do not approve of them." A student said, "Don't ask me about the elections. That's the Government activity that we hate most of all. What we hate is the Government forcing people to vote, then saying, 'All the people are supporting the Government by going to vote.' " And a peasant commented, "The elections are cruel, because they are not the true voice of the people, only the voice of a cruel government." Another peasant recalled how the Front network in the village brought him a message about Government programs, and especially its electoral system:

> Many people who followed the Liberation were always talking politics. . . . Often they talked about the Government and the way the Government was trying to fight the war. Most people thought that the Government was very bad. . . . So everybody was talking about these things all the time. Sometimes the [Front] cadres gave ideas, but usually it was the people themselves, and the people got the idea that becoming involved in Government politics could be very bad.

An agency called the Information Service brought Government political messages to My Thuy Phuong. Information Service cadres from the district headquarters, or the man assigned that function in the village itself, occasionally organized local study sessions. They required each family to send one representative to these events. Inter-family heads made it clear to all that families not represented would be in for problems.

The sessions were usually in the early evening at the communal hall, the *dinh*. Almost invariably, the meetings consisted of readings by information cadres of political statements prepared in Saigon, including speeches by Thieu or the Minister of Information, statements on foreign affairs, or statements denouncing the Front. Sometimes information cadres added their own interpretations to the prepared documents, read documents prepared in Hue, or made comments on regional or even local issues. And very infrequently there were readings of material from Huong Thuy District headquarters, usually reports of Government activities in the area. In a 1972 study session in the village, for example, cadres quoted from a document called Huong Thuy Newsletter. It includes this passage: [13]

> With a correct plan, with enthusiastic hands, and with love for the fatherland and villages as abundant as rivers, mountains, and oceans, Huong Thuy's cadres continue to advance hand-in-hand, despite thousands of difficulties, to beautify the villages, and to bring happiness to the people in a big Huong Thuy District holiday.

The Government organized such study sessions about once a month in the village. Much less frequent were special information events, such as showings of films on outdoor screens. A peasant had this comment on the study sessions:

> Usually we went to these meetings tired from working all day. Sometimes they would talk to us so long about politics, and sometimes it was interesting, but usually it was not. Sometimes we were like prisoners, but we did not dare say anything.

And a tradesman had these recollections:

> They made the people go to the study sessions and listen to speeches about democracy in Vietnam. . . . But we knew that the men who spoke were Government men, so we did not respect them very much. But we listened and usually did not say anything or ask any questions.

If attendance was unavoidable at political study meetings, people often tried to feign busyness, ignorance, tiredness, or illness to avoid deep involvement. In other words, most everyone tried to maintain postures of disinterest.

Leaflet drops constituted another information tactic employed in the village. Over the years, American military units trained Vietnamese in mass production and distribution by airplane of small political leaflets, which time and time again fell on My Thuy Phuong with messages like this: [14]

> All cadre and soldiers in the Communist ranks,
>
> It is time for you to ponder carefully this thought: There is not any reason for you to die in a conflict that sooner or later will be resolved at the conference table.
>
> Now is the time for you to think about your future life as well as your family's.
>
> You should follow the good example of your cadre and comrades. Return to the national just cause; you will have a good chance again to build your life in a generous nation where "love replaces hatred."

There were other expressions of the Government's political development strategy. For example, there were periodic meetings of the village's militia, discussed in Chapter 12, where local information cadres and soldiers gave speeches urging involvement of members in the organization, and urging loyalty to the Government. A wall newspaper at a 1973 militia meeting, which people said was similar to other newspapers of earlier years, expresses it this way:[15]

> To return to the matter of Gia Le women, the majority of this group have husbands, and the majority, like all women in Vietnam who have husbands, sacrifice themselves for the fatherland. In that way, in truth, the Gia Le women's love of country is less than no one's. They encourage their husbands to be eager for military service, for if they did nothing, what would be left of the army?
>
> The men and boys of Gia Le are in general not different from males anywhere else, with hair, ears, throat, and heart, and also "that special thing." So every rank of the men and boys, like the girls of Gia Le, lives in the ricefields, growing up in their place of origin and taking from it a way of life—so they are very strong and healthy. And because they are very strong and healthy their expressions of emotion are also strong and huge. The males of Gia Le also strongly love their country, and because of that invite exploitation, so, the two words Gia Le have a strong personal pull on us. A lot of the people of Gia Le do not follow the Communists as it is believed! There is proof that the people of Gia Le village sacrifice themselves for the nationalist cause more than anything else. . . .

The schools also brought explicit political messages. Teachers frequently delivered pro-Government lectures, organized their students for Government demonstrations and projects, and had them sing the national anthem and salute the flag. Even curricula carried strong political messages. A fifth grade reader used in the village, for example, contains many pro-Government passages. Below an illustration of a day-dreaming boy are the following words:[16]

> Ban lies down on the bamboo bed, anxiously waiting for the sunrise so he can go to join the army. Through the window moonlight falls on the bed, spreads to the middle of the house, and shines dimly on the silent furniture. . . .
>
> Ban draws back the blanket to cover his chest, dreamily looking up into the black sky. A small cloud passes by the window, and he imagines the parachutes of the red beret angels [i.e., Government paratroopers] slowly flying in the wind, and landing in a wild forest or an immense green field.
>
> Ban thinks about the peaceful life of people in the village: The carefree, innocent children playing on the pathways; hardworking, simple peasants working safely under the protection of the patriotic young men.

Unfortunately for the Government, people reacted to appeals such as the foregoing and militia meetings about as they did to the political study sessions. A young Buddhist leader in the village put it this way: "The Government tried hard to propagandize, but it was not very successful. Nobody noticed. Nobody listened. Nobody cared."

A local Government office administered nearly all the economic and political development programs described above.[17] The number of personnel working there increased from about 10 in 1963, including village councilmen and a few extra clerks, to about 20 in 1972.[18] Councilmen, as noted earlier, were the products of elections manipulated and dominated by district authorities. Similarly, those authorities appointed most civil servants working in the village from among those they considered politically reliable. The Government periodically trained all the local civil servants, sometimes at district headquarters, but more frequently in Hue. Training usually consisted of lectures by local or sometimes visiting bureaucrats. Much more occasional were special training sessions, sometimes lasting several weeks, at the National Training Center in Vung Tau. Three or four of the village's civil servants had been there.

As Thieu's Democracy Party emerged in the one-man election-referendum of 1971, the Government gave a choice to civil servants with ties to the three other political parties. "They told us that no one could belong to any party but Democracy," said a former village chief. But the training and enforced party membership did not lessen the problem of local corruption. In fact, most civil servants took bribes, even including low-ranking clerks. Some villagers suggested that such corrupt activities were part of a larger network of shakedowns and payoffs involving district officials. A former village chief had this rather daring statement:

> None of us liked to have anything to do with bad money practices, but we had to. A soldier who worked for the district chief came to every village chief to tell us that we had to instruct all our clerks and policemen that a certain amount of money was expected from our village every month. This was to go first to the district chief, and then, above him, to the province chief.

Some in positions of authority in the village grew prosperous as a direct result of bribes received or by manipulation of Government funds and local resources, including communal land, Self-Development funds, and other programs involving money or material. As repeatedly noted above, no figures are available on resource transfers to civil servants and other local pro-Government individuals. However, there is some solid evidence. Most civil servants had large, relatively comfortable homes—usually of cement and heavy wood beam construction, as opposed to most villagers' wood panel homes. On low salaries, there was simply no way the civil servants could afford such homes without substantial supplemental income. Corruption very likely paid for civil servants' more abundant and higher quality personal possessions, including motorcycles, nice clothing, and comfortable home furnishings. And many people wondered how civil servants could afford to send their children to Hue's private schools if they were not dishonest.

A peasant's comment on the civil servants summarizes the feelings of many: "The Government cadres did not listen. They only caused the people trouble. They became like our enemies." The peasant was generalizing about *all* civil servants in this statement—including the handful of honest, filial, or hard-working individuals assigned by the Government to My Thuy Phuong. Resentment ran too deep for the peasant or most others to differentiate "good" people from "bad" in that village office. And of course the Front made its position on the civil servants clear to all, playing on the resentment and on most villagers' commitment to the movement. A peasant recalled:

> The Liberation always told us that we should not help the Government in any way. They told us that the Government men were puppets, and were corrupt. We knew that they were corrupt, and we knew that they often got rich in their positions. Many people understood that if we helped those men we would be hurting the revolution.

AMERICAN ADVISORS

Supporting the Government's economic and political development efforts in the village were many American advisors.[19] In the years after 1963, and especially after 1967, such Americans played crucial roles throughout South Vietnam. They were involved, first, in actual planning of the Government programs. Second, escalating American involvement in Vietnam led the U.S. Government to create an advisory apparatus in every province and every district. After 1967, this structure included both American military and civilian personnel, and was called Civil Operations Revolutionary Development Support, or C.O.R.D.S. For the province, C.O.R.D.S. offices were in a large compound in Hue, and a succession of U.S. Army colonels and civilian Foreign Service Officers directed C.O.R.D.S. activities as so-called senior advisors. At its peak in the late 1960s, dozens of Americans staffed the C.O.R.D.S. operation in the province, and assisting were large numbers of Vietnamese, Filipinos, and even some Chinese.

The advisory presence became so large, in fact, that once a C.O.R.D.S. senior advisor apparently grew frustrated at the large number of Americans in his province. He reported, "Hue is a special place. Special support is now especially needed to keep it from being loved to death."[20] In Huong Thuy District, there was a large, entirely military C.O.R.D.S. advisory team based in the district headquarters. A succession of U.S. Army captains and majors served as Huong Thuy's senior advisor, and tried to report on and influence Government activities in all 14 villages of the district, including My Thuy Phuong. But sometimes the advisors got ridiculously carried away with reporting responsibilities. For example, once they reported the death of four "friendly ducks" in a military operation.[21] The Americans had so much influence over Government activities that their objections or pressure sometimes brought removal of Government personnel. C.O.R.D.S. even issued a "Questionnaire on Effectiveness of Vietnamese Officials.'' It sent this classified document to many advisors, probably including the Huong Thuy senior advisor, to solicit comments on Government officials. Advisors ranked officials as ''unsatisfactory,'' ''below average,'' ''average or above,'' and ''very high'' in five areas: (1) honesty; (2) demonstrated leadership; (3) effectiveness; (4) potential; and (5) recommendation for retention.[22]

Robert Jones III, formerly of the U.S. Embassy/Saigon, remembered a specific instance of American advisory leverage that affected the village.[23] He stated that once a U.S. Army lieutenant assigned to C.O.R.D.S. charged that My Thuy Phuong's village chief was corrupt and ineffective, and the lieutenant lobbied within C.O.R.D.S. for the man's removal. Jones was unclear as to the outcome of the case. Villagers, however, said that once the Government very suddenly removed a village chief. American pressure may have been behind that particular dismissal.

A peasant commented on the Vietnamese-American relationship:

> We knew how much they [civil servants] needed American support for all their programs. We could understand that, and not criticize that, because we knew that our country is poor. But we also saw that the Americans controlled the Government, and used the Government for American policies. So how could we really respect those men?

A Government soldier said:

> Do you know what it means to lose face in Vietnam? That is so important between our people. Whenever the American advisors went into the Government office, or whenever the Americans were seen in public with our village chief, then the village chief lost face in front of the people. Being with the Americans proved they were not independent.

According to a peasant, ''Whenever I saw Vietnamese soldiers with Americans, I felt sorry for them. They lost face.'' This comment summed up the feelings of many in the village, including many Government soldiers.

In 1969, Thua Thien/Hue's senior advisor wrote, ''U.S. advisors are the key to the entire pacification plan.''[24] In effect, the American advisory apparatus was a parallel government, the closest thing to a colonial bureaucracy the Vietnamese had seen since the French days. And most in My Thuy Phuong disliked the similarities.

My Thuy Phuong's ''quiet war,'' in summary, touched the lives of nearly all villagers and was closely tied to the ''hot war'' being fought by armed men and women. Several comments serve to underline and summarize the main problems and divisions in the village. The last Government village chief stated, ''The people support the Government 100 percent. They see that it is bringing prosperity to them, and they hate the

Communists." A councilman said, "The people here like us very much, because they see what the Government has brought them. They see that they are developing." But an elderly peasant asserted:

> Many years ago, Emperor Khai Dinh taxed the people, and took people from the village to work for him. Emperor Minh Mang did the same. But always they gave us something first, like land, or money, or maybe a new market. It's the same now.
>
> Emperor Thieu and his group give us some things, and we have to be his servants. It's always the same for people in this village.

Another village councilman, a large landholder with a reputation for corruption, had these surprising words:

> The Communists told the people that they should struggle against corrupt officials, try to educate policemen and Government cadres, and try to discover the Government spies. But most important, they told us that we should not pay taxes unless they force us, we should not help the Government Army, and we should not vote in the Government elections.
>
> There are many ways that the Communists told the people to support the revolution, and one of the most important ways was for the people not to support the Government.

Finally, the councilman explained the Front's strategy:

> The Communists would always talk about the need for resisting the Americans, and they told us that it was just part of a large struggle. The struggle to resist the Americans had to come from all the people, and they said that the best way to do that was to resist Government activities in this area.
>
> Many people began to like the Communists very much, and were very happy to unite against the Government.

The councilman spoke these words somewhat sorrowfully, slowly. Then suddenly he looked up, startled. He smiled, perhaps savoring the irony.

NOTES

1. "Thua Thien Report," May 1, 1966, p. 19.
2. "Debrief of a CORDS Deputy Province Senior Advisor: Thua Thien and An Xuyen Provinces; Vietnam; 1967–1968" (Honolulu: Asia Training Center, UH/AID, no. 9682, undated), p. 34; available in University of Hawaii Library.
3. For Vietnamese figures on U.S.A.I.D. assistance, see "Economic and Social Assistance to the Republic of Viet Nam" (Saigon: Government of the Repub-

lic of Vietnam, 1973), p. 26; available through U.S.A.I.D., Washington, D.C. For Thua Thien budget figures, see "Thua Thien Report," November 30, 1966, p. 21. U.S.A.I.D. figures on project aid are reported in "Annual Statistical Bulletin" (Saigon: U.S.A.I.D., 1973); available in East-West Resource Systems Institute Library, Honolulu.

4. In 1971, U.S. advisors reported that I.R. rice grown in Thua Thien provided 2.5 metric tons per hectare, compared to 1.44 metric tons for local rice. In 1972, the figures were 3.0 and 1.2 metric tons, respectively. (See "Thua Thien Report," June 3, 1972, p. 5.)

5. "Thua Thien Report," April 3, 1969, p. 7.

6. *Ibid.*, January 2, 1970, p. 2.

7. See "Economic and Social Assistance," p. 26; *Hearings, Mutual Development and Cooperation Act of 1973* (Washington, D.C.: Government Printing Office, Committee on Foreign Relations, U.S. House of Representatives, 93rd Congress, 1st Session), p. 186.

8. The only budgetary figures available, for 1972, indicate that the equivalent of about U.S.$120,355 was spent in Thua Thien on Village Self-Development. By 1971, the program made the equivalent of about U.S.$1000 available annually to My Thuy Phuong. [See *Dac-San Xuan* (Spring Yearbook) (Hue: Thua Thien Information Service, Spring, 1973), p. 32.]

9. In 1966, the Government's Public Works Service undertook an extensive drainage project in My Thuy Phuong, not part of the Village Self-Development Program. Work proceeded under contract; some people alleged that this project, too, disproportionately benefitted a small number of large landholders. (See "Thua Thien Report," March 25, 1966, p. 10.)

10. See "Thua Thien Report," July 31, 1966, p. 3a; December 31, 1966, p. 3.

11. Villagers also indicated that no livestock disease outbreak occurred that year.

12. See "Special Report on Senatorial Election" (Hue: P.D.D./C.O.R.D.S., undated), p. 3. Also see J.R. Trinchera, "Results of Provincial Council Election" (Hue: PAA/CDO/PDD/C.O.R.D.S., June, 1970), one page. Both documents available in 101st Airborne Museum.

13. *Ban-Tin Huong-Thuy* (Huong Thuy Newsletter), August 12, 1972, p. 2; a publication of the Huong Thuy Information Service.

14. Leaflet made available through the Huong Thuy Information Service.

15. From the single extant page of the 1973 wall newspaper, made available by the Huong Thuy Information Service.

16. *Quoc-Van; Lop 5* (Literature; Grade 5) (Saigon: Canh Hong Publishers, 1974), p. 199; purchased by the author in Hue.

17. For a comprehensive description of Government civil service policies, see Francis X. McCarthy, "The Civil Service System of the Republic of Viet-Nam; A Description and Assessment" (Saigon: U.S.A.I.D., 1969); available in Resource Systems Institute Library.

18. Under Government regulations of 1966, 1969, and 1971, villagers elected nine village councilmen, who shared various administrative functions with a

gradually increased number of appointed civil servants. (See *Huong-Thuy*, yearbook issued by Huong Thuy District headquarters, early 1975, pp. 1–10; obtained by author.)

19. See *Documenting the Post-War War* (Philadelphia: National Action/ Research on the Military Industrial Complex, American Friends Service Committee, 1974), p. 210, for data on support for the Government for calendar-year 1973.

20. "Thua Thien Report," June 3, 1969, p. 8.

21. *Ibid.*, December 29, 1965, p. 1.

22. The questionnaire was known as MACCORDS Form 15, and dated August 28, 1968. It is attached to a file called "Rating of GVN Officials—I CTZ; 1968," which is in folder 1, box 9, no. 71A9237; 19/75:45–3, Center of Military History.

23. Also see "Thua Thien Report," May 4, 1968, p. 7.

24. "Thua Thien Report," March 3, 1969, p. 7.

12

Vietnamese vs. Vietnamese

ARRAY OF FORCES

Government security forces at first supplemented and eventually replaced the U.S. Marine Corps and the U.S. Army—in terms of activities on the ground, *and* as targets for Front forces. Here we briefly examine each Government security branch and reactions to it in My Thuy Phuong.

First was the Government's Army, which in the province consisted of two major branches. There was the main force First Infantry Division, which engaged in widespread operations throughout Central Vietnam. Then there were the provincial forces, consisting of the Regional Forces and Popular Forces. Both were under the control of the province chief. The first of these conducted operations against local guerrillas, while the second guarded strategic installations, such as bridges and important offices. Several Popular Forces platoons operated full-time in the village, guarding strategic points, and sometimes cooperating with Regional Forces on local operations.[1] As noted in Chapter 9, it was Popular Forces soldiers who participated in the Combined Action Platoon, or C.A.P. All provincial forces soldiers served in their home districts, and like main force soldiers were poorly paid.

About 5 percent of the village's draft-age men, usually from more prosperous or prominent pro-Government families, were able to avoid military service through educational, medical, or "family support" draft deferments. Most such deferments required payment of bribes to Government officials in Hue, the district, and sometimes the village. Another 5 to 10 percent of the draft-age men avoided Government service by joining the Front guerrilla force. A few of the 5 to 10 percent group deserted Government units and joined the guerrillas, something that nearly all could do at any time. But because of unattractive alternatives, most young men joined and remained in the Government Army. This was because police arrested and jailed those who refused to serve, and joining the local guerrilla force meant even more certain dangers and interruption of education and family life—sacrifices that few wanted to share. Those who joined the Army were overwhelmingly from poor peasant families, and many were from families which supported the Front but which could not make the sacrifices just mentioned.

A word on the economic impact of the Government draft. The rapid Army buildup in the late 1960s and early 1970s deeply affected 85 to 90 percent of the village's young men and most families. Men who would have otherwise been joining parents in family occupations were, in effect, taken out of the local labor force. While the low Army salaries somewhat offset these losses for most families, significant adjustments were usually necessary. First, field work had to be handled primarily by men over the mid-forties draft age limit, by more women than before, and by children. Most other occupations experienced similar changes. Second, more women than in previous years independently entered the labor force to provide additional family income. Some tried to become small entrepreneurs, buying and selling produce and various dry goods in different markets for small profits. Many others secured jobs at Camp Eagle.

Seventy to eighty percent of those who joined the Army from the village directly entered the First Division, and some went into the newer Third Division, which fought in Quang Tri and later in the Danang area. With few exceptions, these men had very low rank and served in dangerous combat assignments. Draft-age men preferred service in the provincial forces to duty with main force units, for the provincial forces had relatively low casualty rates and permitted service close to home. But because the provincial forces had limited openings, only about 20 percent of the village's Government soldiers could join, and men seeking such assignments usually had to pay entrance bribes to recruiters.[2]

Corruption extended to many Army activities. Important officers of both the First Division and provincial forces assigned enlisted personnel and made many promotions only after receiving bribes. Many officers required bribes for most home leave passes and other special privileges. And even many routine military services required small bribes within the division. Officers often waited for payment before providing military equipment, food, or trucks for units on operations. According to soldiers, First Division personnel on operations often had to pool money to secure such battlefield necessities.

Most Government soldiers, despite their military training, failed to overcome their locally induced dislike for Government policies. Some villagers asserted, in fact, that corruption within military ranks deepened the dislike. As a result, morale within those ranks was poor, and low-ranking soldiers, especially those of the main forces, frequently deserted units to return to families. When they deserted, families protected and shielded them, and felt no shame about doing so. Nearly every soldier of low rank from the village deserted every month or two, for family visits of two to seven days. They called such visits "vacations."

Others sought escape from the military through intellectual efforts. Some kept long diaries, wrote poems, or read novels of romance and adventure. Still others frequented Hue's cinemas or houses of prostitution in the district. One young soldier wrote songs and poems, and on visits home sang to family and friends:

> We are all being raised,
> As sons of a cruel god.
> We are killing our brothers,
> We are killing our souls,
> As sons of a cruel god.
>
> We are all being raised,
> As sons of a cruel god.
> Life must go on,
> Wars never die.

Before 1972, there were few First Division operations in the village, but residents recalled that when the operations came there was looting, rudeness by troops, and excessive use of weaponry and force—phenomena which many said were related to the soldiers' bad training.[3] And off-duty First Division soldiers engaged in armed shakedowns of local tradesmen, people in the market, and travelers on Highway One.

Much more frequently than First Division soldiers, provincial forces personnel came to the village on operations. As noted earlier, Popular Forces soldiers were even assigned there on a full-time basis. Because of proximity, the strengths and weaknesses of these units were clear. Provincial forces activities were flawed in ways similar to those of the First's "regulars." There was corruption, looting, and excessive, sometimes arbitrary use of force. However, these problems were more pronounced during First Division operations, a difference they said was due to the local ties of provincial forces soldiers. Local soldiers were generally more considerate in performance of military tasks than nonlocals. This was due to local soldiers' fear of censure in their home areas for improper behavior. Nonlocal soldiers, in contrast, had little fear of censure in communities not their own.

Members of the provincial forces were worse soldiers than First Division personnel.[4] Regional Forces members could rarely hit chosen targets and preferred to stay close to bases instead of organizing operations. And Popular Forces soldiers could not be trusted to stay awake or protect strategic points when under attack. As with First Division operations, villagers linked these weaknesses to lack of commitment by unwilling soldiers to an unpopular government. For example, a peasant said, "How could the Regional Forces be good? None of the soldiers wanted to fight and die for Mr. Thieu."

One Vietnamese, a Government officer, recalled what sometimes happened when Government military forces came to My Thuy Phuong. "The people in this area sometimes were strange," he said. "I think they liked the Viet Cong very much, because when we had operations in some of these places, the people did very little to help the Army." Here is what he meant by that:

> The people stayed near their homes and answered the questions the soldiers asked them. They did not fight against us, but I knew that they were not friendly. They were probably Viet Cong, but we had no way of knowing for sure.

And this is how the officer acted every time he entered My Thuy Phuong:

> I knew about that place, so I was rather nervous. I never liked to go on military operations there, but sometimes I had to go. At those times, I always behaved well and tried not to make any person angry. But, you know, I still had to be careful. I kept my M-16 ready to fire, and I never took my hand off my pistol, which I wore at my side.

A tradesman in effect verified the officer's suspicions about the village:

> The [Government military] operations came very often, and were very strong. Sometimes they arrested people, and searched houses, and did some things like that. They were looking for the Viet Cong. But, you know, the people did not tell the soldiers anything, and usually did not do anything to help the soldiers. The people were quiet.

The people were quiet indeed, except of course when they aided insurgent attacks. Such Government military "successes" as there were came without much help from ordinary villagers. Rather, it was sheer firepower and coercion that translated into hauls of weapons, suspects, and bodies for Government forces. In the face of large movements of men through their village, and because fighting back was not always possible or advisable, My Thuy Phuong's people often followed the course implied above—minimal cooperation or noncooperation.

There were also various Government paramilitary units in the village.[5] After the Tet Offensive, American and Government planners decided to form a nationwide paramilitary organization, the People's Self-defense Force. Behind this force was the idea that people given guns and some training would willingly defend their homes and villages, and thus improve security for Government activities. Between 1968 and 1972, My Thuy Phuong's Self-defense Force grew to over 2,000 people, including school children, retired Government soldiers, and even women, young and old. Government officials gave guns to only several hundred, classifying them "combat-ready." Most people entered the Self-defense Force for the same reasons they joined the Army—because of coercion by police and the unappealing alternatives of jail or joining local guerrillas. Even though bearing arms for the Government, they were by no means Government supporters or even reliable defenders of Government installations or personnel.

The Self-defense Force was a motley group indeed. Every night small groups of defenders met at the village office, picked up their guns and small amounts of ammunition, and went on their way to patrol specific sections of the village, or to man fixed checkpoints. Self-defense members often indiscriminately fired their guns during patrols or guard duty. Card games impaired their alertness. And their urge to sleep was sometimes stronger than the call of duty. A youth who belonged to the Self-defense Force stated:

> The People's Self-defense Force is so much fun. It gives us a chance to see our friends and play around. Oh, yes, we had some training. We learned how to shoot all the weapons, and they told us when we should do it. But we all agree that if the V.C. ever come, we are going to throw down our weapons and run.

Complementing the Army and Self-defense Force in My Thuy Phuong was the police apparatus. The local police force increased from one in 1963 to two in 1972. In the district, the increase was from 15 to about 30.[6] The policemen were all volunteers. Most people regarded police duty safer than military service, so entrance competition was stiff. There was an entrance exam, but police recruiters also demanded bribes.

The police structure was thoroughly corrupt. Policemen often took a share of taxes collected for the Government, or of rent collected for local landlords. But the corrupt activity that affected most villagers involved the police function of issuing official identification papers and permits. A peasant described what happened when he appeared before a local policeman to request a required family identification paper:

> The policeman said he had many papers he had to take care of, and it might take me several months to get my paper from him. But I knew that I needed it, because when they checked my house they always asked for that paper. We all knew that to give the man maybe 500 piasters we would get the paper right away. We knew that if we didn't give the money, we would have to wait a long time. So I gave the money.

But corruption was but one of the problems brought the village by policemen. There were also occasional police operations. The only one mentioned in available records occurred in late 1967, and was called Operation Thua Thien 230. Its reported objective was typical of many others in later years—"to search for storage areas, specifically to find and confiscate enemy ordnance."[7] People suggested that while such operations were not as disruptive as American or Government military thrusts, they nevertheless brought inconvenience and uncertainty to village life. In addition, the police targeted actual and potential critics of the Government who were not linked to the insurgency. Over the years, policemen from time to time arrested a small number of students, Buddhist activists, and other residents. For example, a student remembered:

> There were some anti-Government demonstrations in 1971. We were opposing Mr. Thieu's election, and there were some demonstrations in Hue. I came home to visit my parents during that period, and the police arrested me. They took me to the district office, and tried to get me to sign a paper that I was a Communist. I would not sign it. And I told them I was a nationalist, and did not like the Communists.
>
> So then they tied my hands, and made me lie with my head in a big metal barrel. Then they hit the barrel with hammers to make it ring and my head hurt. They did this so many times, but I did not sign the paper.

Eventually the police sent the student to prison in Hue, where he spent about a year. Some other local anti-Government dissenters disappeared forever. A peasant described an illustrative incident from 1969:

> The police entered my neighbor's house. He had been active in the Struggle Movement to oppose Mr. Ky. I knew for sure he was not a Communist. The only thing he ever did was to be active in the Struggle Movement. But the police went to his house, and took him away. We never saw him again.

Comments by others emphasized police unpredictability and fearfulness—police terror. These police characteristics were related, in part, to an intelligence function. Like the French and Diem regimes before it, the Government created an intelligence apparatus from the late 1960s linked closely to the police force. It set up sophisticated networks of intelligence agents in the village under the aegis of a program called *Phuong Hoang*, or "Phoenix." Behind Phoenix was the C.I.A., which had proposed it as a way of "neutralizing" the insurgency. Neutralization could mean several things. First, Front supporters could be killed, or "terminated with extreme prejudice," as some C.I.A. advisors used to say. Second, it could mean maintaining pressure on the Front to drive away followers. Neutralization could also mean disgracing the Front or its supporters in the village, or forcing insurgent leaders and guerrillas to withdraw from the village to operate elsewhere. Finally, it could mean arrest.

It was under the banner of Phoenix that local policemen undertook many of their corrupt practices, and engaged in the arbitrary exercise of terror. The Phoenix program, which set monthly neutralization quotas for every village in the province, maintained a so-called Village Intelligence Operations Coordinating Center in My Thuy Phuong.[8]

Exact figures are unavailable for Phoenix operations in the village, and most people did not differentiate between arrests, detentions, and murders by police versus those committed by military units. They spoke of many incidents, however, that were probably connected with Phoenix. The police arrested a few, charged them with "contact with Communism," gave them court hearings, and jailed them. A peasant who attended one of those hearings indicated that written statements by "secret witnesses from the village" brought conviction and a hefty prison sentence for one man, a peasant who allegedly was a local Front official. Others asserted that there were times when people in the village were simply killed, usually by small arms or grenades. According to a peasant, "Always these killings were reported as 'acts of the V.C.' But we all knew that the V.C. usually killed for political reasons, and the V.C. had no reason to kill these people." Such killings—as many as 10 or 20 over the years—bore the unmistakable mark of Phoenix, for most of those killed came from families with close blood ties to the Front. The Phoenix program also meant extortion schemes. A tradesman asserted:

> The policemen threaten people with Phoenix. They go to the people who are poor, and who are most afraid of them, and say, "You are under arrest for suspicion," or, "You are under arrest for contact with Communism." If the people give the police money they are not arrested. If they do not give money, they know they will surely be arrested. The police are so cruel.

Complementing the Phoenix program was an effort called the Provincial Reconnaissance Unit, or P.R.U. This C.I.A.-funded and directed program supported networks of informers in all parts of the province, including My Thuy Phuong, to draw up black lists of suspected Front supporters, and to act directly on information supplied by the informers.[9] When informer reports reached the P.R.U. compound, not far from the village, P.R.U. agents went into action. The agents were tough and cruel, and well paid by their American supervisors. One of them, born and raised in My Thuy Phuong, was a vehement anti-Communist. "My brother was killed by the Communists," he said, "and I want to kill as many Communists as I can. Whenever I heard about Communists, I was happy to kill them." The P.R.U. agents' sometimes demented enthusiasm for their work meant killing was the preferred form of neutralization, and meant killings were not uncommon in the village. "We killed at least 20 here," recalled the agent.

The Front had several responses to all these intelligence activities. At least several Front sympathizers who lived in homes near Government installations were constantly alert to comings and goings, and made lists of people who entered those places. Insurgent leaders studied the lists for possible informers. The Front also uncovered informers through its own local network. According to a peasant, "The Liberation was able to know about spies in the area. We knew who was working for the Americans, and who was working for the C.I.A. and the Government agencies. We always found out." Villagers disagreed on the number of such agents the local Front branch exposed. Some indicated that Front followers ferretted out four or five over the years, while one man said the number was as high as ten.

The Front also used its own intelligence agents. People sympathetic to the movement working as civil servants in My Thuy Phuong, nearby villages, in Government district headquarters, and in the Government military used their positions to gather information about Government intelligence and other types of activities in the area. Such individuals often made verbal reports to local Front contacts in covert meetings, or left written reports at drops in the village or in Hue.

IN AN AMERICAN IMAGE

As time passed, the range of activity undertaken by Government security branches increased throughout the province, and the Government provided better equipment and training to its personnel. This was especially so after 1969, when President Richard Nixon began to emphasize his policy of "Vietnamization." [10] Nixon began his American troop withdrawals in 1969. Between 1969 and 1972, the Government and its American advisors intensified training programs for Government military forces, and departing American units turned over huge amounts of equipment to the Vietnamese. The Vietnamization policy had an impact on My Thuy Phuong, for in and around the village there was an increase in the number of large and small joint American and Vietnamese military operations.

Charles Dyke of the 101st Airborne spoke of the "tremendously close relationship" between U.S. and Vietnamese soldiers.[11] American and Vietnamese squads fought side by side and even maintained joint radio networks. A few Government officers echoed such sentiments. However, on joint operations, Vietnamese clearly played subordinate battle roles. According to many Government soldiers, all tactical planning, requests for artillery and air support, and all transportation requests required American approval.

To illustrate the realities of the Vietnamization effort, Government soldiers and villagers reconstructed a large combined Vietnamese-American military operation, which came to My Thuy Phuong in mid-1971, at the very height of the Vietnamization period. They indicated that three or four others like it occurred in the village between 1969 and 1972. The reconstruction follows.

A joint patrol moved through the village along Highway One. A low-ranking Vietnamese soldier recalled what happened as the patrol advanced:

> The Americans kept yelling, in English, "Don't bunch up, don't bunch up!" It made us mad to hear that, so we kept repeating, "Don't bunch up, don't bunch up!" The Americans got mad, and we laughed. But we had to cooperate with them for a good operation.

The operation began routinely. Vietnamese soldiers entered homes, while 101st troops formed an armed circle—which they called a cordon—around part of the village.[12] Meanwhile, Vietnamese and American soldiers set up a checkpoint along the highway, stopped all vehicles approaching the village boundaries, and Vietnamese soldiers and policemen checked travelers' identification papers. Government soldiers moved from house to house, examining residents' papers, and detaining all men and teen-age boys. Vietnamese soldiers ransacked houses in thorough searches, seemingly more interested in looting prospects than in assigned military tasks. "They stole our chickens and ducks," a peasant woman remembered, "and carried off one of our pigs. Then they found our bags of rice, and said, 'Oh, we must take this. It belongs to the V.C.' "

There were about 20 men and boys detained that day. In what might have been a Vietnamization setback, the Vietnamese soldiers chose not to bother with the detainees. Instead, they walked away, some laden with loot, and turned their detainees over to the Americans. A Vietnamese sergeant assigned as an interpreter to the 101st helped the Americans talk to those being held, who were quiet and quivering with fear. The sergeant asked detainees their names, addresses, occupations, and whether they knew anyone with the "V.C." The Americans, who could not speak Vietnamese, were totally dependent on the sergeant, who culled a few detainees from the group. They were then led away, probably to Camp Eagle.

Many low-ranking Government soldiers living in the village commented on what they learned from the Americans on operations like the one just described, in actual combat situations, and in special training sessions. Comments focused on two major areas. Many remarked, first, on American enthusiasm and combat aggressiveness. "I wish the Vietnamese army could be that strong," said a Government soldier. "Then we would win the war, just like the Americans." Another soldier said, "They were very strong, and always went out on operations day and night. We learned from the Americans that to be good in battle you must have spirit."

The second major area of Vietnamization lessons involved military strategy and tactics. The comments of American and Vietnamese officers suggest that the close command association of American and Vietnamese officers meant that many high-ranking Vietnamese soldiers came to understand American military strategies. Enlisted personnel, however, revealed that the officers incompletely transferred their understanding and acceptance of strategic concepts to the lower ranks. Few low-ranking soldiers, when asked what they had learned from the Americans, could explain such concepts. Instead, they cited these major lessons about tactics, in their own words: "carry lots of equipment," "assume the enemy is everywhere," "maintain communication and supply ties with the rear," "hit with every available weapon," and "don't bunch up."

Something else Vietnamese soldiers learned from Americans was how to use drugs. As an American advisory report put it, "Narcotics, long considered by the Vietnamese to only be a problem of the U.S. Army, has begun to surface as an A.R.V.N. problem." [13] About a third of My Thuy Phuong's soldiers used drugs. A young man who had been drafted into the First Division from a poor family said, "I saw so many of my friends die. The war has no meaning to me. Life has no meaning." Every day for four or five years this soldier injected a heroin-like substance into his arm, and he broke into and robbed homes in Hue to pay for the habit. Once in 1975, he looked at a Government advertisement showing a huge skull dangling a soldier, rope around the neck, over a pit of drugs. The ad read, "The Army Is Determined To End The Peril Of Narcotics." [14] The soldier responded, "Ridiculous."

In effect, Vietnamization aimed at creating a Vietnamese army in an American image—equipped as well as the American army, following American combat strategy, organized in an American fashion, using American military tactics, and full of soldiers as well trained and motivated as American soldiers. Vietnamization was thus in theory the final step in a long process, *Americanization* of an army and of a war. In practice, however, the Vietnamization program at best created a Government army overdependent on direct and indirect U.S. support, and failed to overcome that army's problems of poor training, ineffective leadership, and low morale.

As Vietnamization proceeded, the Front continued guerrilla operations in My Thuy Phuong, but at a generally low level of intensity, and supported less frequently than in earlier years by local tax collections. Contributions made in the irregularly timed collections varied greatly over the years, especially after 1968. In 1970, some suggested, families gave annual contributions equivalent to about U.S.$50.[15] The Front proselyting focus on Vietnamization was reflected in Front strategy on the ground, as by 1971–1972 guerrillas subtly shifted the focus of their military operations away from attacks against Camp Eagle. Guerrillas began to direct their ambush and sniping attacks and laying of booby traps almost exclusively at Government patrols and vehicles.[16]

The Front also spread numerous leaflets in the village on the subject of Vietnamization. Although none of them is now available, this passage from a North Vietnamese pamphlet on Hue is probably similar to what villagers read: [17]

> The people of Hue have for many years seen the obvious cruelty of the U.S. imperialists. The American dollar is still used to "change the skin color of the corpses." In Nixon's plundering "Vietnamization" campaign a lot of traps are ready to lure human beings into sin and suffering. All the dirty reactionary theories of the imperialists build up in the land of the south, of Phu-Xuan [i.e., Hue] to drown the people of the south in slavery. But they still cannot destroy the Hue people's desire for independence and peace. . . .

For My Thuy Phuong, Vietnamization ended on January 17, 1972. That was the date the 101st Airborne formally turned over Camp Eagle to the Government's First Infantry Division. Weeks before the turnover, a steady flow of empty trucks entered Camp Eagle, and left with overflowing loads. The 101st was redeploying, and taking with it huge amounts of equipment. A 101st publication includes this passage: [18]

> All that could be seen were the clean-up crews that removed everything from the staples in the walls of buildings to gigantic stores of munitions and equipment. After making sure the area was up to par, the buildings were boarded shut one by one.

With redeployment, a 101st publication notes, "Camp Eagle closed in peace—a symbol of the efforts and sacrifices of thousands of Screaming Eagles." [19] But as the last American soldiers left My Thuy Phuong, they saw a discouraging sign: Vietnamese soldiers looting the camp. On foot, or using motorcycles, jeeps, or heavy trucks, Government soldiers carried away many items they could use or sell, including roofing, lighting fixtures, and supplies of various kinds. They hauled the loot out by the ton, and sold it in Hue and elsewhere. Eventually, commanders of the Government's First Infantry Division put a stop to the looting, and took over the camp as divisional headquarters. They renamed Eagle "Camp Gia Le," to honor the hamlet it had replaced.

EASTER OFFENSIVE

A dramatic challenge to the "Vietnamized" Government forces came in the spring of 1972. That was the so-called Easter Offensive, which beginning on March 30 again brought a major commitment of North Vietnamese troops to Tri Thien Hue, and which involved local guerrilla forces as well. Events moved rapidly. There was tank warfare in Thua Thien and Quang Tri. The Government shifted commanders. Thousands of refugees fled southward to Danang, and insurgent forces captured Quang Tri Province. The Government lost considerable influence and control in the Thua Thien countryside.[20] Eventually, it reestablished control over the area, but in so doing had to rely heavily upon U.S. air power.[21]

In the village, the 1972 offensive brought several months of uncertainty. Many of those most closely allied with the Government, including most civil servants, joined the southward flow of refugees. Two or three prominent Government supporters were killed during the offensive in individual assassinations. In addition, there were a number of small attacks against Government soldiers guarding bridges and local installations. The strongest memory most people had of the offensive, however, was not of local insurgent attacks, but of retreating Government soldiers. With North Vietnamese attacks north of Hue, the Government's inexperienced Third Division broke and ran. Its soldiers stripped off uniforms and fled, first to Hue, and then through My Thuy Phuong to Danang.

A student recalled:

> We saw the Third Division soldiers coming through here. Some of them walked, some of them came by buses, trucks, or motorcycles they stole. It was very frightening, because those soldiers completely lacked discipline. It made us think that the Government was losing the war.

A peasant woman spoke of the retreating soldiers:

> Two or three of the soldiers of the Third Division came off the road and into my house. One of them had an M-16, and he said, "Give me all of your money, or I will kill you." I was very afraid, so I gave him my money.

Another peasant said:

> All we heard was that Quang Tri had been lost, and that Hue might be lost very soon. We also saw around us that the local V.C. had become very active. There was much shooting here, and the Government soldiers on guard all ran away. It was a little bit scary, but the Government was not protecting us.

Many listened to Liberation Radio during the Easter Offensive. On May 3, 1972, for example, they heard an appeal from the Front's provincial organization, which included this passage: [22]

> The puppet 1st Division in the area was so badly mauled that it has now lost its fighting capability. The enemy in Thua Thien/Hue are panic-stricken. This situation in Tri Thien/Hue occurs at a time when our armed forces and people throughout the south are launching earth-shaking offensives and uprisings. . . . This shows that our people and armed forces' anti-U.S. national salvation struggle is entering a new and extremely favorable phase and is surging forward to score the greatest victories. . . . Our people are launching seething uprising movements everywhere to punish the cruel villains, to smash the enemy's barbarous coercive machinery and to regain power for the people.

But despite its radio broadcasts and a leaflet distribution in the village, the Front failed to involve its local followers in the 1972 attack. The absence of insurgent leaders from the village, and near collapse of the Front network of followers prevented guerrillas from securing much support for their attacks. Though there were weaknesses on the Front side, the 1972 offensive, in summary, presented villagers with dramatic images of Government collapse, retreat, and American rescue. It reminded at least some of the mid-1960s, when the Front was locally most influential. The offensive was thus a reassertion of insurgent strength that in My Thuy Phuong set the stage for the struggle that was to follow: the cease-fire war.

NOTES

1. In early 1975, there were four platoons of Popular Forces troops stationed in My Thuy Phuong.
2. The remaining 10 percent of the village's Government soldiers served with various "elite" units, such as the Marines.
3. On looting, see "Debrief of a CORDS Deputy," p. 41.
4. See "Combat Operations After Action Report," p. 196; "Thua Thien Report," October 3, 1968, p. 3.
5. Between 1963 and 1967, the so-called Civil Reserve Rear Force (*Hau-Bi Quan*) was small and relied entirely on volunteers to patrol village paths and guard Government installations, such as the village office. In 1967, there were only 30 members of the group. (See "Thua Thien Report," August 3, 1967, p. 7.) Also see "Thua Thien Report," February 25, 1966, p. 10.
6. In October, 1966, for example, there were 26 policemen assigned to Huong Thuy District headquarters, and another 10 village policemen, including one in My Thuy Phuong. These numbers varied over the years. In July, 1966, for instance, there were 45 in Huong Thuy headquarters, and 11 in the villages. (See "Disposition of Province Police," PSD Form 334–15, July and October, 1966; available in "Thua Thien Weekly and Monthly Report, 1966;" see note 25, Chapter 9.)
7. From a one-page report on Huong Thuy District, attached to "Thua Thien Report," November 30, 1967.
8. See "Thua Thien Report," January 2, 1970, p. 3; September 3, 1970, p. 3.
9. For background, see Joseph Treaster, "The Phoenix Murders," *Penthouse*, December, 1975, pp. 76–168. For a reference to black lists, see Commanding General, 101st Airborne Division, "Briefing" (Camp Eagle: 101st Airborne, 1969), section 3, p. 3; available in 101st Airborne Museum.
10. See Guenter Lewy, *America in Vietnam* (New York: Oxford University Press, 1978), pp. 162–189.
11. See note 12, chapter 9.
12. See Commanding General, "Cordon and Search Operations" (Vietnam: III Marine Amphibious Force, November 28, 1968); available in 101st Airborne Museum.
13. "Thua Thien Report," July 31, 1972, p. 3.

14. *Chien-Si Cong-Hoa* (Republican Soldier), November 15, 1973, back cover. This magazine, published in Saigon, was obtained by the author in Hue, and is also available in the Cornell University Library.

15. See "Thua Thien Report," May 4, 1968, p. 5; July 3, 1968, p. 6.

16. Casualties among Government and American soldiers continued high throughout the 1970–1972 Vietnamization years, although a larger percentage were related to booby traps. For example, in September, 1971, nearly 72 percent of all Government and American casualties were attributed to booby traps. (See "Thua Thien Report," September 4, 1971, p. 2.)

17. *Hue Anh-Dung,* p. 62.

18. *Screaming Eagle,* March-April, 1972, p. 21.

19. *Ibid.;* also see *Screaming Eagle,* September-October, 1971, p. 3.

20. See "Thua Thien Report," May 3, 1972, p. 1.

21. See F. P. Serong, "The 1972 Easter Offensive," *Southeast Asian Perspectives,* no. 10, American Friends of Vietnam, Summer, 1974, pp. 32–40. Also see Vien, no. 39, pp. 65–82.

22. Liberation Radio, May 3, 1972, in "Daily Report," May 4, 1972, p. L–2.

13

End of the War

CEASE-FIRE WAR

Between January of 1973 and March of 1975, many dramatic events in Thua Thien/Hue and other parts of South Vietnam affected the lives of My Thuy Phuong's people. Some of what happened grew out of the Paris agreement of January, 1973, which represented a major turning point in the long Vietnam conflict. For most Americans, the agreement was important because it led to the withdrawal of the last U.S. troops from Vietnam and return of prisoners of war.[1] While many Vietnamese also hailed the U.S. pullout, for most the agreement represented mainly an end to the fighting, and the hope of political reconciliation—the hope of peace.[2]

The Paris agreement's immediate effect was to further partition the country. It recognized vast areas long controlled by insurgent forces—half or more of South Vietnam—as areas of Front sovereignty, just as it recognized the cities and most of the heavily populated lowlands as areas of Government control.[3] The agreement also established an international commission to report cease-fire violations. It further provided for negotiation between the two rival South Vietnamese political forces and freedom of political activity for Vietnamese of all political beliefs. Many throughout the world hailed the Paris agreement as an important step toward lasting peace in Vietnam. Within several months of the January 28, 1973 cease-fire, however, it became clear that the agreement was not working. Areas of alleged violation of the pact included the following:

> The U.S. undertook massive weapons and munitions deliveries before the agreement's resupply cut-off date. Later, the U.S. resupplied at levels above the "one-for-one replacement" standard set by the agreement, and sent large numbers of retired American military personnel to train Government soldiers, repair helicopters, and assist Government forces in many other ways.[4]
>
> On the Government side, police restricted, harassed, and sometimes arrested anti-Thieu members of so-called "Third Force" Buddhist, Catholic, and press groups.[5] Furthermore, the Government did not permit Front followers to engage in open political activity.[6]
>
> Front guerrillas and small North Vietnamese combat units, for their part, continued harassing attacks against Government soldiers throughout the country.[7] And North Vietnamese civilian and military personnel and enormous amounts of munitions and materiel continued to flow southward from North Vietnam.[8]

By 1974, it was clear to most observers that the cease-fire agreement had succeeded in only one respect: getting U.S. troops out of Vietnam. Throughout South Vietnam, the fighting continued to bring high numbers of casualties to both sides, and all three military forces involved in the war—those of the Government, the Front, and North Vietnam—continued to consolidate rear areas and stockpile weapons.[9]

Closer to My Thuy Phuong, throughout the province, large numbers of Government, Front, and North Vietnamese soldiers continued to fight and die.[10]

On the Government side, there were some minor alterations in military strategy during 1973–1974, but basic problems remained.[11] For example, during the cease-fire period corruption seriously weakened Government military efforts.[12] First, buying and selling of unit assignments debilitated the military personnel system. There was also expansion of black markets in weapons, ammunition, gasoline, and all types of support supplies. Corruption even touched military operations in the province. Many alleged that Government units on operations had to pay officers at headquarters for combat support. Seeing the corruption, and seemingly sensing the absurdity of a cease-fire that meant war, many Government soldiers began to desert their units for longer periods, sometimes flaunted orders, and engaged in petty thievery of military supplies.[13] Morale plummetted.

After the 1973 agreement, American civilian advisors continued to operate in the province, although there were fewer advisors than in previous years—and none in Huong Thuy District.[14] The U.S. expanded the jurisdiction of the provincial advisory office to include the portion of Quang Tri remaining in Government hands, and renamed it Office of the American Consulate Representative. Attached to the office were several American civilians, including a C.I.A. agent, many Vietnamese, some Filipinos and Taiwanese, and even a small group of American soldiers, present under terms of the Paris agreement to search for remains of Americans missing in action.

On the insurgent side, activity in the province was also intense during

1973–1974. The Front tried to consolidate its control in the vast mountainous sections of Thua Thien. Thousands of North Vietnamese laborers built a network of all-weather, mostly two-lane roads through this zone of control, and prepared huge caches of weapons, munitions, and equipment.[15] The Front established administrative organs in many of the scattered, sparsely populated villages of the mountain region.[16] But of most importance, guerrillas and Front followers continued to operate in the populated coastal lowlands and in Hue.

First, small North Vietnamese and Front units launched heavy ground, artillery, rocket, and mortar attacks against Government defenses north, west, and south of Hue, some quite near the village. Insurgent forces also occasionally launched rockets against the city and against installations like Camp Gia Le in My Thuy Phuong, and the sprawling Phu Bai base.[17] And small guerrilla actions—sniping, ambushes, killings, and so forth—occurred sporadically throughout the area.

Complementing the Front military actions were continuing political activities, including small Front meetings, leaflet distributions, and attempts to develop networks of followers in many villages. Clandestine radio broadcasts continued to reinforce messages carried directly by guerrillas and other local Front supporters. Despite guarantees of the 1973 agreement, Front political activity remained mainly covert, but was as widespread throughout the province as during the years 1968–1972. And the People's Revolutionary Party remained largely quiescent, though occasionally party pamphlets circulated through Front channels.

Complicating the pressures most residents of the province felt from the draft and continuing insurgent activities were increasingly desperate economic conditions.[18] With the closing of the numerous U.S. military bases in the area, and with a worldwide economic recession, most everyone in the province began to experience economic difficulties. Unemployment was high. Inflation forced nearly all families to drastically tighten budgets.[19] And many small sources of extra income, such as part-time jobs, began to disappear.

This, then, was My Thuy Phuong's provincial context of cease-fire war—intense fighting, the Government draft, increased Government pressure on critics and potential critics, economic recession, and continued Front political activity.

VILLAGE BATTLELINES

In the village, the period after the 1973 cease-fire brought little alteration in the local balance of military forces, but there were some political shifts. Operating out of Camp Gia Le, the First Infantry Division turned nearly all security responsibilities for the immediate area over to provincial forces, police, and self-defense units. Various types of Government operations thus continued to come to the village, but by 1973, very few of them involved main force units. In fact, main force soldiers participated mainly in defense of the Camp Gia Le perimeter. Like their 101st Airborne predecessors, First Division soldiers in bunkers and on small patrols and ambushes around the camp attempted to prevent sapper attacks and sniper fire.[20]

Four platoons of Popular Forces soldiers, under the command of Government district authorities, guarded local "strategic" points, including two bridges, a dispensary, the market place, and the village office. Regional Forces soldiers periodically came to My Thuy Phuong on operations, searching houses, checking papers, and probing for hidden arms caches or tunnels. Policemen were also active—assisting provincial forces on operations, checking papers, collecting taxes and sometimes rents, and generally trying to keep potential and actual opponents under control.

In 1974, the local police contingent maintained a "Communist Suspect List" of 447 names. A Government captain said that these were names of people "with any connection with the Communists, including anyone with sons or brothers who went to North Vietnam in 1954, or who went into the mountains after 1960." Police periodically questioned those whose names appeared on the list, sometimes jailing them without trial. "We watch them carefully," said the captain. The Government also continued supporting intelligence networks in the area, consisting of paid and unpaid informers from the village.

The People's Self-defense Force continued to expand after the cease-fire agreement. By early 1975, it officially had about 2,300 members in the village, but the Government classified only about 300 as combat ready, or trained and armed.[21] The rest were unarmed women, elderly, and young people trained in first aid and some simple guarding functions—self-defense "supporters" who occasionally stood watch and appeared at Government rallies. Note that the Government maintained tight control of self-defense weapons, collecting them every morning, and limiting distribution of ammunition. Local authorities thought it risky to pass out guns among people they did not fully trust.

After 1973, the Government complemented its security activities in My Thuy Phuong with an attempt to strengthen the administrative branch closest to the people—the village office. This came through the so-called Administrative Revolution, which meant, first, that the Government increased the number of civil servants and soldiers serving in the village.[22] A few extra civil servants joined the local office. Additional policemen did so, too, bringing the total local police contingent to eight. Second, the Government abolished hamlet elections, and the province chief began to appoint hamlet chiefs. Third, the Government required civil servants and many soldiers to join Thieu's so-called Democracy Party—and set up a party office in a Government compound in the village.[23]

Finally, the Administrative Revolution meant assertion of stronger military influence over the local Government apparatus. An Army captain came to the village to coordinate all local security activities. Many Government soldiers and villagers noted that the arrival of the captain brought improvements to the provincial forces patrols, operations, and static guarding assignments. Government soldiers became more alert on duty and improved marksmanship. Discipline tightened. Soldiers engaged in little looting. And desertion became infrequent. But the appointment of the captain caused resentment among most local civil servants, who regarded him as an interloper and threat to their positions.

In 1973–1975, a new Government-sponsored economic development program affected some villagers. This was the Huong Thuy Agricultural Bank, founded in 1973 by the Government and a group of private investors. The bank director said that between 1973 and early 1975 he approved about 200 loans for My Thuy Phuong residents. However, the Government village chief contended there were far fewer. In 1974, the bank's agricultural loans gathered interest at the rate of 29 percent annually, and loans for small businesses at 30 percent. The bank calculated interest on a daily basis, thereby giving borrowers extra incentive to repay the loan premiums sooner. Actual interest rates were therefore less if borrowers quickly repaid their loans. The bank permitted maximum loans equivalent to about U.S.$700. Normally, however, it lent much less.[24]

In the village, the bank's credit policy mainly helped the prosperous. Borrowers had to put up their homes or land as collateral, and the bank considered refugees and landless individuals bad risks. This effectively eliminated many from consideration, including those with the most pressing credit needs. If a family met the basic qualifications it then completed an application, which included specifics on the cost of the proposed project, and which required a loan-guarantee signature from the village chief. Bank employees then visited the family, looked at the proposed project site, and evaluated the proposal.

The requirement that the village chief guarantee loans prevented many from securing credit. Many villagers asserted that only prosperous pro-Government individuals and their friends and relatives received the needed guarantee signatures. A peasant commented, "At first many people here were happy about the bank's lending program, but then we saw that in truth it did not help the poor people. Some people said it showed the Government was lying about helping the people achieve prosperity." A tradesman said, "The bank is a very good example of a program that looks good on paper, but in reality is corrupt and hurts the people." The Huong Thuy Agricultural Bank was thus similar to most other Government economic efforts—it helped relatively few, and generated anti-Government feelings.

Let us briefly pause to examine the ideological and cultural ties which bound most members of the pro-Government minority during the last months of their preeminence in My Thuy Phuong. These were for the most part exactly the *same people,* or from the *same families,* that had been prosperous and influential for so many years. They were bound, first, by anti-Communism. A retired Government village chief said:

> At first we didn't know what Communism was, but we learned quickly. We learned that if we were to keep our jobs, we had to be anti-Communist. Of course we wanted to keep our jobs. There were many advantages to us in our jobs.

Some of those advantages were economic, but others related to power. The former village chief continued, "We were anti-Communist because it was the best way. To be anti-Communist is to be strong. It is very easy to control people if you are strong and anti-Communist." And just as a tiny minority of local civil servants refused to engage in corrupt activities, not all were manipulative and opportunistic in their anti-Communism. A Government clerk from a local prosperous family said, "My father and brother were killed by the Communists, and I hate them with all my heart. I will do anything I can to oppose them." His relatives had been members of the French colonial army, and died fighting the Viet Minh. A soldier who served as a clerk in the Government office, and whose father was a large landholder, spoke of freedom:

> Did you know that in the Communist north there is no freedom? The people are not allowed to make money. They are not allowed to hold money in their hands, but must divide it. There is nothing free and fun to do. It is impossible to go and drink coffee at the cafés, or go to the cinemas, like in the free south. The most important thing about living in freedom is going to the cinema. Under Communism, that is not possible.

One village councilman had long hated the Front, and the Viet Minh before it. He spoke:

> We must have strength to fight the Communists. Communism is the worst evil in our land. It takes away freedom and makes us slaves. Everyone here supports a strong government, because with a strong government the people will be free to have their land, to work, to have families, and to be happy.

Then there were strong beliefs about leadership. The last Government village chief gave his definition of leader:

> The leader must be an honest, good man. He must make decisions for all the people, and must think for the people. The leader knows that the people cannot understand everything about politics, so must make decisions for them.

A tradesman who was a village councilman said, "Vietnam has always had strong, honest men as leaders. They act for the people, and do it with strength." A large landholder had these words:

There is the mandarin tradition. The mandarin always was respected by the people, and could live in a richer manner than most of the people, but his own feelings were always with the people, and he served the people in many ways. Always the people respected him. Those of us who are lucky enough to have more money or more land always remember the tradition of the mandarin in Vietnam. And we always try to be like them.

Historical figures of immense power had long held particular fascination for several. Illustrative is this statement by the captain charged with local security:

Many Vietnamese like Hitler very much. Hitler was a strong leader. He was, above all, a nationalist, and acted in a strong fashion to lead his people. He destroyed all those who did not agree with him. I think that is good. If I could be a good leader like Hitler, I would be very happy.

"The people in Vietnam like strength," commented a village councilman long active in local affairs. "They must have strong, honest men to lead them, to tell them what is right and wrong." Another councilman observed, "In America there is President Nixon. He is another man we admire very much. When everyone was attacking him, he knew what he was doing was right."

Members of the pro-Government minority thus shared a preference for strong, decisive leaders. Many also shared a view of the masses of fellow villagers. For example, a former Government village chief spoke of the people:

Living here is very happy for many of the people. . . . They work and work, and have a good life, and are happy, but have no time to think about politics. . . . So we leaders must act in a strong way to think for the people. We must represent the people, and be honest with them. But we must remember that our understanding of politics is higher than theirs.

A large landholder said:

I love the people in this area. They are good, simple people. . . . But it is very true that the people are not interested in politics. Their experience is too simple for them to understand politics, so they always come to us and ask us, "How should we vote? Should we join this organization, or that organization?" The people do not know. They want guidance. Because I love these people, of course I give them guidance.

Curiously, none of the most important pro-Government villagers ever mentioned democracy or mass political participation while discussing leadership. This suggests that these individuals had not modified notions of paternalistic benevolence to in any way fit the Government's widely circulated claims that leaders in places like My Thuy Phuong were devoted to fostering democracy.

On the Front side in the village, the pattern of 1968–1972 generally persisted during 1973–1974, with people not deeply involved in insurgent activities. Front functional groups did not exist, and the People's Revolutionary Party had no activities, though a few party pamphlets reached local Front leaders. The leaders were for the most part the *same* men who held those positions during 1968–1972. They were capable, dedicated, and experienced, but due to Government security pressure continued to spend most of their time in the jungle and on the move. For this reason, most people saw them as shadowy figures and knew little of them. Their infrequent visits to the village occurred mainly at night. But despite the leaders' absence, they continued to direct insurgent activities. Guerrillas and other Front personnel sporadically collected money and food contributions, and a number of villagers disappeared—most willingly, and some forced—to join local guerrillas. Due to arrests and deaths, the number of guerrillas fell to about 10.

There were also continuing attacks against local civil servants, Government military officers, and their local allies. On at least two or three occasions during 1973–1974, the Front targeted such individuals. Once a grenade exploded in front of the home of a local tradesman noted for his anti-Communist beliefs, and guerrillas fired upon several civil servants. During the period there were no local Front killings, but most civil servants slept either in Hue or in guarded compounds in the village. "It's just to make sure we wake up," said one civil servant. Bullets sometimes fell on Government installations in the village and on Government soldiers guarding or patrolling the area. Along the highway, snipers occasionally harassed military vehicles with gunfire.

There is evidence that during 1973–1974 insurgent leaders brought a new message to the village, complementing the many intertwining messages discussed in Chapter 8. The new message concerned continuation of American aid to Government security forces and alleged Government violation of the cease-fire agreement. There are indications that the Front provided its local leaders with copies of the agreement, which they carefully studied. "These days we do not see the Viet Cong cadres very much," said a peasant, "but when they come they always talk about the peace agreement."

Like those on the Government side, local Front leaders took time out from their struggle in 1974–1975 to discuss their philosophy of leadership—and their views of the people. One Front leader said:

> Leaders must be men who are close to the people. They must always have the needs of the people in their minds, and must sacrifice for national liberation. A leader in Vietnam must have good purpose, and he must be honest. He must listen to the people, and be close to the people.
>
> The best leaders of Vietnam are men of purpose, and they are wise and good. Ho Chi Minh is an example. Chairman Ho had a great purpose, he was wise, and he was close to the people. He is the noblest leader of all.

Still another local leader stated:

> All of the most able leaders in Vietnamese history were men who were nationalists, and fought the Chinese and French, and imperialist America. They were intelligent men, and had very strong beliefs. They always acted very strongly, and always acted in the correct way. The people knew these men were doing the best things for them because they listened to the people, explained their policies to the people, and acted for the people. They were close to the people, like Ho Chi Minh. The people follow them because they have much *uy tin*.

These and other comments suggest that the village's foremost Front members defined leader as an able person, close to the common people, in touch with their aspirations and fears, and willing to learn from them and purposefully act in their interest.

Let us now probe the leaders' views of people involved in the revolutionary movement—their conceptions of revolutionary "followership." One of the leaders said, "The people are most important. They must do what is best for them. The people are very smart, you know. Many of them cannot read or write, but their intelligence is very great, and they know what is best." Another of the men noted:

> Many [leaders] on the Government side are very bad. They think bad things about the people. That is one of the important differences between the two sides. The Liberation is close to the people, and the Government is not. The Liberation would be dead if not for the people's support.

Still another leader commented, "The revolution is the people. The people must do it all—and the cadres only direct the strength of the people." My Thuy Phuong's insurgent leaders thus emphasized the importance of sparking local involvement in movement activities. Their statements came, ironically enough, at a time when they remained virtually absent from the village, except for occasional visits at night.

In summary, the Front had to maintain a low profile during 1973–1974, due mainly to pressure from Government security branches. The cell structure and network of supporters for guerrilla activities, which the Front had so carefully built up in the mid-1960s, remained in disarray. Guerrillas still launched only sporadic attacks from outside village boundaries and continued only low-level proselyting efforts.[25] But the local leaders remained devoted to their cause, convinced that the people were with them. They waited, in the wings.

HOPE, PROTEST, DESPAIR

Feelings ran high during the cease-fire war. For example, a low-ranking Government soldier had this to say:

> Many of us were forced to join the national army. They came to our homes and said, "You must go. You are 18 years old, and you must go." We see that the Government is corrupt, and is doing nothing for the people. So we are in a trap.

Another young soldier asserted, "The Government is very cruel, because it has no compassion for the people. The Government only gives power to Mr. Thieu, and the people are the ones who are suffering." A tradesman had these words:

> The Government's biggest problem is corruption. Corruption weakens the entire country. There are three problem groups in Vietnam today. First are corrupt Government officials. Second there are corrupt businessmen. Third are corrupt military officers.

The tradesman lost a son in December of 1974, when Government forces captured a point southwest of the village, a mountain called Mo Tau. He added, "My son has either been captured or is rotting on Mo Tau. There has been no investigation. No one has come to tell us anything. No one has ever said the Government is sorry. My son just never came home." Many in the village, especially those with sons in the Army, shared the man's dissatisfaction with Government performance.

Others discussed their economic problems in relation to the Government. For example, a peasant asserted:

> We are all so poor, and getting poorer every day. Mr. Thieu wants to raise taxes, and we can hardly afford to buy food. How can we live like this? The Government must do something for the people. If it doesn't, the people will not forgive it, and will curse it for 1,000 years.

And a peasant member of the Cult Committee stated, "The situation is so bad in our country now, and the Government so corrupt, that many people remember an old saying to gain strength. We say, 'If we fail, hope passes to our sons.' That is the hope for Vietnam."

Frustrated by the cease-fire war, two or three villagers became active in the primarily Catholic People's Anti-Corruption Movement, which had a small branch in Hue, and which organized small anti-Government demonstrations, quickly broken up by police.[26] A few local Buddhist leaders joined in meetings at Hue pagodas, demanding an end to corruption and implementation of the cease-fire accords.[27] Others felt that protest was futile, so engaged more energetically than usual in traditional pursuits. They busied themselves improving family graves, shrines, and the village pagoda. Several peasants indicated that they simply tried to work harder, for long hours spent tilling ricefields or gathering firewood in the hills brought temporary distraction along with extra income. And two elderly men, retired peasants, often got together for several hours to recite Vietnam's long, cherished narrative poem of love, honor, and struggle—"The

Tale of Kieu." One of them said, "This story gives us hope that there will be peace." [28]

Still others felt such despair that they turned to drugs. Several young people began experimenting with marijuana, and many soldiers continued occasionally to inject heroin-like substances into their arms. A small number literally destroyed themselves, as suicide began to take a toll, including one or two young men approaching draft age and a grieving young widow. Others found escape in creative endeavors. For example, a member of the Government's Self-defense Force composed a poem called "Our City": [29]

> What do you see in this city?
> After work it's crowded with cars and people.
> They push each other because they're hungry,
> because they have so many children.
>
> What do you see in this city?
> The children after a drunk American.
> They ask for money because they're poor,
> because their country is at war.
>
> What do you see in this city?
> In the hands of a tired stranger,
> she sells her body because she wants to live,
> because she doesn't care for the future.
>
> What do you see in this country?
> Dancing clubs, bars and crazy music.
> The customers try to laugh,
> because they are afraid they will cry,
> Their soul will be deserted and bitter.
>
> What do you see in our city?
> They say: "Peace will come to our country,"
> even though the mines explode every morning,
> and at night the sounds of cannon are everywhere.

But there was another response to lingering war in My Thuy Phuong: renewal of passive support for the Front. As noted above, the Front continued to operate much as it had during 1968–1972—from a distance and sporadically. But its ties to the past were clear. One peasant put it this way:

> Many people still remember the Liberation, because when the Liberation was strongest the people had happy hearts. After the Paris agreement we have not seen the guerrillas or the cadres very often. Sometimes they come for taxes, and sometimes for very small meetings. But many people remember them, and many people think the Liberation ideas are better now than before.

Front messages continued to reach many through the occasional visits by insurgent leaders and guerrillas. Front followers sometimes distributed leaflets and small flags, and clandestine radio broadcasts continued during the entire period. Many included timely responses to speeches by President Thieu, or to Government reports on military operations in the province. One radio feature reached many in the village every night at 11 o'clock. According to a tradesman, "The Communists play tapes of captured soldiers, who give their names, names of parents, and village names. This is the most popular program." The program was *so* popular, in fact, that it brought sales to one local tradesman: many bought small radio earphones.

"We always remember President Thieu's words," said a village tradesman. "He said to watch the Communists' acts, not listen to their words. We can see how bad the Communists are by looking at their acts." A Government soldier contended, "Every day the people hate the Communists more. They are so cruel in disregarding the Paris agreement." And a student, son of a civil servant, stated, "No one likes the Viet Cong side any more. To follow them is to betray our nation and our families."

But most villagers had different views. For example, a peasant said:

> The most important idea the people had after the Paris agreement was that the Government was very strong. We saw the Government flag everywhere. But we felt that the Communists were still very strong, and some people knew that the Communists controlled an important part of the country.
>
> Furthermore, the people began to think that the Americans were becoming very weak. America had to worry about problems of its economy, and about the Watergate matter, so more and more people began to think that the Communists might win.

A low-ranking Government soldier noted:

> The people's attitude toward the Viet Cong was very special after the Paris agreement. Some of the people then thought that the Viet Cong was going to win. Others did not, but the majority came to think that it might happen.
>
> So the majority began to be very careful about the Viet Cong. Of course the Viet Cong cadres sometimes came here for taxes and to make propaganda, and so the people, to guarantee their future, listen and are polite.

A peasant said:

> The people know that the Government is bad and is going to lose. The people have supported the Liberation side for a long time. They support the Liberation 100 percent, and after 1973 the support for the Liberation has increased, in truth, because of the Government's corruption, and because the war continues without end. So the Liberation is still strong.

And another peasant noted:

> Many of us never really understood what the National Liberation Front meant. We now understand clearly what it is like under the Government of the Republic of Vietnam. For the poor people of Vietnam, could it be any worse under the Liberation side?

In summary, My Thuy Phuong's revolutionary potential actually seemed to increase during 1973–1974. Passive support for the Front increased, so altogether about 70 percent of the people favored that side. And Government supporters and the politically uncommitted dipped to about 10 and 20 percent, respectively. Pressure of the cease-fire war brought these changes on, along with increasing corruption of the local Government apparatus, and people's memories of Front ascendancy in the 1960s—memories in some cases perhaps clouded by nostalgia.

A contrast with this picture of Front strength comes in the computerized assessment of Government pacification in My Thuy Phuong. In March of 1974, the village was classified between "B" and "C," meaning that it was in general a safe place for the Government.[30] Curiously, the hamlets far from the highway in the ricefields, which villagers described as virtual Front strongholds, were chalked up as "B" by the computers in Saigon!

VICTORS AND VICTIMS

In early January of 1975, North Vietnamese and Front forces initiated a massive campaign, the Ho Chi Minh Offensive. It directly and dramatically touched My Thuy Phuong.[31] Most of the early attacks, however, were in Phuoc Long Province and other points distant from the village and Thua Thien/Hue.[32] One exception came on February 21, when the Government organized a village council election. During the voting, guerrillas set off a large explosion some distance from the polling place, causing no casualties or property damage. Everyone heard the explosion. The district chief stated, "It is a reminder that the Communists do not approve of the election."

Another reminder came toward the end of February. Eight high school students on guard with the local Self-defense Force disappeared—abducted, according to Government officials, and "gone to the mountains with the Liberation," according to several of their friends.[33]

By March 9, 1975, military pressure by North Vietnamese and Front forces was widespread throughout South Vietnam, especially in the Central Highlands, and also in the strategic Tri Thien Hue sector.[34] In Quang Tri, insurgents launched a heavy attack near the My Chanh river crossing, Government troops counterattacked, and 3–4,000 refugees fled southward to Hue, according to an American official's estimate.[35]

In Thua Thien, the 1975 offensive began in a place called Ap Hoa Binh—"Peace Hamlet"—to the north of Hue near the Quang Tri border. There a company of Front forces, 60 to 80 guerrillas, came in from the mountains and attacked Government positions. On the same night, Front forces attacked two other locations north of Hue, and hit Government Marine positions with what the *New York Times* estimated at 1,100 rounds of mortar, rocket, and artillery fire.[36]

Also on March 9, there began a series of small Front operations south of Hue, including the village area. For example, small guerrilla forces entered the village of Thuy Thanh, east of My Thuy Phuong, and Thuy Phu, to the southwest. Mortars hit Camp Gia Le the same night.[37] It seems likely that North Vietnamese and Front commanders planned their widely scattered attacks in the province as tests of Government defenses.[38] And it must be emphasized that the early March attacks in Thua Thien met with vigorous resistance by Government forces, including Marines, the First Division, and provincial forces.

The Government's province chief estimated that his forces killed about 150 Front guerrillas in Phu Thu, east of the village. North of Hue, a variety of Government forces, including about 45 tanks, killed and captured many more guerrillas. In the Vinh Loc area south of My Thuy Phuong, provincial forces attacked guerrilla positions, supported by air and artillery fire.

The initial guerrilla attacks and Government counterattacks drove many people from their homes into Hue. According to Huong Thuy District officials, about 14,000, mainly from Phu Thu District, sought shelter in the Thua Thien Stadium. And the fighting brought very wide destruction to the contested hamlets. In Phu Thu District, there were several days of heavy bombing and use of helicopter-borne rockets. Commenting on Phu Thu, photojournalist Jean-Claude Labbé said, "There is not one village left."[39]

With heavy fighting very nearby, My Thuy Phuong was far from quiet during early March, 1975. On March 9, when guerrillas launched attacks to the south and east, about one company of guerrillas infiltrated the ricefield hamlet area. These were some of the same guerrillas who had been operating in the village and other parts of Huong Thuy District for many years, augmented by numerous North Vietnamese soldiers clad in guerrilla garb. The guerrillas attacked the provincial forces guard points by the hamlet bridge, and Self-defense checkpoints in the hamlet. All the Government defenders fled. From March 9 to 12, Government forces counterattacked, employing battalion-size provincial forces ground operations, dropping in paratroopers, and using helicopter support. Eventually, Government forces drove away or killed all of the guerrillas, but not before nearly all of the hamlet's 750 residents fled to other parts of the village or to Hue. Only a few elderly women stayed behind in the hamlet, hoping to prevent looting by Government troops.[40] After the Government counterattack, a peasant woman stood by the highway, wringing her hands in dismay, her head thrown back. "My son. Oh, my son," she moaned. "My life has ended. There is nothing left for me." Her son, a Regional Forces soldier, died in the Government assault.

On March 13, several of the hamlet's residents went back to visit homes, and came out wearing face masks and carrying slings. They bore the badly mutilated bodies of six guerrillas, including one woman. They temporarily laid the bodies near Highway One, and buried them that same afternoon—in unmarked graves. Dozens came to the site, and stood silently watching their neighbors prepare the bodies and dig graves. Front pressure in the village during the first half of March did not end with the death of those guerrillas. Early in the morning on March 12, about a dozen sappers attacked Camp Gia Le's munitions storage areas. All were killed. On March 14, several guerrillas wounded two provincial forces soldiers in a fire fight near the highway.

By mid-March, tensions throughout the province had increased significantly. According to the *New York Times,* about 100,000 Quang Tri and Thua Thien refugees jammed Hue.[41] Fighting, which the *Times* characterized as "persistent though scattered," continued throughout Thua Thien, especially north of Hue.[42] And in the village, guerrillas and other Front followers grew active—spreading leaflets and telling people that a General Uprising was near. Local insurgent leaders planned these and other actions in the area, although they did so under careful direction of the provincial Front organization and, according to two men close to the Front, North Vietnamese commanders.

A dramatic Front action came in broad daylight on March 15, when a guerrilla or guerrillas shot and killed a policeman serving in the village. The Government's village chief reported that guerrillas had infiltrated the village and were responsible. The policeman, who had served in the village for a few years, had a reputation for corruption and cruelty. Front leaflets and rumors had repeatedly warned him that his behavior did not meet with the people's approval. So no one shed tears when the policeman fell victim.

The Government responded as it usually did to such incidents of selective violence. It organized a large combined military-police operation. Field force police, provincial forces, and Self-defense members from the village searched every home in the area of the killing. The Government personnel thoroughly ransacked houses in the search, and frisked people from head to toe. The troops were disspirited, however, and clearly would have preferred to be elsewhere. "I'm hungry, let's go home," complained a young soldier shuffling along on the operation, his M-16 slung low on his shoulder. "Get your guns up! Guns up!" shouted a captain. "Act like soldiers now!"

Early on March 16, those same reluctant soldiers killed a man near the place the policeman had been shot. Later officers claimed that the man shot was a guerrilla. The soldiers tied their victim's feet with rope, and dragged him out to the highway.[43] A retired Government soldier, who often boasted that he had worked for the C.I.A., took up a long vigil by that spot on the highway, and made little anti-Communist speeches to any passers-by who would listen. He moved in a slow, trance-like dance around the corpse. "This is a V.C. He is from North Vietnam, and he came here to kill the policeman. Ha, I'm glad we killed him! We are leaving him here to scare the people. They are all V.C. here, you know." The body lay by the highway for two days.

On about March 17, North Vietnamese and Front pressure increased all around Hue, paralleling a substantial increase in other parts of the country. As Frank Snepp writes, the North Vietnamese drive against Government positions in the Central Highlands prompted Thieu to order withdrawal to Saigon of the Airborne Troops guarding Hue.[44] This was part of Thieu's revised strategy following setbacks in the Highlands, which in effect wrote off the entire northern section of South Vietnam. Thieu vacillated when it came to ordering the defense of Hue. One day it was to be defended at all costs, the next day not.

The Airborne pullout, fighting in the province, and general uncertainty sparked rumors in Thua Thien/Hue of imminent massive attacks and Government abandonment. Thousands began packing up personal belongings and heading about 60 miles south to the coastal city of Danang. Most everyone regarded it as invulnerable to attack.[45] Most of those who fled were Hue residents, residents of Quang Tri refugee camps, and rural provincial civil servants, police, and military officers, as well as others allied with the Government. The first to go were people who could afford commercial air flights or large charter vehicles for carrying belongings. Among them were the wives and children of high-ranking Government military officials. Buses, trucks, and taxis—piled high with furniture, motorcycles, sacks of rice, chickens, dogs, and people—began to move southward.

Between about March 17 and March 22, Hue residents and Quang Tri refugees in Hue saw friends and neighbors packing and leaving, and most seemed gripped with an uncontrollable desire to do the same.[46] An elderly woman said:[47]

> We began to realize that the government offices were moving away and that the army was moving out. So the people just started to move, too—government and soldiers' families first, and then many others. People just didn't want to be left behind, with everyone else going.

"We are leaving because we are afraid of the fighting," said another Hue resident, a tradesman. The man continued, "We all remember Tet Mau Than." A Government soldier stated, "We are afraid of the Communists. We must leave and be safe in Danang." A man interviewed on Highway One asserted:[48]

It's so strange and terrible this time. In the other bad times, in 1968 and 1972, lots of us became refugees too. But this time there's no fighting, no reason. Hue is being shelled a bit now, but that's not why we are leaving. We are leaving because the Government is giving our home to the Communists.

And a fleeing taxi driver said, "I think the Communists will be all right. But it's no good to be caught in the war zone between one side and the other. That's where you can be killed." [49] For an elderly Hue tradesman, the realization that the Americans were leaving came as a shock:

We saw the American advisors closing up their offices and burning papers. Then we knew that America was betraying our national government, and that it was giving over Hue and Quang Tri to the Communists without a fight. We knew then we had to leave.

Contributing to the panic were rumors about a meeting organized March 18 by the province chief, during which he "gave permission" for all noncrucial civil servants, women, children, and the old to leave if they felt it necessary, but urged all others, especially those with weapons, to stay behind and fight. And apparently few in the province heard or were convinced by President Thieu's broadcast of March 20, which assured that the Government was "determined to safeguard our territory at all costs." Thieu also characterized rumors about abandonment of the province as groundless.[50] On that statement, a Hue student said, "It's a lie. They withdrew the airborne division yesterday." [51]

With the advance of North Vietnamese and Front forces, Government soldiers and civil servants began to join the flow of refugees, with many of the highest ranking officials the first to run. Among them were the deputy commander of all Government forces in northern South Vietnam, and the commander of Camp Gia Le.[52] The First Division's deputy commander had these words: "My commanding officer ran away two days ago, but there were never any orders. No orders to fight, no orders to withdraw. I don't even know where my wife is. Why should I care about my unit?" [53]

Hundreds of thousands took to Highway One and headed to Danang—on every conceivable type of vehicle, including buses, taxis, jeeps, motorcycles, ambulances, sound trucks, and bicycles. Many hundreds walked, some dragging carts or carrying market baskets loaded with possessions. The deserting Government soldiers were angry, embarrassed, and sometimes desperate. Some commandeered vehicles at gunpoint, while others robbed, looted, and even killed to get money for passage. Not far south of My Thuy Phuong, a family of four fleeing to Danang was knocked from its motorcycle and crushed beneath the wheels of a truck. For a while, refugees moved around the family, too panicky to stop. Finally, someone laid the four corpses on a mat by the roadside.[54] There were numerous other fatal traffic accidents along Highway One, especially on the treacherous Hai Van mountain pass between Hue and

Danang. Several trucks and a bus overturned. Vehicles lost brakes and plunged over cliffs.

The refugee movement of 1975 was the largest in Thua Thien/Hue history, and one of the largest refugee movements of the entire war. About 95 percent of the permanent residents and Quang Tri refugees evacuated Hue.[55] As the refugee flow continued, military pressure from insurgent forces increased. Rocket and artillery fire repeatedly hit Hue. According to Hanoi's General Van Tien Dung, the 304th, 324th, and 325th North Vietnamese divisions, including hundreds of tanks and a number of technical units began advancing on Hue from north and south.[56] And in the villages local guerrillas began positioning themselves and preparing for their "opportune moment." Notice of it came on March 22, 1975. Clandestine transmitters broadcast an appeal of the provincial National Liberation Front Committee and People's Revolutionary Committee:[57]

> Dear compatriots: Although the Americans and Thieu have sustained setbacks and are in a critical situation, they are still very stubborn and crafty. In many areas of our province, the enemy is rounding up our compatriots and forcing them to leave their native land, their ancestors' tombs and their ricefields, orchards and homes and go with him to live an extremely miserable wandering life so that he can continue to carry out pressganging and troop upgrading activities and use their blood and bones as a shield to protect himself.
>
> Let all of our compatriots resolutely and firmly stay close to their ricefields and orchards in the liberated areas, refuse to leave, struggle fiercely against the enemy's people-herding activities, refuse to side with the enemy, build shelters to protect themselves against enemy bombing and shelling and, together with all of our people, fight the enemy to protect their villages.
>
> The People's Liberation Armed Forces is launching a fierce offensive against the U.S.-Thieu clique's nibbling troops, giving direct support to our compatriots who are rising up to liberate their country and win back their right to be masters and defeating the clique's people-herding schemes.
>
> Let all of our compatriots rise up in vigorous struggle.

In My Thuy Phuong, guerrillas responded by launching one of the heaviest attacks in the province. At first, a few random rockets hit Camp Gia Le, but later hundreds of rounds of rocket, mortar, and artillery fire rained down on the installation.[58] During one attack, a university student cried out, "What if they miss! What if they miss!" But North Vietnamese and Front gunners were on target and there was little damage done anywhere outside the base.

On about March 20, several guerrillas and other Front followers left copies of a small flyer near the village market, by wells, and along paths—places people were sure to find them. The flyers contained words describing "the suffering of the people," and calling upon the people to prepare for the fast approaching "final liberation of South Vietnam from the hands of the Saigon puppet authorities." The message was signed

"Youth Liberation Forces." [59] It was unclear how people reacted to the flyer. They were clearly more interested in the rapid flow of events before their eyes. About 400 reacted to what they saw and heard by packing bags and joining the refugee movement south. These were civil servants, policemen, military officers, some panicky enlisted men and students, and those larger landholders and tradesmen with close ties to the Government. With their departure, the Government apparatus effectively ceased to exist. The date was March 22. The village office stood empty, and no one guarded strategic points in the village.

Like most other rural residents of Thua Thien Province, about 95 percent of My Thuy Phuong's people chose to remain close to home. Many who remained, however, were nervous or fearful, uncertain of what fighting lay ahead in the village, or of what the retreating Government soldiers and advancing North Vietnamese and Front soldiers would do. Several dozen people sat and stood in front of homes, watching the flow of refugees. Others continued working in the ricefields as usual, and several men chose the period of panic and Government collapse to work on repair of an ancestral shrine. Many children continued to play in front of homes and fish in village streams. A few children even studied lessons, though schools were closed and teachers gone. And a small number of Government personnel remained behind to the end, staying close to families and choosing not to fight. One of them, a young enlisted man who worked in the village office, wanted his photograph taken and sent to his parents. For him, the war was over. He said:

> Don't take my picture in front of the [Government] flag, and don't take it in front of the village office. They have no meaning. Take the picture in front of the spirit house. Only it has meaning for me now. . . . We are all going to die here. Try to remember us as good men, and try to tell people we are sorry.

Another who chose not to flee was one of the low-ranking local policemen. He stayed close to home, loaded a gun, and wrung his hands nervously: "America brought this war to Vietnam, and now it is abandoning its responsibility. The Vietnamese people have enough resolve and strength to fight the Communists. We only need weapons."

On March 22, guerrillas or North Vietnamese forces sabotaged the Truoi Bridge south of the village, and the refugee flow came to a complete halt.[60] According to the last Government province chief, between March 22 and 24, about 10,000 Government soldiers moved south through the village, most of them on foot.[61] Only about 3,000 of them somehow managed to flee the province. The rest crossed Huong Thuy District and ended up at a distant coastal point called Vinh Loc, which a narrow but treacherous channel of water separated from the escape road to Danang. Massing at Vinh Loc, the soldiers grew disorderly, and then came under mortar attack.[62] Finally realizing that escape was impossible, the trapped soldiers began to move northward back toward home villages. As they walked, they threw down weapons and shed uniforms.[63]

Other residents of the province, including at least several from My Thuy Phuong, evacuated from a place called Thuan An, on the coast east of Hue.[64] A small armada of ships waited off the Thuan An beach, picking up soldiers from an ocean of people.[65] Many remembered that there was much shelling in the area, and that half-crazed soldiers fought each other. They swam desperately out to waiting boats, clawing over floating corpses. A Government soldier from My Thuy Phuong remembered, "I got onto a boat, and the boat was so full that some of the soldiers had to shoot other soldiers swimming out. Some other soldiers threw grenades. The water around us was red from the blood."

"We have fought for 20 years, and our fight will end in a few days," said an elderly peasant. As the Government collapsed around him, the man, formerly a Viet Minh guerrilla, seemed excited and happy. Another peasant, who had previously appeared cynical about the war, spoke of the Front's "correct policy for the past 20 years." He was suddenly enthusiastic about the cause of revolution. Still another peasant commented, "Our family never liked the Front, or Mr. Thieu, but now we are happy it is almost over. Of course we support the Liberation now."

As they worked repairing an ancestral shrine, two peasants commented on the change they saw coming. "It may make a difference to the poor people of Vietnam if the Communists win," said one man. "We will support them and give them a chance. We will see. It is good that the fighting and the difficult times are almost over." The other peasant concurred and predicted, "The Liberation Front will form a new government and will be very good. There will be no more rich group in Vietnam, and the farming people like us will live better."

A man who had a small rice plot near the highway watched the retreating soldiers as he weeded his land. He said, "Oh, yes, it looks like the V.C. is going to win. I always thought they might win. If they win, good, then there will be peace, and I will be able to work in the ricefields. I will be happy, like a bird let out of a cage!" In mock amazement, a student asked, "How could I be surprised that we won? We were fighting the Americans, and the puppet Thieu, and we always knew they would lose, and we would win. We have always known that. Everybody knows that." Another student contended:

> The Liberation Front will give the soldiers of the old army a chance to join us. We will not give any of their big men any important work, and we will watch them carefully. But if they agree to ask forgiveness for the past, and go to political study meetings, then there will be no problem.

A peasant concurred, and added that the Front would probably not long retain Government civil servants, police, and military personnel in important positions of local authority. "How can they work like us?" he asked. "They need to take breaks at least three times a day for tea and coffee, and they gossip like women!"

A few had specific ideas for future governmental policies. "Our government will be a government of the people," said a student. "We will organize meetings of the people, and ask for ideas from the people on everything we do. We always want all the people to support us." A peasant commented: [66]

> The comrade Liberation fighters always sacrifice for the fatherland, and we think everyone should do that. I expect that everyone will support the Liberation policies, and help carry them out. Anyone who is lazy, or who opposes the people, will be in trouble, and Liberation cadres will have to visit him, to talk to him, to convince him. But the people will all support the Liberation. Definitely.

On March 24, the last battle was clearly over in My Thuy Phuong. Small numbers of Front guerrillas patrolled freely through the area, and some of them talked and joked with villagers. A few even stood by the highway and waved to Government troops shedding uniforms and moving back to home villages. Along a path near Highway One, someone posted a handwritten cardboard sign. It read, "Victory Without Bloodshed." As the guerrillas prepared to take over, they perhaps joined those quoted above, and others of the 95 percent who remained in My Thuy Phuong, in realizing what had happened in their village: Due to many fundamental weaknesses, the Government apparatus had collapsed before their eyes and disappeared forever. And most villagers, including those long hesitant to align themselves with the revolution, were ready to support the victors.

NOTES

1. See *Far Eastern Economic Review* (hereafter cited as FEER), January 29, 1973, pp. 11–28; Bernard & Marvin Kalb, *Kissinger* (Boston: Little, Brown, 1974); "Documentation on the Viet-Nam Agreement" (Washington, D.C.: Office of Media Services, Bureau of Public Affairs, U.S. Department of State, 1973); Gareth Porter, *A Peace Denied: The United States, Vietnam, and the Paris Agreement* (Bloomington: Indiana University Press, 1975); Tad Szulc, "How Kissinger Did It; Behind the Vietnam Cease-Fire Agreement," *Foreign Policy,* no. 15, Summer, 1974, pp. 21–69; Vien, no. 39.

2. U.S. advisors described the mood of Thua Thien/Hue at the time of the cease-fire in "Thua Thien Report," February 1, 1973, p. 1. The *New York Times* (hereafter cited as NYT) reported that many in Hue were nervous that the city and province would be "given up" to insurgent forces. (NYT, March 24, 1975, p. 6.) Also see James Jones, "In the Shadow of Peace," NYT, June 10, 1973, VI, p. 15 and NYT, September 1, 1973, p. 2.

3. See "The Provisional Revolutionary Government," *Indochina Chronicle,* no. 32, April 17, 1974; NYT, January 24, 1973, p. 1, map.

4. Fred Branfman, "Indochina: The Illusion of Withdrawal," *Harper's Magazine,* May, 1973, pp. 65–76; *Documenting the Post-War War.* Also NYT, February 25, 1974, pp. 1, 10; April 18, 1974, p. 2.

5. See *Dai Dan-Toc* (Saigon newspaper), March 9, 1975; "The Third Force in South Vietnam" (Philadelphia: American Friends Service Committee, 1975), pamphlet. Also NYT, February 18, 1973, p. 3; March 25, 1973, p. 3; September 15, 1973, p. 2; September 27, 1973, p. 39; August 9, 1974, p. 17; August 18, 1974, pp. 1, 22; August 19, 1974, pp. 1, 12; August 21, 1974, pp. 1, 14; October 10, 1974, p. 11; October 11, 1974, p. 4; October 21, 1974, pp. 1, 13; October 23, 1974, p. 4; November 2, 1974, pp. 1, 5; November 4, 1974, p. 3.

6. See NYT, January 5, 1974, p. 2; January 29, 1973, p. 1; January 30, 1973, pp. 1, 10; February 11, 1973, p. 6; February 13, 1973, p. 17; February 21, 1973, p. 18; February 27, 1973, pp. 1, 8; March 13, 1973, p. 14; April 7, 1973, p. 8; June 1, 1973, p. 7; May 15, 1973, p. 3; October 24, 1973, p. 3; January 6, 1974, p. 3; July 15, 1974, p. 2. Also John Spragens, "1974 'Communist Atrocities,' " *Indochina Chronicle,* no. 33, June 24, 1974, pp. 14–17; "Father Chan Tin's View of 'Political Prisoners': A Case Study of Militancy Overriding Objectivity" (Saigon: Department of State Airgram, December 26, 1973), released by Department of State, Washington, D.C.

7. NYT, January 28, 1973, p. 18; February 18, 1973, pp. 1, 6; February 21, 1973, p. 18; February 28, 1973, pp. 1, 10; March 29, 1973, p. 18; May 15, 1973, p. 3; October 24, 1973, p. 3; July 16, 1974, p. 7.

8. NYT, October 25, 1973, p. 16; October 31, 1973, p. 13; March 28, 1975, p. 6; December 14, 1973, pp. 1, 5; May 7, 1974, p. 3.

9. See NYT, January 27, 1974, pp. 1, 24; January 28, 1974, p. 27.

10. See NYT, January 1, 1974, p. 6; November 4, 1974, p. 3.

11. See NYT, May 7, 1973, p. 3.

12. See *Tia Sang* (Saigon newspaper), December 18, 1974.

13. NYT, December 15, 1973, p. 3.

14. For information on Government operations in the province during 1973–1974, see *Dac-San Xuan, 1973* and *Dan-Van* (Hue: Information Service); Government yearbooks. For Huong Thuy District data, see *Huong Thuy,* pp. 52–59. Also see NYT, February 9, 1973, p. 3; March 20, 1973, p. 17; March 31, 1973, p. 6.

15. See NYT, May 6, 1973, pp. 1, 4; May 7, 1974, pp. 1–3; August 24, 1973, p. 3; January 8, 1974, pp. 1, 4.

16. See NYT, March 31, 1974, p. 3.

17. See "Thua Thien Report," February 1, 1973, p. 2. Also NYT, January 29, 1973, p. 12; April 5, 1973, p. 15; April 6, 1973, p. 5; April 7, 1973, p. 8; May 6, 1973, pp. 1, 4; May 19, 1973, p. 6; May 31, 1973, p. 8; June 1, 1973, p. 7; August 18, 1973, p. 6; August 19, 1973, p. 6; August 20, 1973, p. 7; August 22, 1973, p. 14; August 24, 1973, p. 3; August 26, 1973, p. 7; September 7, 1973, p. 8; September 13, 1973, p. 6; October 14, 1973, p. 8; October 24, 1973, p. 3; June 22, 1974, p. 8; June 25, 1974, p. 4; July 28, 1974, p. 9; November 3, 1974, p. 3.

    Also see *Bulletin d'Information* (Paris: Service de Presse, Permanent Mission of the Provisional Revolutionary Government of South Vietnam in France), September 11, 1974, no. 8, p. 8; October 1, 1974, no. 10, p. 4; April 1, 1975, no. 26, p. 2; in Cornell University Library.

18. See *Newsweek,* October 15, 1973, p. 48. Also NYT, January 26, 1973, p. 12; April 7, 1973, p. 10; September 14, 1973, p. 2; April 20, 1974, p. 11.

19. The inflation rate was estimated at 80 percent. (See NYT, May 7, 1974, p. 3.)

20. According to Government civil servants, First Division soldiers had "operational authority," along with provincial forces, in roughly the southern fifth of the village.

21. According to district officials, there were 174 male and 118 female "combat" members in the village in early March, 1975, armed with 80 M–1 and 20 M–2 carbines and 38 rifles of various types. The figure of 2,300 self-defense members represents most of the able-bodied villagers.

22. See *Huong-Thuy,* pp. 1–10; NYT, November 28, 1973, p. 2.

23. Also see NYT, March 29, 1973, p. 19; June 12, 1973, p. 3; January 20, 1974, p. 12.

24. This data provided by the director of the Huong Thuy Agricultural Bank.

25. An "official" view of the village was provided by Robert Jones III, for many years employed by the U.S. Mission/Vietnam. He offered the following description of the village, based on the April, 1974 computerized H.E.S. evaluation:

> "There is a V.C. infrastructure (functioning); portions of populated areas are penetrated by cadre/guerrillas on a fairly regular basis during hours of darkness. V.C. taxes are collected from sympathetic households. Police and some officials travel to neighboring areas to sleep. GVN military control is total in populated areas day and night; however, political orientation of population is mixed. NVA/VC military units have safe havens in Western extremity of village, but generally don't appear except at time of rice harvest. Least secure hamlet is Dong Tien [i.e., central My Thuy Phuong]."

District officials provided H.E.S. scores for all villages of the district. As indicated earlier in the text, the most favorable scores for the Government are "A". "B" and "C" are progressively less so. The following H.E.S. scores are as of March 1, 1975:

Village	Hamlet Ratings			Hamlet Total	Village Overall
	A	B	C		
Thuy Bieu	1	3	—	4	B
Thuy Xuan	3	5	—	8	B
Thuy Truong	1	1	—	2	A
Thuy Phuoc	1	1	—	2	A
Thuy Van	3	1	—	4	A
Thuy Thanh	—	3	—	3	B
Thuy An	2	4	—	6	B
Thuy Duong	1	2	—	3	B
Thuy Chau	2	5	—	7	B
Thuy Luong	6	3	—	9	A
Thuy Phu	1	1	—	2	A
Thuy Tan	2	1	—	3	A
Thuy Phu	—	—	5	5	C

26. See NYT, September 21, 1974, p. 11; *Chinh Luan* (Saigon newspaper), March 4, 1975.

27. See NYT, October 21, 1974, pp. 1, 13; *Doc-Lap* (Saigon newspaper), February 6, 1975.

28. See Nguyen Du, *The Tale of Kieu* (New York: Vintage Books, 1973).

29. The poem was written by a student, and appeared on the single extant page of a 1973 wall newspaper prepared for a meeting of self-defense members; obtained from the Huong Thuy Information Service.

30. Information provided by Robert Jones III.

31. The best book in English on the 1975 offensive is Frank Snepp, *Decent Interval* (New York: Vintage Books, 1977). Also see Alan Dawson, *55 Days; The Fall of South Vietnam* (Englewood Cliffs: Prentice-Hall, 1977); FEER, September 12, 1975, pp. 35–39.

    For a Vietnamese interpretation of the offensive, see Van Tien Dung, *Our Great Spring Victory* (New York: Monthly Review Press, 1977); another translation of this appears in "Sen Gen Van Tien Dung Article: 'Our Great Spring Victory,' " in "Daily Report," supplement, vol. II, July 7, 1976, and for details on fighting in Thua Thien/Hue, see pp. 48–50. The Vietnamese language original on Thua Thien/Hue appears in *Tin Sang* (Saigon newspaper), April 28, 1976, p. 6. Vo Tien Dung and Vo Nguyen Giap wrote another less vivid account of the offensive; see *Saigon Giai-Phong*, July 6, 1975, p. 3; July 8, 1975, p. 3. Also see NYT, April 26, 1976, pp. 1, 16; April 29, 1976, p. 12; May 31, 1976, p. 2 for English language highlights of the Dung article.

32. See NYT, December 11, 1974, p. 6; December 15, 1974, p. 11; December 16, 1974, p. 15; December 18, 1974, p. 2; December 24, 1974, p. 3; December 26, 1974, p. 5. Also see FEER, September 12, 1975, p. 35; January 17, 1975, pp. 10–12.

33. Front followers indicated that those who left the village had received assurances that they would not be armed by the Front, but would be sent to a rear area for political study sessions.

34. The pressure was so intense that the Government issued extremely strict mobilization orders, ordering more searches for deserters, tightening of draft deferments, etc. In the village, the new orders had a demoralizing effect on most male high school students—most of whom were over 18 years of age and thus eligible for the draft under the new regulations. Also see *Chinh Luan*, March 4, 1975; *Dai Dan-Toc*, March 14, 1975.

35. The official was Roger R. Kelling, senior advisor, Tri Thien Hue; interviewed in Hue on March 10, 1975. The author believes his estimate was accurate.

36. NYT, March 12, 1975, pp. 1, 12.

37. Information on the Front attacks of early March was provided by former Government province chief Nguyen Huu Due, and also is based on the author's observations. (Ex-Colonel Due was interviewed in Birmingham, Alabama, September 27, 1975.)

38. *Chinh Luan*, March 13, 1975, p. 10. Also see NYT, March 12, 1975, pp. 1, 12; March 13, 1975, p. 3.

39. This statement was made to the author in Hue on March 16, 1975.

40. Most residents of the ricefield hamlets returned to their homes on about March 18, 1975.

41. NYT, March 14, 1975, pp. 1, 10.

42. *Ibid.*

43. A photograph of a woman and girl passing the corpse, taken by Jean-Claude Labbé, was published around the world. See Associated Press (hereafter AP), photograph, *Newsday*, March 20, 1975, p. 5.

44. See Snepp, *op. cit.*, pp. 170–216.

45. For a summary of events in and around Hue, see *ibid.*, pp. 205–229; Dawson, *op. cit.*, pp. 83–150. Also see "Sen Gen Van Tien Dung," p. 48.

46. The March 19, 1975 evacuation of Quang Tri prompted many to leave. See AFP Hong Kong broadcast (in English) of March 26, 1975, in "Daily Report," March 26, 1975, p. L–6.

47. NYT, March 26, 1975, p. 14.

48. NYT, March 22, 1975, p. 9.

49. NYT, March 26, 1975, p. 14.

50. *Dan-Chu* (Saigon newspaper), March 22, 1975.

51. The withdrawal of this division to Saigon occurred on March 19, 1975, according to the author's observations and NYT, March 20, 1975, p. 18.

52. This information was provided by the ex-province chief of Thua Thien/Hue. (See note 37.)

53. NYT, May 25, 1975, VI, p. 36.

54. See AP, photograph, *Newsday*, March 22, 1975, p. 1.

55. On March 24, 1975, the American Broadcasting Co. reported that only 10,000 remained in Hue of an original population of about 200,000. (ABC broadcast heard in Danang by the author.) The estimate of 95 percent evacuation from Hue was by the former Government province chief. See *Dan-Chu*, March 21, 1975.

56. "Sen Gen Van Tien Dung," p. 50. Also see "Daily Report," March 26, 1975, p. L–5, and *Chinh Luan*, March 21, 1975; "Combined News Services," *Newsday*, March 22, 1975, p. 5. For articles on the Thua Thien/Hue military situation, see *Chinh Luan*, March 21, 1975, pp. 1, 9; March 24, 1975; March 25, 1975. Also see NYT, March 23, 1975, pp. 1–2; March 24, 1975, pp. 1, 4; March 26, 1975, pp. 1, 14. Also *Trang Den* (Saigon newspaper), March 27, 1975, pp. 1, 8; March 30, 1975, p. 1. Also FEER, September 12, 1975, p. 36.

57. "Daily Report," March 24, 1975, p. L–11.

58. Camp Gia Le was attacked first on March 21, 1975, then repeatedly during the next several days. See *Chinh Luan*, March 23, 1975, p. 1; *Saigon Post* (Saigon newspaper), March 24, 1975; *Trang Den*, March 28, 1975, p. 1; also BBC broadcast, March 22, 1975, heard by the author in Hue.

59. The author has lost the flyer, and cannot recall the entire text, but does recall the portions quoted.

60. See *Chinh Luan*, March 25, 1975, p. 1.

61. Also see NYT, March 28, 1975, p. 6.

62. See Tiziano Terzani, *Giai Phong! The Fall and Liberation of Saigon* (New York: St. Martin's Press, 1976), p. 31.

63. See Liberation Radio broadcast, March 25, 1975, in "Daily Report," March 25, 1975, p. L–9.

64. See AFP Hong Kong broadcast (in English), March 25, 1975, in "Daily Report," March 25, 1975, p. L–8.

65. AP, photograph, *Miami Herald,* March 27, 1975, p. 1; NYT, March 27, 1975, pp. 1, 16; United Press International (hereafter UPI), photograph, *Newsday,* March 26, 1975, p. 1.

66. It must be noted that in his final visit to My Thuy Phuong, on March 24, 1975, the author heard no comments strongly favorable to the Government, unless the comments of the policeman included in the text might be so construed. Most strong Government supporters had by then departed, leaving behind only a few who wanted to flee but could not, the local Front supporters, and most of those who had previously assumed uncommitted stances.

Epilogue: What Kind of Peace?

On March 24 or 25, 1975, North Vietnamese tanks advanced through My Thuy Phuong toward Hue.[1] On March 26, a new flag flew over the Hue citadel, and the Front issued a victory statement and appeal.[2] Simultaneously, North Vietnamese and Front forces advanced on Danang, which was choked with hundreds of thousands of refugees. The city began to collapse in a self-inflicted orgy of panic, looting, and killing.[3] On March 29, North Vietnamese and Front forces captured Danang, encountering no resistance.

By early April, Quang Tri and Thua Thien/Hue refugees, many of whom were probably apprehensive about life under the new regime, began the long northward trip back to homes they had abandoned.[4] As North Vietnamese forces began pressing down the coast of Vietnam toward Saigon, capturing province after province and city after city, a Military Management Committee and a People's Revolutionary Committee, consisting of military officers and civilians, became Thua Thien/Hue's new governing bodies.[5] With considerable North Vietnamese influence, the new authorities set up people's revolutionary committees in all villages, presumably including My Thuy Phuong.[6] According to a radio broadcast from Vietnam, there were rallies of local residents, where officials explained the new regime's policies.[7] The *Washington Post* reports that somewhat later the authorities organized people in villages like My Thuy Phuong into "solidarity cells" of 10 to 20 families each. These emerged as important institutions for political proselyting and control.[8]

Young people joined Liberation Youth Groups, and women joined the Women's Liberation Associations.[9]

There was an emphasis in all of the early official pronouncements on the correct behavior of North Vietnamese and Front troops. In fact, the Front established a 10-point code of conduct for its personnel.[10] The new authorities disarmed former Government soldiers, required civil servants and soldiers of the collapsed Government apparatus to register, conducted a census, and sent some higher ranking former officers for extended stays at special guarded political study or reeducation centers.[11] In later months, the authorities organized reeducation sessions in schools, offices, and meeting halls for most former civil servants, soldiers, and for citizens of all strata in the province.[12] Many others were sent to the reeducation centers, some for terms of three years or longer.

The new regime's political messages for people in places like My Thuy Phuong presumably followed the pattern set in other provinces. There was most likely a heavy dose of anti-Americanism mixed with an emphasis on the heroism of Ho Chi Minh. The messages also promoted revolutionary ideas and emphasized the reunification of Vietnam.[13] Such messages came in many forms. The official newspaper *Giai Phong*—"Liberation"—began to bring political messages to the Vietnamese people, certainly including My Thuy Phuong villagers. One article includes a number of revolutionary folk ballads from Thua Thien:[14]

> [A ballad] points to the anti-aggression opposition to imperialist America:
>
> When Americans come,
> American ghosts are all over the streets.
> In the sky the birds rarely twitter.
> Instead the helicopters fly. . . .
>
> Speak up so they can see the struggling spirit of the Vietnamese people, never slowed before the power of modern weapons brought here with the intention of conquering and annexing this country:
>
> Americans boast of modern civilization.
> Coming to our country,
> they get hurt by bamboo spikes.

Schools provided new textbooks to students, probably including students in My Thuy Phuong, and the books carried many political messages. Illustrative is this passage, from a fourth grade mathematics text:[15]

> On only one day (31-10-1972) there were 50,000 people of the Cuban capital, 10,000 people of the Italian capital, 7,000 people of the Japanese capital, and 8,000 people of the American city of Boston demonstrating to condemn American aggression in Vietnam. How many people in the four above countries do you calculate demonstrated that day to support the Vietnamese people and oppose American aggression?

In August of 1975, a primarily symbolic Thua Thien/Hue People's Congress met and prepared an appeal, which very likely reached many of My Thuy Phuong's people. It includes these words:[16]

> Dear compatriots, cadres, and combatants: The path on which we are advancing is clear and our future is very bright. The Thua Thien/Hue People's Congress calls on all the compatriots throughout the province and cadres and combatants to initiate an emulation movement to engage in productive labor and economically build their province and their fatherland. . . .
>
> Let the peasants of both sexes develop their role as the main force troops of the revolution, work hard, increase land productivity, scrupulously implement the party's land policy, unite and help each other in advancing along the path of collective work to build their native province as well as a new life.

And a cartoon serial from a privately owned Saigon daily, which probably reached the My Thuy Phuong area, depicts the struggle of a young Vietnamese boy against American soldiers. In one day's strip, the boy confronts an American, saying in English, "You no come Vietnam, V.C. no shoot you. You go combat over here, V.C. shoot you dead, dead."[17]

Among the first acts of the new Thua Thien/Hue authorities, according to the *New York Times,* was reopening of markets and shops, where they fixed prices of essential commodities and prohibited excessive profit taking.[18] North Vietnamese and Front troops, police, and new militia-like units maintained law and order in villages—and, according to a broadcast, thwarted "several attempts at sabotage by the reactionaries."[19] The new authorities also launched campaigns against "decadent," "reactionary," and "depraved" culture. They banned many books.[20] Male long hair and flamboyant Western dress came in for criticism.[21] Western popular music was also banned.[22] And workers removed information displays of the former regime.[23] Later, schools, banks, medical facilities, and Hue University reopened, and cinemas began to show North Vietnamese films.[24] Free literacy classes began in the area, probably including My Thuy Phuong. And according to an American journal, there were significant improvements in health care in Hue.[25]

In September, 1975, the Provisional Revolutionary Government introduced a new South Vietnamese currency. People could exchange only certain amounts of old currency, and credit the value of additional old piasters to savings accounts in nationalized banks.[26] And as reported in a private Vietnamese newspaper, during 1975–1976 in Huong Thuy District, presumably including My Thuy Phuong, there was a land redistribution. The authorities divided at least 8,000 acres of communal land which had previously been controlled by "the dishonest and wicked Vietnamese group." Families of war dead and those who aided the Front received top priority, and large, poor families received extra allocations. Former Government soldiers who had completed reeducation courses and had "reestablished their rights as citizens" were also eligible for land. The average allocation was .60 *mau* per family—increasing average landholdings by about 50 percent.[27] At the same time, the authorities organized peasants in My Thuy Phuong and other villages of the district into hundreds of production groups, each of which had about 80 members. These began to bring new land into cultivation and purchase water buffalo and agricultural tools.[28]

In late 1975, the new authorities combined Thua Thien/Hue, Quang Tri, and Quang Binh Province of North Vietnam into a single new province, Binh Tri Thien, and established several new provincial people's groups, such as the Ho Chi Minh Youth Workers' Group.[29] In April of 1976, My Thuy Phuong residents participated in Vietnam's election for a national assembly. According to Radio Hanoi, they joined more than 99 percent of Binh Tri Thien's voters in going to the polls.[30] In July, 1976, Vietnam's new assembly formally reunified the country.[31]

But reunification has not brought the period of healing, rebuilding, and peaceful change that many expected in Vietnam.[32] While there are signs that there has been some redistribution—wider sharing—of economic resources, there have been problems which overshadow that advance. First of all, the economy is in a shambles and there is simply less to redistribute. Unemployment is high in cities and towns, commercial activities everywhere have drastically slumped, and money is tight. Some of those problems grew out of government efforts to tax profits and eliminate a separate southern currency. When the government converted old to new piasters, in one fell swoop it eliminated much wealth, for the conversion was in effect a 90 percent devaluation of banked savings.[33]

Since 1977 in Central Vietnam, there have also been serious natural calamities—floods and droughts. These have led to costly crop failures and acute rice shortages. Exacerbating the problem were cuts in special grain allocations to Central Vietnam, which for years has been a rice deficient area. It therefore seems likely that the people of My Thuy Phuong have encountered extraordinary hardships simply finding enough to eat.

There are also the so-called new economic zones. These are large tracts, often remote and full of unexploded ordnance, which the government is trying to develop for agriculture—and the urban unemployed. Many thousands from the cities, sometimes unwillingly, have settled the zones. According to refugee reports, many settlers have faced food, water, and housing shortages. The work has been heavy and exhausting. Diseases have run rampant in some zones, and many have perished.

Then there is the pressure of continuing warfare. With Soviet arms and financial help, Vietnam has embarked on extensive and destructive military activities in Cambodia, Laos, and the Chinese border region. Large numbers of young Vietnamese have fought and died at those distant fronts, particularly near the Chinese border. In 1979, China invaded and temporarily occupied parts of northern Vietnam, supposedly as "punishment" for Vietnamese moves at the border and elsewhere. All these military involvements led Vietnam to institute a nationwide mobilization and draft, surely touching the lives of young men in My Thuy Phuong. Among them there have very likely been casualties.

The economic, social, and political adjustments occurring in Vietnam, plus the draft, have driven many to flee. These are the refugees known as "boat people." Since 1975, there have been hundreds of thousands, mostly ethnic Chinese from the cities, who have paid huge exit bribes to Vietnamese authorities, hired boats, and fled the country. Their first destinations have usually been Malaysia, Hong Kong, or any other shore they think will receive them. Thousands have met tragic ends at sea, victims of storms, unseaworthy boats, or pirates. Most who have finally landed hope to move on to the U.S. for a new chance.

It is indeed possible that some of My Thuy Phuong's people have fled the country, and some may have made it to refugee havens and then the U.S. But even the village's most prosperous residents are probably not prosperous enough to hire boats and pay all the necessary bribes. It is thus a safe bet that virtually all of My Thuy Phuong's people have stayed put and tried to adjust to new conditions, however difficult.

But worries very likely plague the village—worries about shortages, about social and economic changes, about the draft, and about fighting that could claim the young men. So true peace, peace of mind, probably eludes most villagers. In that sense, My Thuy Phuong perhaps remains a village at war.

NOTES

1. See AFB Hong Kong English language broadcast, March 24, 1975, in "Daily Report," March 24, 1975, p. L–4.

   On the loss of Hue, Arthur McTaggart, last director of U.S.I.S./Hue, commented, "It is embarrassing. The least President Ford could have done was to issue a statement." (Interviewed March 25, 1975 in Danang.) Roger R. Kelling, senior advisor in Tri Thien Hue, said, "It is very tragic. We were just getting started in Hue. I was just establishing a good relationship with the province chief. We had just gotten some good projects started. Very tragic." (Interviewed March 29, 1975, in Danang.)

2. There is some disagreement on the date of this event. (See NYT, May 25, 1975, VI, p. 36; *Chinh Luan*, March 31, 1975.) Also see Liberation Radio broadcast of March 26, 1975, in "Daily Report," March 27, 1975, p. L–14–16.

3. See *Saigon Giai-Phong*, May 1, 1976, p. 3; May 4, 1976, p. 3.

4. See NYT, March 30, 1975, p. 13; Liberation Radio broadcast, April 7, 1975, in "Daily Report," April 9, 1975, p. L–14. For an account of conditions under the new regime in a province in Central Vietnam, see Earl Martin, *Reaching The Other Side* (New York: Crown, 1978).

5. See *Trang Den*, March 21, 1975; FEER, September 12, 1975, pp. 35–39; Liberation Radio broadcast, April 15, 1975, in "Daily Report," April 21, 1975, pp. L–24—L–28; Saigon domestic radio broadcast, May 15, 1975, in "Daily Report," May 16, 1975, p. L–2.

6. Liberation Radio broadcast, March 26, 1975, in "Daily Report," March 28, 1975, p. L–13; NYT, September 21, 1975, p. E3

7. See Radio Hanoi broadcast, April 5, 1975, in "Daily Report," April 8, 1975, pp. L–14—L–15; Radio Hanoi broadcast, April 23, 1975, in "Daily Report," April 23, 1975, p. L–10; Liberation Radio broadcast, April 24, 1975, in "Daily Report," April 28, 1975, pp. L–16—L–22; Radio Hanoi broadcast, May 3, 1975, in "Daily Report," May 5, 1975, p. L–12; Saigon domestic radio broadcast, May 15, 1975, in "Daily Report," May 16, 1975, p. L–2.

8. Washington Post Service, *Sunday Star-Bulletin and Advertiser* (Honolulu), April 25, 1976, pp. B–1, B–4.

9. See *Tin Sang,* September 16, 1975, p. 9.

10. See Liberation Radio broadcast, March 28, 1975, in "Daily Report," March 31, 1975, p. L–28.

11. See NYT, March 30, 1975, p. 13; FEER, June 27, 1975, pp. 13–14; *Indochina Chronicle,* no. 42, July-August, 1975, p. 23, photograph; *Time,* February 16, 1976, pp. 30–37; FEER, May 14, 1976, p. 20; *Honolulu Advertiser,* June 11, 1976, p. C–11; NYT, June 12, 1976, p. 6.

12. See Liberation Radio broadcast, April 3, 1975, in "Daily Report," April 3, 1975, pp. L–1—L–2.

13. See FEER, June 6, 1975, p. 15; August 1, 1975, pp. 20–21. Also NYT, December 29, 1975, p. 5; January 20, 1976, p. 5.

14. *Giai-Phong,* August 10, 1975, p. 3; available on microfilm from Indochina Resource Center, Berkeley, Ca.

15. *Toan; Lop Bon; Pho-Thong* (Math; Grade 4; Universal) (Vietnam: Nha Xuat-Ban Giao-Duc Giai-Phong, 1973), p. 71; released by the Provisional Revolutionary Government of South Vietnam, and in the author's possession.

16. See Hanoi Radio, August 28, 1975, in "Daily Report," September 2, 1975, p. L–4.

17. *Tin Sang,* November 3, 1975, p. 10.

18. NYT, September 28, 1975, p. 6.

19. Radio Hanoi, June 27, 1976, in "Daily Report," June 28, 1976, p. K–12; Radio Hanoi, August 28, 1975, in "Daily Report," September 2, 1975, pp. L–2—L–5.

20. *Cf. Saigon Giai-Phong* article of May 31, 1975, broadcast on domestic radio, May 30, 1975, in "Daily Report," June 2, 1975, pp. L–1—L–2.

21. *Cf.* NYT, July 13, 1976, p. 3.

22. Radio Hanoi broadcast, April 15, 1975, in "Daily Report," April 17, 1975, p. L–12.

23. *Ibid.*

24. According to a newspaper account, banks reopened in the province and began to emphasize loans to peasants. (*TinSang,* August 11, 1975, p. 4.) Also see Giai-Phong Agency report on Radio Hanoi, June 3, 1975, in "Daily

Report," June 13, 1975, p. L–3; *Tin Sang,* January 21, 1976, p. 4; Radio Hanoi broadcast, April 15, 1975, in "Daily Report," April 17, 1975, p. L–12.

25. *Indochina Chronicle,* no. 49, May-June, 1976, pp. 7, 12, 14–16. Also see Douglas Pike, "The Veteran in Vietnam," paper for Association for Asian Studies meeting in New York City, March 27, 1977.

26. See NYT, September 22, 1975, pp. 1, 11; September 28, 1975, p. 6. Also UPI, *Honolulu Advertiser,* October 8, 1975, p. A–16.

27. See *Tin Sang,* September 16, 1975, p. 9; October 17, 1975, pp. 1, 10. Also Tiziano Terzani, "Vietnam: The First Year," *New York Review of Books,* July 15, 1976, p. 6; Hughes Tertrais, "Back to the Land," *The Guardian,* February 8, 1976, quoted in *Indochina Program Newsletter* (Philadelphia: American Friends Service Committee, no. 35, April 16, 1976), pp. 19–20; NYT, March 3, 1976, pp. 49, 57.

28. *Tin Sang,* October 17, 1975, pp. 1, 10.

29. *Tin Sang,* July 13, 1976, pp. 3, 8; also see NYT, March 6, 1976, p. 40.

30. See Radio Hanoi broadcast, June 30, 1976, in "Daily Report," July 1, 1976, pp. K–1—K–2; *Tin Sang,* May 11, 1976, p. 8.

31. NYT, July 3, 1976, p. 1.

32. For detailed articles on Vietnam's tasks of reunification and reconstruction, see *Vietnam Quarterly* (Cambridge, Mass.: Spring, 1976). For continuing coverage of developments in Vietnam, the best sources in English are FEER, NYT, and "Daily Report."

33. See NYT, July 15, 1979, p. 15.

Bibliography

1. ***Vietnamese Publications***

Anh, Toan. *Lang Xom Viet-Nam* (Vietnamese Villages). Saigon: Phuong Quynh, 1968.

Ban-Tin Huong-Thuy (Huong Thuy Newsletter), 1972. Huong Thuy: Information Service.

Chien-Si Cong-Hoa (Republican Soldier), 1973. Saigon.

Chinh Luan (newspaper), 1975. Saigon.

Dac-San Xuan (Spring Yearbook). Hue: Information Service, 1973.

Dai Dan-Toc (newspaper), 1975. Saigon.

"Dai-Nam Nhat-Thong-Chi; Thua-Thien Phu" (General Geography of Dai Nam; Thua Thien Province). Saigon: Ministry of Education, no. 10, 1961.

Dan-Chu (newspaper), 1974–1975. Saigon.

Dan-Van (Information). Hue: Information Service, undated.

"Dia-Phuong Chi; Tinh Thua-Thien" (Local Guide; Thua Thien Province). Hue: Vietnam Information Service, undated.

Doc-Lap (newspaper), 1974–1975. Saigon.

Duong, Pham Cao. *Thuc-Trang Cua Gioi Nong-Dan Viet-Nam Duoi Thoi Phap Thuoc* (The Situation of Vietnamese Peasants Under the French Period). Saigon: Khai Tri, 1967. Available in Cornell University Library.

"Economic and Social Assistance to the Republic of Viet-Nam." Saigon: Government of the Republic of Vietnam, 1973. Available through U.S.A.I.D., Washington, D.C.

Giai-Phong (newspaper), 1975. Saigon.

Hue Anh-Dung Kien-Cuong (Heroic and Strong Hue). Hanoi: Ban Lien-Lac Dong-Huong Thanh-Pho Hue, 1971. Available in Cornell University Library.

Huong-Thuy. Huong Thuy: Information Service, 1975.

Huong, Vu et al. *Co-Do Hue* (The Old Capital of Hue). Hue: Sao Mai, 1971.

Khiem, Thai Van. *Co-Do Hue* (The Old Capital of Hue). Saigon: Ministry of Education, 1960.

Muc Luc Chau Ban Trieu Nguyen (Complete Table of Contents Nguyen Dynasty). Hue: Uy-Ban Phien-Dich Su-Lieu Viet-Nam Vien Dai-Hoc Hue, 1960. Available in Cornell University Library.

Phuong, Tran et al. *Cach-Mang Ruong-Dat o Viet-Nam* (Land Revolution in Vietnam). Hanoi: Nha Xuat-Ban Khoa-Hoc Xa-Hoi Viet-Nam, 1968. Available in Cornell University Library.

Quoc-Van; Lop 5 (Literature; Grade 5). Saigon: Canh-Hong, 1974.

Saigon Giai-Phong (newspaper), 1975–1976. Saigon.

Saigon Post (newspaper), 1975. Saigon.

Son, Pham Van et al. *The Viet Cong "Tet" Offensive (1968)*. Saigon: Printing and Publications Center, Republic of Vietnam Armed Forces, 1968.

Song Than (newspaper), 1975. Saigon.

South Viet-Nam National Front for Liberation: Documents. South Vietnam: Giai Phong, 1966. Available in Cornell University Library.

Tia Sang (newspaper), 1974–1975. Saigon.

Tin Sang (newspaper), 1975–1976. Saigon.

Toan; Lop Bon; Pho-Thong (Math; Grade Four; Universal). Vietnam: Nha Xuat-Ban Giao-Duc Giai-Phong, 1973.

Trang-Den (newspaper), 1974–1975. Saigon.

Vietnam Bulletin, 1973. Washington: Embassy of the Republic of Vietnam. Available in East-West Resource Systems Institute Library, Honolulu.

Vietnamese Studies, undated. Hanoi.

2. ***French Publications (all in the Cornell University Library).***

Bulletin des Amis du Vieux Hue, 1916–1919.

Bulletin d'Information, 1974–1975. Paris: Press Service, Permanent Mission of the Provisional Revolutionary Government of South Vietnam in France.

Chaigneau, Michel. *Souvenirs de Hue*. Paris: L'Imprimerie Imperiale, 1867.

Cordier, Paul. *Notions d'Administration Indochinoise*. Hanoi: Imprimerie d'Extreme Orient, 1911.

Cury, Louis. *La Societe Annamite; Les Lettres—Les Mandarins—Le Peuple*. Paris: Faculte de Droit de L'Universite de Paris, Jouve & Co., 1910.

Gourou, Pierre. *L'Utilisation du Sol en Indochine Francaise*. Paris: Centre d'Etudes de Politique Etrangers, Travaux des groupes d'Etudes, Paul Hartman, 1940.

Henry, Yves. *Economie Agricole de l'Indochine*. Hanoi: Gouvernement General, 1932.

Taboulet, Georges, ed. *La Geste Francaise en Indochine*. Paris: A. Maisonneuve, 1955–1956, 2 vols.

Thomazi, Auguste. *La Conquete de l'Indochine*. Paris: Payot, 1934.

"Tombeaux Annamites dan les Environs de Hue." *Bulletin de la Societe des Etudes Indochinoises,* no. 1 & 2, 1958.

Vinh, Nguyen Van. *Les Reformes Agraires au Viet-Nam*. France: Librairie Universitaire Uystpruyst, 1961.

3. ***Books and Special Studies.***

Betts, Russell. "Viet Cong Village Control: Some Observations on the Origin and Dynamics of Modern Revolutionary War." Cambridge: M.I.T. Center for International Studies, August, 1969.

Boyle, Richard. *Flower of the Dragon; The Breakdown of the U.S. Army in Vietnam*. San Francisco: Ramparts Press, 1972.

Browning, Frank and Dorothy Forman, eds. *The Wasted Nations*. New York: Harper & Row, 1972.

Burchett, Wilfred. *Vietnam; Inside Story of the Guerrilla War*. New York: International, 1965.

Buttinger, Joseph. *Vietnam: A Dragon Embattled*. New York: Praeger, 1967.

———. *Vietnam: A Political History*. New York: Praeger, 1968.

Caputo, Philip. *A Rumor of War*. New York: Holt, Rinehart & Winston, 1977.

Chagnon, Jacqui and Don Luce. *Of Quiet Courage: Poems From Viet-Nam*. Washington: Indochina Mobile Education Project, 1974.

Chinh, Truong and Vo Nguyen Giap. "The Peasant Question (1937–1938)." Ithaca: Southeast Asia Program, Department of Asian Studies, Cornell University, data paper no. 94, January, 1974.

Dang, Nghiem. *Viet-Nam; Politics and Public Administration*. Honolulu: East-West Center Press, 1966.

Davison, W. "Some Observations on Viet Cong Operations in the Villages." Santa Monica: RAND Corporation memorandum RM-5267/2-ISA/ARPA, May, 1968.

Dawson, Alan. *55 Days; The Fall of South Vietnam*. Englewood Cliffs: Prentice-Hall, 1977.

Documenting the Post-War War. Philadelphia: National Action/Research on the Military Industrial Complex, American Friends Service Committee, 1974.

Donnell, John and Charles Joiner, eds. *Electoral Politics in South Vietnam*. Lexington, Mass.: D. C. Heath, 1974.

Du, Nguyen. *The Tale Of Kieu*. New York: Vintage Books, 1973.

Dung, Van Tien. *Our Great Spring Victory*. New York: Monthly Review Press, 1977.

Fall, Bernard. *Viet-Nam Witness; 1953–66*. New York & Washington: Praeger, 1966.

______. *Street Without Joy*. New York: Schocken Books, 1972.

Fitzgerald, Frances. *Fire In The Lake: The Vietnamese and the Americans in Vietnam*. New York: Atlantic-Little, Brown, 1972.

Halberstam, David. *The Best and the Brightest*. New York: Random House, 1972.

Hammer, Ellen. *Vietnam; Yesterday and Today*. New York: Holt, Rinehart and Winston, 1966.

Han, Vo Luan. "Thua Thien Agricultural Development Problems and the Result of Investigations of 411 Thua Thien Farmer Households." Saigon: Joint Development Group, 1967. Available in Cornell University Library.

Hayden, Tom. "A Vietnamese View of Human Nature." Santa Monica: Indochina Peace Campaign, undated.

Henderson, William. *Why the Vietcong Fought: A Study of Motivation and Control in a Modern Army in Combat*. Westport, Conn.: Greenwood Press, 1979.

Hickey, Gerald. *Village in Viet-Nam*. New Haven: Yale University Press, 1964.

Hoa, Nguyen Dinh. *Vietnamese-English Dictionary*. Rutland, Vt. & Tokyo: Tuttle, 1966.

Kahin, George and John Lewis. *The United States in Viet-Nam*. New York: Dial Press, 1967.

Kalb, Bernard and Marvin Kalb. *Kissinger*. Boston: Little, Brown, 1974.

Lamb, Alastair. *The Mandarin Road to Old Hue; Narratives of Anglo-Vietnamese Diplomacy from the 17th Century to the Eve of the French Conquest*. Hamden, Conn.: Archon Books, 1970.

Lewy, Guenter. *America in Vietnam*. New York: Oxford University Press, 1978.

Long, Ngo Vinh. *Before the Revolution; The Vietnamese Peasants Under the French*. Cambridge: M.I.T. Press, 1973.

Marr, David. *Vietnamese Anticolonialism 1885–1925*. Berkeley: University of California Press, 1971.

Martin, Earl. *Reaching the Other Side*. New York: Crown, 1978.

McAlister, John. *Vietnam: The Origins of Revolution*. New York: Knopf, 1969.

McAlister, John and Paul Mus. *The Vietnamese and Their Revolution*. New York: Harper & Row, 1970.

Meyerson, Harvey. *Vinh Long*. Boston: Houghton Mifflin, 1970.

Oberdorfer, Don. *Tet*. Garden City: Doubleday, 1971.

The Pentagon Papers as Published by the New York Times. New York: Bantam, 1971.

Pike, Douglas, ed. "Documents on the National Liberation Front of South Vietnam, 1959–1966." Wason microfilm 1562, Cornell University Library.

———. *Vietcong; The Organization and Techniques of the National Liberation Front of South Vietnam.* Cambridge: M.I.T. Press, 1966.

———. *War, Peace, and the Viet Cong.* Cambridge: M.I.T. Press, 1969.

———. "The Veteran in Vietnam." Paper for Association for Asian Studies meeting in New York City, March, 1977.

Popkin, Samuel. *The Rational Peasant: The Political Economy of Rural Society in Vietnam.* Berkeley: University of California Press, 1979.

Porter, Gareth. *A Peace Denied: The United States, Vietnam, and the Paris Agreement.* Bloomington: Indiana University Press, 1975.

Race, Jeffrey. *War Comes to Long An; Revolutionary Conflict in a Vietnamese Province.* Berkeley: University of California Press, 1972.

Rose, Dale. *The Vietnamese Civil Service System.* Saigon: Michigan State Advisory Group, 1961. Available in East-West Resource Systems Institute Library, Honolulu.

Schell, Jonathan. *The Village of Ben Suc.* New York: Knopf, 1967.

Scott, James. *The Moral Economy of the Peasant: Rebellion and Subsistence in Southeast Asia.* New Haven: Yale University Press, 1976.

The Senator Gravel Edition; The Pentagon Papers; The Defense Department History of United States Decisionmaking on Vietnam. Boston: Beacon, 1974.

Shaplen, Robert. *The Road From War; Vietnam 1965–1970.* New York: Harper & Row, 1970.

Snepp, Frank. *Decent Interval.* New York: Vintage Books, 1977.

Tanham, George. *Communist Revolutionary Warfare; From the Vietminh to the Viet Cong.* New York: Praeger, 1967.

Terzani, Tiziano. *Giai Phong! The Fall and Liberation of Saigon.* New York: St. Martin's Press, 1976.

Thai, Nguyen. *Is South Vietnam Viable?* Manila: Carmelo & Bauermann, 1962. Available in East-West Resource Systems Institute Library, Honolulu.

Thai, Nguyen Van and Nguyen Van Mung. *A Short History of Viet-Nam.* Saigon: Times Publishing Co., 1958.

"The Third Force in South Vietnam." Philadelphia: American Friends Service Committee, 1975.

Vennema, Alje. *The Viet Cong Massacre At Hue.* New York: Vantage Press, 1976.

Vien, Nguyen Khac. *Tradition and Revolution in Vietnam.* Berkeley: Indochina Resource Center, 1974.

Vietnam Veterans Against the War. *The Winter Soldier Investigation: An Inquiry into American War Crimes.* Boston: Beacon Press, 1972.

West, F. J. *The Village.* New York: Harper & Row, 1972.

Woodside, Alexander. *Community and Revolution in Modern Vietnam.* Boston: Houghton Mifflin, 1976.

Wolf, Eric. *Peasant Wars Of The Twentieth Century*. New York: Harper & Row, 1969.

Zasloff, J. "Origins of the Insurgency in South Viet-Nam, 1954–1960." Santa Monica: RAND Corporation, item RM-5163/2-ISA/ARPA, May, 1968.

4. ***United States Government Documents.***

"After Action Report, Offensive Operations 17 May–28 February 1969." Camp Eagle: Headquarters, 2nd Brigade, 101st Airborne Division, March 5, 1969. Available in Museum, Ft. Campbell, Ky.

"Analysis of V.C./V.C.I Related Activity in Thua Thien—1970." Camp Eagle: 101st Airborne Division, February 21, 1971. Available in Museum, Ft. Campbell, Ky.

"Annual Statistical Bulletin." Saigon: U.S.A.I.D., 1973. Available in East-West Resource Systems Institute Library, Honolulu.

"Briefing." Camp Eagle: Commanding General, 101st Airborne Division, 1969. Available in Museum, Ft. Campbell, Ky.

Captured Documents. Washington: Office of Media Services, Bureau of Public Affairs, Dept. of State, 1968. Available in Cornell University Library.

"Civic Action Priority List." Camp Eagle: AC of S, G-5, 101st Airborne Division, December 14, 1969. Available in Museum, Ft. Campbell, Ky.

"Combat Notes Number 10." Camp Eagle: 101st Airborne Division, March 5, 1968. Available in Museum, Ft. Campbell, Ky.

"Combat Operations After Action Report." Camp Eagle: 1st Battalion (Airmobile), 501st Airborne Infantry, 101st Airborne Division, March 1, 1969. Available in Museum, Ft. Campbell, Ky.

Commander in Chief, Pacific. *Report on War in Viet-Nam*. Washington: Government Printing Office, 1968.

"Cordon and Search Operations." Danang: III Marine Amphibious Force, November 28, 1968. Available in Museum, Ft. Campbell, Ky.

"Debrief of a CORDS Deputy Province Senior Advisor; Thua Thien and An Xuyen Provinces; Vietnam; 1967–1968." Honolulu: Asia Training Center, UH/AID, no. 9682, undated. Available in University of Hawaii Library.

"Disposition of Province Police." Hue: PSD form 334–15, July and October, 1966, in "Thua Thien, Weekly and Monthly Report, 1966." Available in folder 35, box 17, no. 71A–5365, Center of Military History, Dept. of the Army, Washington, D.C.

"Documentation on the Viet-Nam Agreement." Washington: Office of Media Services, Bureau of Public Affairs, U.S. Department of State, 1973.

"Economic Impact of 101st Abn Div (Ambl)." Camp Eagle: 101st Airborne Division, October 14, 1970. Available in Museum, Ft. Campbell, Ky.

"Fact Sheet on the Combined Action Force." Danang: III Marine Amphibious Force, March 31, 1970. Available in Historical Branch, Headquarters, U.S. Marine Corps, Washington, D.C.

"Father Chan Tin's View of 'Political Prisoners': A Case Study of Militancy Overriding Objectivity." Saigon: Dept. of State Airgram, December 26, 1973. Available through the Dept. of State, Washington, D.C.

"G-5 Activities." Camp Eagle: AC of S, G-5, 101st Airborne Division, 1969–1970. Available in Museum, Ft. Campbell, Ky.

Hearings, Mutual Development and Cooperation Act of 1973. Washington, D.C.: Government Printing Office, Committee on Foreign Relations, U.S. House of Representatives, 93rd Congress, 1st session, 1973.

"Leverage Policy Statement." Saigon: COMUSMACV memo, MACCORDS-PP to Senior Advisor, I CTZ, January 30, 1968. Available at National Records Center, Suitland, Maryland; no. P & P 0642–67; (CORDS 149), 1/49:23–4, 71A7502.

The Marines In Vietnam; 1954–1973: An Anthology and Annotated Bibliography. Washington: History & Museums Division, Headquarters, U.S. Marine Corps, 1974.

McCarthy, Francis. *The Civil Service System of the Republic of Viet-Nam; A Description and Assessment*. Saigon: U.S.A.I.D., 1969. Available in East-West Resource Systems Institute Library, Honolulu.

"101st Airborne Division Press Release." Camp Eagle: 101st Airborne Division, 1970–1971. Available in Museum, Ft. Campbell, Ky.

"One Year Later . . . The Rebirth of Hue." Saigon: Vietnam Feature Service, U.S. Information Service, [1969]. Available in Museum, Ft. Campbell, Ky.

"Operational Notes Number 7." Camp Eagle: 101st Airborne Division, November 10, 1969. Available in Museum, Ft. Campbell, Ky.

"Operations Note Number 10—Field Expedient Target Locator." Camp Eagle: 101st Airborne Division, April 1, 1970. Available in Museum, Ft. Campbell, Ky.

"Province Report, Department of the Army, Thua Thien Province, I CTZ, MACV Advisory Team 18, APO 96258." Hue: C.O.R.D.S., 1967–1973. Available in Center of Military History, Department of the Army, Washington, D.C.

"Rating of GVN Officials—I CTZ: 1968." Danang: C.O.R.D.S., 1968. Available in folder 1, box 9, no. 71A9237; 19/75:45–3, Center of Military History, Department of the Army, Washington, D.C.

"Report for Month Ending . . ." Hue: U.S.A.I.D. Reports Officer, 1966. Available in "Thua Thien Papers, 1966," folder 10, box 10, Center of Military History, Department of the Army, Washington, D.C.

"Senior Officer's Debriefing Report." Camp Eagle: 101st Airborne Division, May 11, 1970. Available in Museum, Ft. Campbell, Ky.

"Significant Activity Since January 1970." Camp Eagle: 101st Airborne Division, 1970. Available in Museum, Ft. Campbell, Ky.

Sloan, T. for Mr. Cross. "Methods of Leverage on G.V.N. Officials." Danang: Deputy for CORDS/III Marine Amphibious Force, undated. Available at National Records Center, Suitland, Maryland, no. CORDS–159, 1/49:23–4, 71A7502.

"Special Intelligence Study NR33–68 on the Hue Tet Offensive . . ." Camp Eagle: 101st Airborne Division, December 29, 1968. Available in Museum, Ft. Campbell, Ky.

"Special Report on Senatorial Election." Hue: Chief, PDD/CORDS, June, 1970. Available in Museum, Ft. Campbell, Ky.

"Status of Police Personnel." Hue: PSD form 334–1, October, 1966, in "Thua Thien, Weekly and Monthly Report, 1966." Available in folder 35, box 17, no. 71A–5365, Center of Military History, Dept. of the Army, Washington, D.C.

"Synopsis of the Battle of Hue." Camp Eagle: 101st Airborne Division, January 10, 1969. Available in Museum, Ft. Campbell, Ky.

"Thua Thien—Terrorist Activity, 1967–1968." Danang: U.S.A.I.D., Public Safety Division, undated. Available in folder 60, box 19, 19/66:23–7, 71A5365, Center of Military History, Dept. of the Army, Washington, D.C.

"U.S. Marine Corps Civic Action Effort in Vietnam; March 1965–March 1966." Washington, D.C.: Historical Branch, Headquarters, U.S. Marine Corps, 1968.

"U.S. Marine Corps Civic Action Effort in Vietnam; April 1966–April 1967." Washington, D.C.: Historical Branch, Headquarters, U.S. Marine Corps, 1970.

5. ***Serials and Important Articles.***

A. *Serials.*

Daily Report; Asia & Pacific, 1965–1976. Springfield, Va.: National Technical Information Service, Foreign Broadcast Information Service, U.S. Dept. of Commerce.

Far Eastern Economic Review, 1971–1976. Hong Kong.

Honolulu Advertiser, 1975–1976. Honolulu.

Indochina Chronicle, 1973–1976. Berkeley.

Indochina Program Newsletter, 1976. Philadelphia: American Friends Service Committee.

Miami Herald, 1975. Miami.

Newsday, 1975. Long Island, New York.

Newsweek, 1973. New York.

New York Times, 1960–1979. New York.

Rendezvous With Destiny, 1969–1971. Camp Eagle: 101st Airborne Division. Available in Museum, Ft. Campbell, Ky.

Screaming Eagle, 1970–1972. Greenville, Texas: 101st Airborne Division Association. Available at the Public Affairs Office, Ft. Campbell, Ky.

Sunday Star Bulletin and Advertiser, 1976. Honolulu.

Vietnam Quarterly, 1976. Cambridge, Mass.

B. *Important Articles.*

Branfman, Fred. "Indochina: The Illusion of Withdrawal." *Harper's Magazine,* May, 1973.

Chomsky, Noam. "The Remaking of History." *Ramparts Magazine* reprint (undated). Available through Indochina Program, American Friends Service Committee, Philadelphia.

Huntington, Samuel. "The Bases of Accommodation." *Foreign Affairs,* July, 1968.

Popkin, Samuel. "Corporatism and Colonialism; the Political Economy of Rural Change in Vietnam." *Comparative Politics,* April, 1976.

Race, Jeffrey. "Toward an Exchange Theory of Revolution." *Peasant Rebellion and Communist Revolution in Asia.* John Lewis, ed. Stanford: Stanford University Press, 1974.

Scott, James and Benedict Kerkvliet. "How Traditional Rural Patrons Lose Legitimacy: A Theory With Special Reference to Southeast Asia." *Cultures et Developpement,* vol. 5, no. 3, 1973.

______. "The Politics of Survival: Peasant Response to 'Progress' in Southeast Asia." *Journal of Southeast Asian Studies,* September, 1973.

Serong, F. "The 1972 Easter Offensive." *Southeast Asian Perspectives,* Summer, 1974.

Szulc, Tad. "How Kissinger Did It; Behind the Vietnam Cease-Fire Agreement." *Foreign Policy,* Summer, 1974.

Terzani, Tiziano. "Vietnam: The First Year." *New York Review of Books,* July 15, 1976.

Treaster, Joseph. "The Phoenix Murders." *Penthouse,* December, 1975.

Vien, Nguyen Khac. "Myths & Realities." *Bulletin of Concerned Asian Scholars,* December, 1973.

Index